D0443828

CONVERSATIONS

WITH A

MASKED MAN

CONVERSATIONS
WITH A
MASKED MAN

My Father,
the CIA, and Me

JOHN HADDEN

Arcade Publishing • New York

First Edition

Arcade Publishing books may be purchased in bulk at special discounts for sales promotion, corporate gifts, fund-raising, or educational purposes. Special editions can also be created to specifications. For details, contact the Special Sales Department, Arcade Publishing, 307 West 36th Street, 11th Floor, New York, NY 10018 or arcade@skyhorsepublishing.com.

Arcade Publishing® is a registered trademark of Skyhorse Publishing, Inc.®, a Delaware corporation.

Visit our website at www.arcadepub.com.

10 9 8 7 6 5 4 3 2 1

Library of Congress Cataloging-in-Publication Data is available on file.

Cover design by Laura Klynstra
Cover image: Shutterstock

Print ISBN: 978-1628725919
Ebook ISBN: 978-1628726329

Printed in the United States of America

To Beatrice
From her grandfather

Contents

Timeline

1923—JLH Born 1923, New York City

1927—Collapse of German economy

1929—JLH Attends Buckley School, NYC

 Great Depression Begins

1935—JLH Attends Groton School

1939—Germany Invades Poland

1941—JLH Attends Harvard University; Japan Attacks Pearl Harbor

1942—JLH Attends US Military Academy at West Point

1945—US Drops Atom Bombs on Hiroshima and Nagasaki; End of
  WWII; JLH is US Army Engineer in Germany

1948—Arab-Israeli War Begins

1949—JLH Joins CIA, Base Berlin

1952—JLH Marries Kathryn Falck

1953—Rosenbergs Executed; CIA-Backed Coup in Iran; JLH, Jr. Born

1954—JLH Establishes CIA Base Hamburg; CIA-Backed Coup in
  Guatemala

1956—JLH at CIA, Washington DC; US Tests First H-Bomb over
  Bikini Atoll

1958—JLH at CIA Salzburg, Austria, 1958-1961

1961—JLH at CIA, Washington DC; Berlin Wall Erected; Bay of Pigs
  Invasion, Cuba

1963—JLH is CIA Station Chief, Tel Aviv, Israel; JFK Assassination

1964—Gulf of Tonkin Resolution: Vietnam War Begins

1967—Arab-Israeli Six-Day War; JLH at CIA Middle East Desk under
  Angleton, Washington, DC

1968—MLK Assassination

1970—Students Killed at Kent State University by National Guard Officers

1972—Nixon Exposed for Watergate Break-In

1973—JLH Retires from CIA, Teaches History, Woodberry Forest School, VA; CIA-Backed 9/11 Coup in Chile

1975—JLH Retires: Lecturer, woodworker, Brunswick, ME

1991—Persian Gulf War

2001—Trade Center Attack; Global War on Terror Begins

2013—JLH Dies in Brunswick, ME

2014—Birth of ISIL

Preface

My father spent the last few years of his CIA career in Washington, DC, during the Nixon administration. He didn't like being in Washington; he'd managed to be posted overseas for most of his early career. But now he'd achieved too high a rank to be sent out again. Uncomfortably hemmed in, he quit just before Watergate broke, collected his thirty-year retirement package, and moved to Maine.

He liked to talk. But not about himself and rarely, if ever, about his work. He was a private man. Growing up, he and I were often at odds. I wanted very much to make sense of his worldview—or debunk it. I loved him very much and I believe the feeling was mutual, but I wanted this love to mean something, to provide answers, to show the way. These three particular motivations, however, were so absent from his own way of thinking that there was no way he could satisfy me.

Not long after 9/11, I asked my father if I could interview him on tape and write a book about his life in and out of the CIA. To my surprise—or to surprise me—he agreed, as long as he could edit the results. Of course: there was no other way he could talk freely. We recorded long conversations. He demolished my interrogations. Each new turn he took wiped out whatever dossier I was foolishly trying to assemble. Sometimes reluctant, sometimes bitter, or cynical, or uproarious, he told mesmerizing stories, laced with surreal black comedy, some very hard facts, and a labyrinth of clues and deceptions. Even at his most rigorously accurate, my father was a contradictory character, the kind we love in the theater.

I've kept our interviews in dialogue form to let the reader be lulled and misled, as I was, and to arouse skepticism. I want readers to *hear* it, as a play, in which the puzzle is to be solved, as often as not, by what is *not* said, to hear the tone of voice, to trust the sound more than the words.

In our conversations, which were more fragmented and wayward than I have presented them here, he talked about his travels—in different countries, different bureaucratic circles, politics, factions—but he wanted me to know that he didn't go anywhere really, that the whole exercise was useless and absurd. Any sense of his journey as a spiritual destiny, fighting the good fight, or adding-up of any kind was out of the question.

While reworking this material after a long hiatus, I've found a deeper sense of the cruel stupidities he was faced with for most of his time in the CIA—and the deadening of his sense of belonging to a cause, or even a country, or even a species. And I feel a deeper sympathy for him than I did when he was alive. (There are simpler reasons for my admiration, too: I'm proud that he was there to stop the bombing of Cairo, for instance.)

My father refused to look at the evidence of his life except in the most literal way, which to me was meaningless. My own experience of our travels, as a family, was that they were remarkable, laden with meaning and destiny. But his stubborn dismissal of anything remotely metaphorical was suspect: he played himself as a character, as my foil. He encouraged the differences between us and reveled in the fact that The Way, which I kept hoping he would help me find, was entirely up to me. He was the Mad Hatter at the tea party.

In his talks with me, always aware of the tape recorder, my father left rabbit holes at every turn, often pointing the wrong way. I think he wanted to demonstrate that we have been listening too reverently to byzantine, powerful men like him. In any case, he gave a performance, and it behooves me to be a good audience and follow his lead. I have no moral resolutions or answers of any kind. Therefore I can offer no inside knowledge about what the fabricators and guardians of the secrets have done to us or to themselves. No one will ever know, and none of it will make any sense.

About ten years ago I wrote a draft of this book, sent him a copy, and followed up with a visit to his house in Maine. I found him in bed with a bad cold, looking at me sideways with a miserable face. In a small reedy voice, he said, "Hi, big guy. I don't think you're going to like what I have to say."

He had gone through the material, making careful marks with a red pencil, crossing out a name here and there, or a procedure—small stuff—for the first fifty pages. Farther in, whole paragraphs fell to the red pencil, and later still, three or four pages at a time were crossed out. He'd given up before reading to the end. He couldn't let it be published. He was afraid. He didn't want to be hounded by lawsuits or worse. After he was dead and gone, I could do whatever I wanted with it.

At the time I didn't believe that he was actually afraid. I'd never seen fear in him. Mostly, he conveyed a kind of ironic fatalism. I felt hurt and disappointed, but I told him I understood, and left the room. Ten minutes later he appeared downstairs, fully dressed, saying in a hearty voice that we should go for a walk with my dog, Leo. In spite of himself, he was a sucker for birds and dogs and other living things—and they liked him too, unaccountably. I had to laugh at this miraculous transformation, which I knew was genuine.

We had a nice afternoon, but I simmered inside. I'd worked for many months on the book and I'd begun to like it. The country was then reeling from the revelations at Abu Ghraib, and my father had expressed his disgust over the affair. As a sometime interrogator himself, he knew that torture was not only abhorrent but counterproductive. Intelligence-gathering relies, paradoxically, on trust, and maintaining a semblance of moral high ground. When you've lost moral ground *and* you've proved that no one can trust you, your contacts dry up.

At dinner I reassured him that I would wait on the book but wished he would add his voice and his credibility as a professional to the debate about American policy in the Middle East. He refused to talk about it, except to grumble about whistle-blowers. They were egotists who were only out to blow their own horns, he said, and they did no one any good at all. In the next few years this animus against whistle-blowers grew into a small obsession. He was in conflict about what he knew and what he might say out loud.

Pop died on a sunny day in May 2013. He was at home, surrounded by his family. In his last two weeks he claimed to feel no pain, though the cancer that was killing him had taken over. But he had bouts of troubled restlessness that were impossible for us to understand. I think he had too much going on in his mind to notice the physical pain.

My son Reilly and I sat with him on one of his last fully lucid days. He had a small list of things to tell us. He wanted to be sure that we were okay to let him go. We said we were. He wanted us to take care of my mother—in particular, to make sure the CIA sent the pension they owed her; we said we would. He wanted no fuss about his death, and he named several good friends who might "raise a jar" to him. I took down the names and read them back to him. He nodded. He also wanted me to gather all his files in the attic, and to publish the book. "Print it!" he said, raising his wild eyebrow.

CONVERSATIONS

WITH A

MASKED MAN

CHAPTER 1

Travels

"Goddamn bastards!"
"Never trust anybody."
"Bongo, bongo, bongo."
—John Lloyd Hadden, Sr.

I was born an American overseas, the first of four children. As we grew up, everything around us changed regularly: climates, cultures, houses, schools, landmarks, and circles of friends. Only the furniture was constant. We didn't know what our father did except that he wore a suit, went to work during the day, and attended cocktail parties at night. Now I know: his job was to get people to tell him things they shouldn't have—to gain their trust while keeping his own loyalties deeply hidden: the craft of espionage. His big presence, his love of making things, his scary intelligence and a syncopated rhythm of curses, mottoes, and nonsense noises framed our understanding of who we were and what this transient life of ours was all about. We accepted the universe according to Poppa or rebelled against it—but we never questioned the basic framework until much later.

When people ask me where I'm from I still don't know quite what to say. Living outside "the States," I was equally proud and confused about who we were. Americans abroad stand out from other people. Our limbs are rangy, we have bigger mouths than other people, and the way we talk has a flat, grating sound, like the machinery we make. We have a manifest destiny in our gait and a blank expression in our eyes. People think of us as friendly but false. I thought we were better than they were. I roved the countryside with other American kids on our superior American bikes.

In 1963, after ten years of living mostly in German-speaking cities (nearly twenty years for my father), with brief periods in the States
for home leave, we moved to Israel. Not long after our arrival in Tel
Aviv, one Saturday night, I went with a small crowd of young Americans to see a movie about Marco Polo that was playing at the embassy.
Ten years old, I was thrilled to hang out with the American kids. The
Saturday night movie was the social event of the week. It was the
beginning of a brand-new life in a brand-new world. The embassy
itself seemed like a very important, brand-new place. Access to it made
us important. After the movie we waited outside the embassy's front
entrance for our rides with our embassy mothers.

We didn't know it, but President Kennedy had just been killed.
A crowd of Israelis had gathered on the sidewalk in front of the
embassy, peering in through the virile architecture of the entrance,
straight planes of concrete and glass. "Look on my works, ye mighty,
and despair!"[1] the building said to them. We were on the cusp of our
Ozymandian moment. We had pushed the Soviets and they'd backed
off; we were winning the space race and Kennedy had promised we'd
be on the moon by the end of the decade. We'd made rock 'n' roll and
the Ford Mustang.

The Israelis on the street recognized us as the children of the
wounded nation and left a discreet semicircle around us, watching
us as though we embodied the riddle of power and violence that
had been posed by Kennedy's assassination. We paid no attention to
them—they were foreigners. But they knew something we didn't: JFK
was dead.

Marco Polo (Gary Cooper), heroic discoverer of the East, had
filled us with swashbuckling urges. Young boys will always test a new-
comer with small violence, to determine the new boy's place in the
pecking order. One of them, the son of the Air Force attaché, came
dive-bombing toward me two or three times, punching me in the
stomach with his imaginary rapier. On the third pass I hit him back,
and then we were on the ground, flailing about not far from the feet
of the Israeli onlookers.

---

1 Percy Bysshe Shelley: "Ozymandias."

Later my father reprimanded me. He was a new boy himself and didn't want to attract undue attention. He was the new CIA station chief here, but his cover was as a mid-level diplomat, a second secretary. He said I should have taken the other boy around the corner and "beaten the crap out of him," but since we'd fought in public, I was forbidden to go to the movies at the embassy for the next two years. My social prospects at the American embassy suddenly declined.

We joined the club at the Sharon Hotel and things began to look up. The Sharon was a gorgeous stucco building right on the Mediterranean shore that had tennis courts and a big saltwater pool with a high dive. All kinds of privileged people, mostly non-Americans, mingled there. It was a good place for my father to meet people unobtrusively. He arranged a family membership. It suited him to have his kids spend time there—lavish living and having one's kids at the pool were part of the cover. This was a departure from Pop's Spartan mode of child-rearing. His house was TV-free till he was in his eighties, comics were not allowed, and mindless pleasure of any kind was frowned upon. Even so, over the next four years I practically lived at the Sharon Hotel. We lived only a few blocks away, in Herzliya Pituach, ten miles north of Tel Aviv, and I could walk to the hotel or ride my bike.

There was a trail that led to the beach through a fissure in the cliff that rises on that part of the shoreline. I spent many evenings

wandering along the beach at dusk or up to the mosque on top of a neighboring bluff. Sometimes I rode on old roads I'd never seen before. I remember once riding slowly through an ancient Arab neighborhood, mysterious, old, and crumbling, and then a mile or two later, coming upon a cluster of white South African houses, sparkling with new money and optimism. The Arab kids my age must have thought I had been superimposed on their ancient landscape, like a strange, modern ghost. I didn't think about it much. I lived in the modern world and hung out with my modern friends. In the daytime I learned to play tennis and Ping-Pong and I tried not to stare at women from France or Greece who wore bikinis and were married to wealthy Israelis or to diplomats. I drank Orange Tempo and went bodysurfing.

Lying on the beach, I watched the Mirage jets do their daily aerobatics, streaking in from the horizon faster than sound and splaying straight up at the last minute into the stratosphere to avoid crossing the border into Jordan. Before the Six-Day War in 1967 and the occupation of the West Bank, the country was shaped like a wasp. We lived at its waist, eight miles wide. The jets were nearly out of sight directly overhead when the sonic booms hit the cliff. I loved it. I nursed fantasies of becoming a fighter pilot. I played in the dunes. I turned brown and wore flip-flops. I tried not to look too American.

Dancing in the warm waves and getting pickled in the saltwater of the Mediterranean is my idea of heaven, even now. Maybe that's where I'm from. The Sharon Hotel.

* * * *

My father was a well-built man of average height. His features were stern but beautiful, almost feminine, except for his twice-broken nose. When we were young and he was still with "the Company," his hair was black and neatly slicked back. He smelled of Vitalis. He projected intelligence, urbanity, and wit. He was a wonder to some, invisible to others. He showed a generous interest in those who were most unlike himself. He made friends easily; it was a part of his job he genuinely enjoyed.

At home he was typical and weird, like any father—a living paradox. But he could be intense. His mood dictated the atmosphere in the house, and he was often irritable or explosive. In the early days he taught us to play chess and took us camping and sailing, and we had fun. But he was a tough disciplinarian who required absolute quiet, shouting "RUHE!" ("Quiet!") and banging the table when he read the paper or listened to radio broadcasts. He loved us in a deep, rough way, but he was so absorbed by his work that he sometimes seemed annoyed by our presence in the house. He always brought a newspaper, a reference, or a history book to add to the stack of reading material at his end of the table, left over from dinner the night before. My mother backed him up in any decision he made or any quarrel that broke out, as though life was nerve-racking enough, and the less she had to do with questions and outcomes the better. She worked in the CIA before he joined up and I think she missed the independent life she'd led in her twenties. She'd worked in Tokyo and Rome before she got to Berlin. She enjoyed social scenes and had a serious career as an international horse show jumper.

Kathryn Falck, or Betty, was thirty-something when they married. She provided for all her husband's personal needs and protected him for over sixty years. Pop often upset her with his hard manner and his foul language—she was a good Catholic girl—but she kept it to herself. She admired him and wanted to thwack him, by turns. But she stayed in the background, did all the chores, and kept everything neat

and clean. She loved him, and was tenacious in her love. She was the only person in the world who could do it. My father utterly depended on her. I imagine she bore the worst of his many frustrations when just the two of them were in the house. He flirted with her sometimes; he was unpredictable. A few years ago she complained that he never said good morning to her. Every day from then until he went into the hospital, he came down the stairs for breakfast and shouted a large, singsong "Good Morning!" to the whole house. She rolled her eyes, partly in grudging humor, partly in exasperation.

Now she lives in a small retirement community not far from the house. She misses him more than she thought she would, she says almost every time we speak. She regrets that she didn't realize "what a wonderful man, what a catch" he was. Without the constant hard work of keeping him fed and fielding his outrageous whims and irritations, she has lost much of her sense of purpose. Her short-term memory is ebbing too. But she talks a lot more than she did, and she's comfortable showing sides of her personality I'd never known. She invites me for dinner, forgetting that I am on a job in California and have been for over a month, and mentions that she is beginning to confuse my father and me. It was a mistake to call me by the same name as his, she says. I agree completely.

When we were little kids we lived in our own worlds, interrupted only slightly to make brief appearances as "such good children" when cocktail parties occurred at our house. My sister Barbara, two years younger than me, watched everything with a wary eye. She became a wonderful painter/photographer with a fine, cynical sense of humor. Alex, who arrived three years later, was the darling, the butt of all jokes and teasing. Barbara and I treated him as if he were a pet, or our adopted child. We adored him, as did everyone. He listened wide-eyed to everything and said very little. He became a deep-thinking wooden-boat builder and a perfectionist. The youngest was Jamie. He was a baby when we got to Israel. He did most of his schooling later, in Maine, and spent more time on his own with our parents than any of the rest of us did. He took on some of our father's mannerisms and became a bronze sculptor, painter, and metalworker. All four of us work with our hands; all of us are more than a little wary to be out in the open; we work hard

and we make relatively little money. We get along with one another
better than most siblings I know. We each have different tastes and tem-
peraments but we all share a relatively dark worldview. As the current
recession was getting under way, Pop said, "You know, I'm beginning to
think I did pretty well by you four. None of you have a sixteenth floor
to jump out of."

When I was about twelve, he and I started shouting at each
other, mostly about politics, across the dinner table. The others
endured years of this contention in silence. Toward the end of our
stay in Israel, he proposed that I go to a boarding school—Groton
School, the same tiny upper-crust institution for boys in the middle
of Massachusetts that he and many of his male relatives and forebears
had endured. I had a bad four years there before I got out and discovered Vermont, where I worked in a factory, on a farm, and with
carpentry crews, wandered about the East Coast in a '66 Chevy, and
finally embarked on a career in the theater. I carved out a shaky
existence as an actor/director, on the edge of poverty and on the
move most of the time. The rhythm of change accelerated and I
rarely stayed in one place more than a few months. I fell in love with
Shakespeare and made my living working with his plays. I had a small
family of my own, full of love and wonder, which fell apart, unlike
my father's, which was made of tougher, more traditional stuff. Eventually I found my way back to the Vermont woods, where I'd built an
octagon house, and somehow kept doing my theater work. I made
a life for myself that was far removed from the one I'd begun, but
many unanswered questions, along with a good deal of restlessness
and confusion, remained. I felt I would never know my place in the
world until I knew more about who my father was and what he had
seen and done in his travels.

*   *   *   *

As I was driving up to Maine for the first interview, having stopped off at
a Radio Shack for a twenty-dollar tape recorder, batteries, and tapes, my
head began to ache. I noticed, as I pulled into the driveway, that I was on
time, which was unusual, and that I was more than usually anxious.

We sat at the dinner table, where we'd often sat to read or talk, only now we were in Brunswick, Maine, and the table had stayed in one place for decades. It would never again be packed up carefully and flown to other hemispheres along with the rest of the furniture. He was in his usual position where he could see everything. I sat alongside, facing him. I remembered angry things we'd said to each other at this same table, at this same angle, about Vietnam, Communists, free love—or just about anything.

My mother puttered around in the kitchen, where she could keep an eye on us, over the counter he'd made for her. Soon after they moved into the house he knocked out the wall between the dining room and the kitchen, supported the load with a timber frame beam, and installed a broad counter with cabinets between the two rooms so they could be always in touch and yet remain in their separate realms.

At eighty years old his hair was white and disheveled, and he wore clothes that were comfortable, frayed, and stained with woodworking materials. He raised an eyebrow at the tape recorder and started to talk:

FATHER: Well, I never took the work that seriously. For a lot of people it was their whole life. In 1972, when I left, a retired officer received an average of eighteen monthly installments of his pension. The average retiree was dead in a year and a half. But for me, other things were much more interesting. Playing squash, for instance, or making things out of wood. Which is another reason I wasn't very good at spying, because I didn't think it was a serious line of work. It really wasn't. . . . It's a game. A puerile occupation. People die, and your career is on the line and people get mad, and . . . there's a lot of uproar. There's a lot of uproar. But that doesn't mean it's serious, does it?

SON: You said sometimes you weren't sure it was worth it.

FATHER: You watch and you see what happens. For example, the so-called missile gap during the Cuban Missile Crisis.[2] I was between posts, stuck in Washington, in the war room, keeping track of things. I had pins all over the walls on maps that showed where everything was, the warheads, the

---

2 The Cuban Missile Crisis in October 1962 was a testosterone-filled game of chicken between Kennedy and Khrushchev, compounded by all the testosterone-filled politics surrounding both men, played with nuclear bombs.

ships, the blockade. All of our reporting showed that there was no crisis, and certainly no missile gap, but they needed a crisis for political reasons. There was an election on. As there always is; it's an ongoing circus. And this just went on and on and on and on. The whole Bay of Pigs operation, which never should have happened. And Vietnam, which never should have happened—and now, Iraq and Afghanistan—it never stops.

There's the case of a Chief of Station we had out in Indochina in the sixties who was an unrepentant blowhard.[3] The day he arrived he said, "From now on I want all reports cut in half, so type up two reports for every one turned in by our case officers." At the end of thirty days, he could announce that he had doubled the output of his station. Just to take up more air. And he got away with it, you know, and got to be one of the very top people in the Agency. Totally amoral. But then he got mixed up with a double agent[4] who had been dealing with the Libyans under the table. And that did him in. Also, he got involved in the Ollie North conspiracy. And that . . . that stupid admiral, who's still . . .

SON: Poindexter.[5]

FATHER: Poindexter. Who's still in the government.

SON: He just got kicked out.

FATHER: I don't think he did.

SON: For running a gambling pool for assassinations on the Internet?

FATHER: That's the kind of thing that I found discouraging. Everything got more and more corrupt, as I watched. There was a progression of corruption in every aspect of American life, and of course it was as much within the Agency as it was within the Pentagon, as it was within the Congress, as it was within the presidency—it was everywhere. Pervasive. Bush isn't the cause of any of this; he's just a symptom of a country that's very sick. I saw it more clearly afterward, of course, but that was part of what was going on, and part of why I didn't take it very seriously, because

---

3 This must be Ted Shackley, a name I remember hearing occasionally in side-conversations between my parents, usually without much heat, as in, "Yeah, that was Shackley . . ." CIA station chief in Miami during the Cuban Missile Crisis and in Laos and Saigon, 1966–1972. Widely associated with "black ops."

4 Edwin Wilson.

5 John D. Poindexter was an admiral in the Navy and the national security advisor under Reagan.

the intelligence wasn't achieving anything. People weren't paying attention to it. That reached its height under Casey and Reagan, when all
intelligence became politicized—as it has remained ever since.

SON: You became a high-ranking officer by the time you retired. What
kept you going? Did you have a deep feeling for your country?

FATHER: I used to.

SON: Where did that come from?

FATHER: I went to West Point, didn't I?

*   *   *   *

One day after school in Israel, I was sent to the embassy to visit him, for
a reason I have long since forgotten. It was the only time I remember
going there after the Marco Polo incident. I went up the elevator.
Low-ranking officers must work farther away from the lobby than the
important people, I thought. When I emerged from the elevator on
the top floor, there were armed Marine guards on either side of me, in
puttees, standing at attention, carbines held vertically in front of their
noses. That seemed odd; no other floor had Marine guards. The office
suite was spacious and airy, with a pleasant view of Tel Aviv and the
blue sea. My father ushered me in and said he had to go across the hall
for a moment to see the ambassador, and he left me alone, instructing
me not to look in *that file*, pointing at the one that was left open. I
looked. There was a huge, fat folder, and on the tab it said, in his neat
block handwriting: *Kim Philby*. I didn't know who that was but I'll
never forget the name. I later discovered a racy, bohemian magazine
at home (*Evergreen*) that featured an article about Philby, the Soviet
mole. I didn't get it. I didn't realize there was anything to get. Eleven or
twelve years old, I was mesmerized by the hip counterculture allure of
the magazine and by photographs of beautiful and mysterious women.

Nowadays, having been a father myself for thirty-some years, I
know the keen wish to have my son understand something of my
deepest interests. Had it been me, I would have brought him into
that office purely to let him know that I was more important than I
seemed, hoping he would figure out what I was up to without badly
compromising my position. I never thought about what the big office

meant, or why I should know about Kim Philby. My young American classmate at the time, Ryan Golding,[6] figured it out. Ryan asked his father about it. Golding senior, a rising diplomat who had pictures of himself shaking hands with Kennedy on the wall at their house, said, "Yes, you've got it right. But don't tell anybody. Especially Johnny." So he never did, and I remained in the dark.

I opened a bureau drawer full of handguns one day when I was alone at home, probably looking for more magazines. I pretended I didn't see them. I didn't want to get caught snooping, even by myself.

My childhood abroad ended when we were evacuated during the Six-Day War. At last, I thought, we were going home. I spent an uneventful summer in a Maryland suburb of Washington, and then my father drove me up to Massachusetts and dropped me off at the boarding school.

I was embarking on my first solo adventure. I felt excited and optimistic. Every turn in the past had brought new openings, and this move was surely the best of all. But after I arrived at the school I slowly understood that my life would be less delightful than it had been, and that the America I thought I belonged to was a fantasy. We were not smarter than other people, nor more beautiful. We were simply more powerful. Groton School was there to demonstrate this.

In my third year there I turned sixteen. While Nixon bombed Cambodia, I struggled to get through the days. I was a social misfit and I faltered in my studies, which no longer illuminated the world as they once had. When I could get away with it, I escaped into the woods surrounding the school. At night I crawled into a trench in the underground bowels of "Hundred House" with one or two deeply loved friends where we smoked Camels, railed against the war and injustice, talked about our heroes—Dave Van Ronk, Jimi Hendrix, Janis Joplin, and the writers—Hesse, Silone, Beckett, Malcolm X— and tried to make sense of our upside-down world. There were a few special places at the school that offered me solace and a feeling of safety: the chapel, the woods, and that dank place in the dirt under Hundred House.

---

6 Ryan Golding is not his real name. Throughout, I have changed the names of everyone except members of my family, and figures who are in the public record.

One afternoon in the spring of 1970—Parents' Weekend—I found myself in a crowded room at the Headmaster's House. My parents, who rarely came to these events, were there. I stood in the game room holding a can of orange soda, waiting in line: the headmaster had a bumper pool table!

It was about the time of the killings at Kent State: four students slightly older than me had been shot to death at Kent State University, in Ohio, by young men from the National Guard; the students had been watching a demonstration on the campus green to protest the illegal war in Cambodia.

A woman in her midforties approached me. She was dressed unfashionably, like a dowdy flapper, seeming as much out of time as out of place. She was the new wife of my faculty advisor. I think she felt awkward, out of place. Perhaps she felt some kind of kinship with me and wanted to show it. But she had nothing to say, so she said, "Isn't it marvelous that your father and Neddie were in the CIA together all those years ago in Berlin?"

Despite the fact that I'd been in trouble since the day I arrived at the school, Neddie (my advisor, her husband) and I had never talked to each other more than twenty perfunctory minutes per year. He had no children of his own, and outside of class he had no idea how to talk to one. His wife must not have realized that Neddie had taken a vow of silence on this topic. Perhaps she wanted to be part of her husband's earlier life, which must have thrilled her. Or, excluded from conversations with other masters' wives, she just wanted to talk to somebody, and the only one who'd listen was an acne-ravaged rag of a boy, a fellow creature from the bottom of the heap.

Neddie and my father had been classmates at Groton, which was then, I imagine by looking at the old sepia photos, even drearier than now. They ran into each other again in Germany. My mother had told the story of how Neddie had ridden hundreds of miles on his motorcycle through the pouring rain across the ruined countryside—the Soviet Zone—to appear at their wedding in Berlin. The picture of this tweedy, myopic man on a motorcycle seemed farfetched, if not impossible.

Neddie's wife and I stared at each other. She thought I'd known. We stood there in a numb silence.

The idea seeped into me. Poppa. Berlin. The CIA. Neddie's wife's smile faded away, as did her entire self, like a Cheshire Cat trick in reverse, and my mother slipped into view, peering at me. She was tall and smoked a cigarette, very sleek. Neddie's wife must have confessed her indiscretion to Neddie and he must have passed it on to my father. My father must have dispatched my mother from the next room. She and I had the following exchange:

"Is he in the CIA?" I asked.

"Yes, isn't it marvelous?"

"Yes."

It was indeed marvelous, but not in the colloquial sense. I couldn't think clearly. I'd never thought there was anything unusual about our lives, but in that moment things started falling into, and out of, place. During our stays abroad we never lived in embassy housing (we always knew someone's father's rank by the kind of house they lived in), nor did we stay in any one place long. Instead we moved from house to house at yearly intervals, something nobody else in the diplomatic corps found necessary to do. We children were told at the end of each year that something had gone wrong with the plumbing, but it must have been because it would have taken about a year to bug every room in the house. Ah, I get it now, the plumbing!

Among other things that suddenly made sense, I remembered a long drive out into the desert in his Ford Falcon. We stopped in the middle of nowhere. Pop got us all out of the car and passed out peanut butter sandwiches wrapped by my mother in wax paper. He dove into the trunk and withdrew a small pruning shears. I'd never seen him handle a garden tool. He darted about quickly, clipping bits of shrubbery, keeping a lookout on the horizon. There was a fantastic dome a mile or two in the distance beyond some barbed wire. It was the nuclear reactor at Dimona,[7] I learned later. He tossed the clippings and the shears into the trunk, banged it shut, herded us into the car

---

7 Israel's nuclear reactor sits in the desert not far from the city of Dimona.

again, turned around and drove the three or four hours back home. I hadn't thought much about any of these oddities at the time. Now I was standing in the Headmaster's House in my jacket and tie, hanging on to my can of Orange Crush, staring at my mother's face. Bits of memory were knocking loose like old plaster, revealing the bricks underneath.

Chapter 2

A Soldier in Training

"Perpend, and give ear."

—Fool, *Twelfth Night*

My father loved to tell stories, crammed with facts and references, and driven by passionate conviction. They were tall tales that sounded almost true. These days, watching what's going on in the world, when I hear or read stories that sound raucously false, I feel reassured—I'm in familiar territory; I can go to work deciphering the story. It's the smooth, quiet stuff that I've come to mistrust. In any case, I liked hearing my father tell the same old implausible mythologies.

We came from a line of Scottish cannibals. (There were cannibals in the Highlands well into the 1700s—didn't I know that?) Along the way some of these bogtrotters, so he called them, lumbered down from the Highlands and became prosperous textile merchants in Aberdeen. After a century or two of doing very good business, the other mill owners discovered that the Haddens had over time diverted a great deal of river water toward their own mills. They were promptly run out of the country.

In America, undeterred, they got into the China trade, clipper shipping, and made their way to social prominence in New York City. To make the most of it, they imported worthless trinkets packed in reams of the finest silk. The trinkets were carefully tallied, taxed, and thrown away. The silk packing got through untaxed and made their fortunes.

When clipper shipping waned, no Hadden would so dishonor himself to make the switch to steam. The last of the fortune ran out during the Depression. My grandfather, who had a firm with employees to pay but no jobs to do, kept a town house on the Upper East

Side and a country house in Connecticut, and he sent five children to the most expensive schools. My grandmother claimed the only phone book she needed was the Social Register. Their style of poverty was not dire. But it was a change. No longer did footmen who attended coaches-and-eight wear silver buttons bearing the family crest. The sum of my father's inheritance was a handful of silver buttons. He affixed them to pepper grinders that he made and gave away as Christmas presents. On the crest, a snarling griffin's head floats over a bar with stripes, and a scroll beneath reads, *Suffer*. All of this seems hardly plausible to me now, even though I have held the buttons in my hand. They were real. But reality is an ephemeral thing. I can't find a picture of the crest anywhere.[8]

*   *   *   *

When I was very young, my father and I played chess. He crushed me every time. I had no instinct for the extended logic of defense and attack. Later, when we taped these rather formal conversations, the angle of observation and the position of our limbs were much the same as they always had been. It occurred to me one sleepless night that these interviews were like those chess games. He talked about the history of espionage, making obscure references that I didn't recognize, and seemed to get a little bored by my questions. He downplayed the significance of his work, a "puerile occupation." Was my interest in his work, by extension, puerile? When I came down the next morning, all I knew was that I wanted him to stay in the game. Maybe if I could seem less interested, it would provoke him to reveal something more than a detached and dystopian overview. I chose a King's Pawn opening—simple and conventional; I asked him about his childhood. He drew a slow breath and began:

---

8 According to *Aberdeen, 1800–2000: A New History*, edited by W. Hamish Fraser and Clive Howard, the Haddens were tightfisted and incestuous oligarchs that controlled not only the textile industries but also the city councils and the banks. They lost their influence by making bad investments overseas, and failing to upgrade the equipment in their factories. No wonder I dislike oligarchs. I come from the worst of them.

FATHER: My earliest memory, a kind of snapshot in my mind: going downtown to watch the riots[9], with Mishu, my grandmother's chauffeur. He drove this great big shiny car, you know, the kind where the chauffeur sat in front—he was in the open air, rain or snow— and the rest of the vehicle was covered over, where my grandmother would sit with her rug, in the back. Let's see, it was the Depression, so I was at least six years old. I remember very distinctly, when no one was paying any attention, being taken by this guy Mishu, this Russian chauffeur—I'd sit in the front seat with him, 'cause that was a lot more fun—and he would drive me down to Union Square, where the riots took place. The unions against the scabs, you see . . . and there they were . . . Christ, throwing things and beating each other up, with brickbats and anything that would come to hand, really having at it. It was fantastic. And here I was, standing outside this huge limousine, a Pierce-Arrow, with this chauffeur in uniform, cap and black boots. The two of us standing there . . . watching the riots! It was . . . [*he erupts in wheezy bubbles of laughter*] . . . it was just like going to a Broadway show!

These people . . .

"These people . . ." The small phrase gives me a chill. The way he says it leaks contempt for this rabble or those brainless clods; he is above the fray, dissociated and indifferent. I was used to the sound of this phrase but only later, transcribing our conversations, did I become aware of the chill. Maybe I could gauge what he was saying by noticing the temperature of my reactions to his language.

FATHER (cont'd): . . . these people never spilled out into the street. They stayed in the square fighting each other and kept it there so bystanders could watch without getting hurt. It was very civilized. Riots were very civilized in those days. Nobody got shot, nobody got hurt. The rioters got hurt, obviously, taken off to the hospital and whatnot, but the cops would

---

9 In March 1930, a demonstration by 35,000 people against unemployment and evictions was broken up violently by the police. Union Square was a major locus of dissent all through this period and beyond.

stand around and watch. Why get mixed up in it? Looking back on it, it was just amazing. . . .

SON: Did Mishu have any political sympathies?

FATHER: I hadn't the foggiest idea; I had no idea.

SON: And you?

FATHER: I just thought it was a fantastic thing to watch. I had no feeling one way or the other about it. The world was the way it was and you were the way you were, and you didn't think that it could be different. Or should be. I went out to school in the morning, and I went by bus to play football, across the bridge. And I'd roller-skate in the park on the weekends, or ice-skate when the pond froze over . . . coast on a sled . . .

SON: Do you miss the city?

FATHER: The city doesn't mean anything to me anymore. But back then, the city was like a little village. Within the few blocks, everybody knew everybody. Everybody knew the cop who walked the beat, everybody knew Mr. Pieczik, the garbage man, who had a horse, for God's sake. And a two-wheeled wagon that would tip up at the dump. And Mike, the coal man, who would come and open the manhole cover in front of the house, and coal would chute right down into the cellar, from the truck . . .

SON: Did you enjoy that kind of thing?

FATHER: Oh, yeah, wide-eyed, you know, watching what was going on [*laughing gently*], on 72nd Street, yeah, it was great.

Pop had taken one of my bishops already. I looked up the 1930 riots to find that the cops were not a benign presence—they wreaked bloody havoc on the workers.[10] But I didn't think to question it. He had pegged me as a forgiving audience. And so I was, especially when the words warmed up. Now he could slip through the rest of his child-hood without talking, for instance, about his acute loneliness. Or if it showed up, it would simply be there. It wouldn't be due to anything; it wouldn't mean anything.

FATHER: I went to Buckley when I was six.[11] I wasn't really interested in anything particularly. I was a very lazy person. Geometry . . . Geometry was a lot of fun, because you came out with a QED; you could prove something. That attracted me . . . Life was bearable if you worked hard. They made it hell if you didn't. You'd look up in the air for a moment, not paying attention, and there was Mrs. Stoddard's ruler right across your hand. Whack! [*laughs*] But no, I think you have the wrong impression of me, I was a very average student.

MOTHER: Oh, not every eight-year-old is sitting there reading the history of the Great War.

FATHER: Well, my father had the *London Times History of the Great War.* Pffft—it was all right there: Von Kluck, K-L-U-C-K, what a name, huh? Kluck . . . He was the general who almost made it. He was on the right wing of that great swing through France. Up to the Battle of the Marne—which, had he gone west of Paris instead of east of Paris, would have ended

---

10 *New York Times*, March 6, 1930: "Hundreds of policemen and detectives, swing-ing nightsticks, blackjacks, and bare fists, rushed into the crowd, hitting out at all with whom they came into contract, chasing many across the street and into adja-cent thoroughfares and pushing hundreds off their feet. From all parts of the scene of battle came the screams of women and cries of men with bloody heads and faces."

11 Buckley School is an exclusive boys' school in Manhattan. My father was there from the age of seven to twelve, and then was sent to Groton, following his three older brothers, Gavin, Arthur, and David, in descending order. The youngest, their sister Gay, is often omitted from the family narrative. My father was in boys' schools, if you include West Point, for sixteen out of his first twenty-three years.

the war—in 1914. Maybe. If he could have kept some connecting link between himself and a man named Von Bülow, who had the next army over. As the door swung. [*He gestures with his hand: the swinging door of an army.*] But when he came inside, the garrison in Paris attacked his flank, and so he had to pull back, and when he pulled back, the whole thing fell apart. The Battle of the Marne, so-called . . .

Two years before Pop died I put together a solo show with some of this material, omitting anything he'd crossed out before, showing the two of us going at it, a little like an elaborate Punch and Judy show. Von Kluck at the Marne became my opening monologue, a way for me to warm up into his eccentric mannerisms, practice his undulating eyebrows and the way he might land on a certain word like the growl from a tuba, with several dozen layers of irony—of the MAAR-RNE—and give the audience a taste of things to come.

I wanted him to see the show before I took it around, so I booked a performance at a small theater in Brunswick. The place was full. The local TV station came to tape it. I played for laughs whenever I could find them, but it was a little horrifying. On the video I can hear my father chuckling at what he later called my cartoon version of him. He seemed to appreciate the fact that I was tough on both of us. Softening our relationship would have been somehow disrespectful. The audience liked his character. He felt appreciated, and I got what I wanted. I could go ahead and play it elsewhere with a clear conscience. I'd taken my first pawn.

FATHER (cont'd): . . . and that was my introduction to military history. I think I was about eight. I would read it in the summer. During the summer we lived in Connecticut at the end of a dirt road in a wooden clapboard house. It was an old house, mildly comfortable . . . but it had no heat or anything. There was a chain in the lamp over the dining room table, this long chain, and on Sunday—we had a chicken every Sunday— we'd put a wishbone into one of the links of the chain, and after about twenty years it looked like some dinosaur had died! [*he laughs uproariously*]

I once met my grandfather, but I was too young to remember him. He had been wounded in the Great War. Had he been fighting against Von

Kluck's battalions east of Paris? I don't know. He was dying behind a curtain in some medic's station near the front, when a society lady happened by, volunteering as a nurse. She asked who was behind the curtain. A Lieutenant Gavin Hadden. *Gavin Hadden? Have him sent to Paris at once.* But he's a goner. *Do as I say.* Yes, ma'am. So he was saved by a society connection. But when he came home from the war he was not the dashing, vigorous young man that my grandmother, Rebecca Lloyd, had married. By the time my father was born, in 1923, my grandfather had gone quiet.

Gavin was a civil engineer and architect who loved curves. His great accomplishment was designing and building the Cornell Stadium. He took my father to a football game in order to study the question of stadium design. He saw that people generally gathered around the fifty-yard line, not necessarily to get the closest seat. So he built the stadium with parabolic curves that reflected the natural geometry of a football crowd.

The Depression was under way and these contracts dried up. My grandfather kept his people employed until his own money ran out. That, and a series of bad real estate investments, sank him. Then the story gets murky. He took a job with the Manhattan Project, developing the atom bomb. His old friend General Groves, who ran the project, hired him as an engineer, and as someone to talk to, someone to do his writing for him. My grandfather was the general editor of the official history of the project, in thirty-six volumes, about a third of which remains classified.

The fact that my grandfather worked on the bomb was never talked about at home. Even during these interviews I didn't ask a lot of questions about this, and if I had, I'm not sure my father would have known the answers. My grandfather was taciturn in any case; his involvement in the bomb made him almost mute. My father thinks his father died of pent-up anxiety, unable to speak and, finally, unable to breathe.

An irony exists: my father spent much of the last third of his career assembling a report on the development of the Israeli bomb based on his experience as the Tel Aviv station chief. Key to the report was the fact that the Israelis had funneled enough weapons-grade uranium (100 kg) from a plant in Apollo, Pennsylvania (NUMEC), to fuel some of the first atomic bombs in what would become one of the top five nuclear arsenals in the world.[12] The plant was run by Zalman Shapiro, a man who had very close ties to the Israeli secret services, including the Mossad. My father traced the disappearance of the uranium, confirmed that the isotopic signature of radioactive deposits he collected on plants near the Dimona reactor was consistent with material processed at NUMEC, and found that there had been deep collusion by American corporate and federal entities that were working with the Israelis. A brief mention of my father's report (author unnamed) appeared in a declassified document about the NUMEC investigation that was released in March 2014, but the report itself has not been seen. I thought there might be a copy in the attic, but the NUMEC box I retrieved from under other boxes of endless papers, though it contains dozens of essays and reports gleaned from newspaper reports and other public sources, carefully typed, duplicated, and filed, holds nothing like a classified report. Of information he'd gathered himself, I found only cryptic notes, handwritten in pencil on legal pad paper. There is also a pile of correspondence, including a letter from CIA director Stansfield Turner authorizing him to deliver his report to selected members of the Department of Energy in 1979, well after his retirement. He must have delivered the report orally, with these notes. It was his habit to leave as little trace behind as possible.[13]

More of this anon; for now it is enough to note that both my father and my grandfather toiled on important atom bomb reports. After sixty years in hiding, my grandfather's report was recently declassified by the Department of Energy and is available on the web. The CIA still denies the existence of my father's report.

Son: Who were the shining figures of your childhood?

---

12 The story is beautifully told in Roger J. Mattson's book *The Apollo/NUMEC Affair: A Nuclear Insider's Account of Israel's Alternative Path to the Bomb*. Mattson is a safety engineer and a former official of AEC and NRC. He led NRC investigations of the Three Mile Island accident, the Chernobyl disaster, and the Apollo/NUMEC affair.

13 See appendix for these notes on NUMEC.

FATHER: I never had any . . . shining lights.

SON: No heroes?

FATHER: Heroes? I only had one real hero, ever, and that was General Marshall. He struck me as pretty heroic. [*Pause*] Napoleon was quite a guy. Caesar was quite a guy. Those were the great guys. General Grant was quite a guy, and General Sherman was quite a guy . . .

SON: Sherman? And his scorched-earth policy?

FATHER: Look into it. He was a great man.[14]

SON: You said you were impressed by E. B. White. How did you first come across him?

FATHER: Oh, when I was a boy, reading the *New Yorker*—but at the time I was a lot more interested in Charles Addams and the cliché expert, Dr. Arbuthnot. E. B. White was really beyond me. All that stuff about the Blue Flower and the peace that was going to come after World War II—that struck me as totally nutty.[15] I didn't see that in the cards at all. But I came to see that he was an extraordinary man. And a brilliant writer. My father loved the *New Yorker*. The humor of the thing appealed to both of us.

SON: Well, it's still just about the only place . . .

FATHER: No, it's no good anymore.

SON: . . . the only place in American publications where . . .

FATHER: After World War II the humor disappeared.

SON: What about Booth? You know, the guy in the armchair and the crazy dogs? Steinberg? Feiffer? Steig?[16]

---

14 I did; from everything I read, though Sherman was the father of *Blitzkrieg*, he was a great man, far more complex than I would have thought. His job was to beat the South. In my opinion the North should have let the South secede. Slavery, if that's what the war was about, was on its way out in any case, hastened by European embargoes, industrialization, and the fact that slaves were a far greater economic asset to the South as free people. Our unwieldy and contentious political climate today is still clouded by the effects of having given the South a vicious beating. "Indivisibility" is not necessarily a virtue, especially when delivered at such a cost—and beatings do not teach wisdom.

15 My father was referring to *The Last Flower*, a story by James Thurber, another of my father's favorites, about the aftermath of WW XII, in which only a man, a woman, and a flower remain alive. White praised the story in the *New Yorker*, writing about the "beauty and fragility of this earth." He has mixed up the title and the author.

16 I happen to know that my father loved these guys.

FATHER: Nothing's as good as it used to be, that's a given. Everybody knows that things aren't as good as they used to be. West Point has gone down the drain; look what's happened to the old boarding school! Harvard College is gone now—I mean, nothing is left. I'm a typical old geezer and I know it. [*hard laugh*]

SON: Okay.

I stopped breathing. It struck me that the interview form was very familiar to me. All my conversations with my father were interviews. They were not reciprocal; they took place on his turf. We were like the father and son in Lewis Carroll's *Father William*:

"You are old, Father William," the young man said,
    "And your hair has become very white;
And yet you incessantly stand on your head—
    Do you think, at your age, it is right?"

"In my youth," Father William replied to his son,
    "I feared it might injure the brain;
But now that I'm perfectly sure I have none,
    Why, I do it again and again."

I noticed he wasn't breathing either. I was not the only one suffering here. We both took a long, cautious breath, and continued.

SON: Were you afraid of anything as a boy?
FATHER: I was afraid of Dr. X.
SON: Who was Dr. X?
FATHER: Dr. X was a mad scientist in this Gothic castle, where the scientists were, and he had one hand missing. And one after another in this Gothic castle people were being murdered—strangled, you see. And you saw this figure in a cloak and a mask. But it wasn't a mask. What it really was, coming out of a panel in the back—*Kkkkkwwhhh!* [*the sound of neck vertebrae snapping*] was this mad scientist who didn't have a hand. He had invented a thing called synthetic flesh. And so he has this hand, in a . . . It looked like a . . . Oh my God, I'll never forget this, in this thing that looked like a fishbowl, and it was alive! The hand by itself was alive, and he would reach in, and put it on like a glove. And when the moon was full [*he bursts out laughing*], he would go from room to room and just go— *Kkkkkwwhhh!* And he would put synthetic flesh on his face, to turn him so that nobody would know who he was. And then he'd come out and start murdering people. Incredible . . .
SON: And this frightened you. This was a horror film?
FATHER: Yes, my cousin Pam took me to see it. Oh God, I couldn't sleep.

My father's cousin Pam Symington was one of my favorite people. She was older than my father by two or three years. She once told me that the other cousins were a little intimidated by him. He was younger than they were, yet he arranged them into squads of Napoleon's armies, each commanded by a different officer. He was Marshall Ney.[17] Pam loved his weirdness, and he loved hers, I think. She always had a sense of infinite possibilities. Even in her nineties, she exuded a lightness of being and flower-girl sexiness that reminded me of a lost world.

---

17 Ney was a cavalry officer whose father was a cooper. Napoleon called him "the bravest of the brave" for his actions during the retreat from Moscow. He was one who forced Napoleon's abdication, and was later executed for it.

Pam took me in too, when I was wandering around in my late teens. We went on long walks in Vermont, near her house in the woods. She pointed out the way a tree was wrapped around a rock formation, or she would suddenly listen to something that I couldn't hear, and smile. She gave me books about Celtic legends and mysticism. She and my father couldn't have been more philosophically—or temperamentally—opposed, but they were two parts of a whole.

Not long ago she asked me to make her a pine box for her green burial, which I did. She pinned some of her favorite photographs on the inside of the lid, which she held balanced upright next to her wheelchair, and said, "Well, what are we waiting for? Put me in the box!"

FATHER: Yeah. She lived nearby. 66th, 68th Street, four blocks away. We really grew up together. Pam and I would listen to *The Lone Ranger*, and *Chandu the Magician*—BONG! And then there was a wonderful program, it had something to do with stomach powder or something, and you got the murder on Tuesday [*laughing*] and the solution on Wednesday. That was a great program. There was a whole fall when my mother was going to teach me by the Calvert System to save money by not sending me to Buckley. She was going to do homeschooling, and so I was out at the Symingtons in Cold Spring Harbor all of September, and all of October, and probably part of November, out there on Long Island waiting for my mother to crank up and get started. But she never did [*laughing*], so I went back to school late.

MOTHER: Who cooked the food and who took care of things?

FATHER: Oh, there was a cook; there was a cook.

SON: You were by yourself, with the servants?

FATHER: Yeah, there was Mishu, the chauffeur. There was a big staff out there, a guy taking care of the horses . . .

MOTHER: But the cousins weren't there.

FATHER: They were and they weren't. I didn't pay much attention to things like that; I was wandering around nailing two sticks together down on the beach. I remember horrifying my mother, because Mishu was an Irishman and he got terribly drunk I guess, and he wandered into a pond and fell over and drowned. And I remember telling my mother that he didn't drown, he was murdered! And my mother almost lost her mind, because she was worried that I might tell Aunt Elizabeth that she better get on the stick and find out who killed Mishu [*laughing hilariously*], and I remember her horror, trying to shut me up, telling me to forget it and go away!

SON: Do you think he had been murdered?

FATHER: Oh, I was convinced, as a little boy, yes. How else would he have gotten out into the middle of the pond and drowned? I mean, what an implausible story. Mishu. He was such a funny, funny man . . . I think he was Russian. And this riot in Union Square. Of course that was a bright shiny memory because those were such incredible cars, and for a little boy, it was unforgettable. I mean, if people are having all this uproar, how could we just sort of stand there and watch? I can remember—even as a little boy—thinking, this is a strange business.

SON: It was being fought by poor people.

FATHER: Oh yeah, workers and scabs, you know.

SON: And there you were with this enormous limousine.

FATHER: A perfect target, for mayhem.

SON: Which remained untouched.

FATHER: Absolutely, people paid no attention to it. Crazy. Civilized man! And we think the dinosaur is a funny creature . . . who didn't make it! Christ, he was here for a hundred and eighty million years. What are we? Fifty thousand? At the most. We're in our terrible twos. And there's no nanny around to tell us "No, don't do that! No! Put that down! Yes, the bomb: put it down! And, don't disembowel your little brother, what do you think this is?" *WHACK!* Hopeless.

* * * *

A few years ago I took my son Reilly camping in France. We criss-crossed the farmlands and spent all our money on cheese and café-au-lait in ancient villages. At night we drove our tiny rented car into out-of-the-way fields and put up a tent, and were as happy as trespassers can be. Only once, at the beaches of Normandy, did I think about the two wars that hammered France. It was only a trick of time that gave us the luxuries of peace and beauty in the same countryside where millions of boys had met their deaths or witnessed senseless carnage in earlier years.

Satan of Verdun, a pit bull mutt, who was said to have saved the French at Verdun by delivering a crucial message across enemy lines, surviving multiple gunshot wounds and dying in the effort, was one of a million dogs who were put to work carrying messages across the lines, dragging corpses, taking medicine to wounded men, locating mines, and a variety of dangerous tasks they could do far better than any human. Most of these dogs were killed during the war, and many of the survivors were put to death afterward, as unfit for civilian life.

In ages past, my father's side of the family did not produce many soldiers, nor any artists I ever heard of. They were inclined to choose comfortable occupations—business and the Episcopal Church. John Lloyd, my father's uncle for whom he was named, was a notable exception. When the US entered the Great War, Lloyd was studying at the theological seminary in New York, but he felt a calling to go overseas and minister to the troops. The seminary's administrators held him back, possibly because he was the only remaining son of a bishop[18] whose older son had died in childhood. So young Lloyd quit the seminary, enlisted, and was sent to the trenches as a foot soldier, where he carried a rifle and ministered to the men, to his father's horror and sadness.

I picture John Lloyd sitting in the freezing muck of a forgotten trench, cradling the head of a wounded soldier in his lap. The man's eyes drift away as death comes to relieve him, and John Lloyd is alone again, holding a useless bag of blood and bones. He sits in the eerie silence before dawn, before the shelling begins. When the shells come in, they howl in his ears, pushing at the edge of his sanity.

He survived the shells, the gunfire, and the terror, but was hit with mustard gas in France at the very end of the war. Opposing commanders of one more battle had not heard the news that the armistice had been signed and the war was over. He died six grueling years later of the effects of mustard gas.

During the war John Lloyd wrote his mother long, beautiful letters describing his comrades, to cheer her up. There was much he left

---

18 Arthur Selden Lloyd, author and Suffragan Bishop of New York, 1921–1936, was known for his high regard for children.

out of his news. Many years later my father took these letters and bound them into a book with oiled endpapers and green leather that he burnished carefully.

My father adored his uncle. John Lloyd, in his dying years, had played with his toddler nephew, and my father remembered accounts of these moments. His own parents did not provide this kind of attention. My father joined the army as soon as he could, following his uncle's footsteps to the next war. It was a tremendous disappointment to him to miss the actual fighting. He always thought of himself as a soldier—and I think some part of him wanted to establish a line of soldiers.

As my father's eldest son, I was given his and his uncle's names to carry on, but they never felt like my names. When I did not pass them on to my own son, my father was quietly distraught. I thought his concern was a matter of pride, or arcane tradition—my cousin, the third of the Gavin Haddens, was called "G3." The story of John Lloyd had not yet made a deep impression on me.

Now it does. I treasure the secondhand memory of my great-uncle. Imagining my father as a boy on the soldier's knee, his eyes looking up with trust and adoration, I am sorry he didn't get more of that. Picturing him as a boy lets me see things in him now that I either missed or deliberately turned away from when he was alive. He made beautiful gestures toward me, hand-binding a copy of *Romeo and Juliet* for me, for instance, after he'd seen me play it. Pop often surprised me in the later years with whimsical, generous impulses but I was too guarded to pay proper attention. I didn't realize there was no longer anything to be afraid of.

But though I kept an emotional distance, I felt an insatiable need to find out about this man, this father. I was curious about his keen interest in war—and I wanted to know the source of his anger. His expression of it was something I knew all too well, but what was its source? My own anger had grown to its peak during my years at Groton School. I wondered if he had found his at the school as well, when he was a boy, a little older now, after his uncle's death.

* * * *

SON: Was there any sort of violence at the school?

FATHER: No. The occasional guy would get beat up and there'd be the towel fights and the usual hugger-mugger, but . . .

SON: And how did you fare in all that?

FATHER: Oh, I'd join in with everybody else. Everybody beat up on everybody—I wasn't singled out. Except once. Once they made the mistake of stealing my sneaker. I remember picking up a lead pipe and chasing this guy and I was going to kill him. And you know, if three or four others hadn't jumped me, and . . . and held me back . . . I would have killed him. They left me alone after that.

SON: Why, though? Why did you . . . ?

FATHER: They stole my sneaker. That was enough, and I just went . . . I was absolutely out of my mind. I remember now, to this day, being so maddened, that I had no idea what was going on. I remember that very distinctly. It frightened them so that they left me alone . . . nobody ever bothered me again. [*He breathes hard, then laughs.*] I was—I was going to kill him.

SON: Yeah.

FATHER: So. I was lucky. [*laughs*]

SON: I got to that point once, one night. But with me it had been building up.

FATHER: Oh, no, I don't think I obsessed about anything, no. Except that I didn't like the school. I didn't like being there.

Many children suffer in their schools, by violence and the pack mental-ity of the playground, and by drudgery, damaging their creative minds. Private schools are not much different from public schools in that regard, except that boarding schools allow no escape for months at a time, which is hard, especially in winter. Especially in an all-boys, *Lord of the Flies* world. But in both cases children sit at their places and are told what to think for forty minutes at a time, with small breaks, for most of the day. Our method of education is primitive at best; it does not allow children the freedom nor give them the tools to become keen learners and collaborators. This is a great shame. Considering the unimaginable challenges we will face, our children should far exceed us in every way—and would, given the chance. And often do, miraculously.

What I object to primarily about the separation of rich and poor in our system is that it lavishes resources on one side and deprives the other, teaching young people on both sides that class divisions in this culture reflect the intrinsic truth of who we are, and that the separa-tions are mostly insurmountable.

When I was dropped off at the school at fourteen I had no idea how to conduct myself. I was used to an easy, unsupervised life in a land of the sun and the warm, rocking sea, and I did not make a quick adjustment to the frigid culture of a New England prep school. My guess is that my father and I, had we been thrown together there, would not have been friends. He was a Manhattan boy, closed and savvy, and a little dangerous. I was an odd duck, dressed in polyester, ugly ties and all. (My mother and I went to Sears one afternoon and bought all my clothes according to a list sent home to incoming new boys. There was no mention of Brooks Brothers on the list, though that's what most of the Grotties wore.) When I got to the school and watched my father drive away,[19] on a beautiful fall day in Massachu-setts, I was wide open and vulnerable. I wanted too much to have friends, and I was helpless in a fight. I came from a family that was supposed to have money and clout, but didn't. I knew nothing about this world; I was a perfect target.

---

19 Listen to William Hurt's reading of Tobias Wolff's story "Nightingale" for an exquisite rendering of a father's experience of this moment.

Neither my father nor I were happy there. My fifth form (eleventh grade) roommate owned a heavy bullwhip from Spain, which I borrowed late at night. I went outside to a clearing in the woods and cracked the whip in circles above my head until I was exhausted and drenched in sweat, the anger appeased for the moment. I remember lying in my cubicle knowing that it would be all right to die. Ever since then I have not been afraid of death, nor have I particularly tried to avoid it, though I have fallen in love again with life and, generally speaking, the living. I'm not sure my father ever did.

SON: So this kid stole your sneaker . . .

FATHER: . . . and I lost my temper.

SON: . . . and you chased him with a lead pipe. And you wanted to kill him.

FATHER: I would have killed him.

SON: Was that was the only time?

FATHER: That was the only time. I have a bad temper, it's true, but nothing like that, no.

SON: It seems to me that your temper was worse when you were working in the CIA.

FATHER: Of course. Look, you're always trigger-happy when there's any stress at all, sure. Of course I was.

SON: So how would you process that?

FATHER: By quitting. [*laughs*]

SON: You lost your temper all the time at home—how would you process it?

FATHER: It doesn't . . . help much to think about it at all. Just forget it, move on, do better next time. You can't live the day over again, can you?

SON: You say that you didn't take it all that seriously. That for instance, squash was more important to you than . . .

FATHER: You get rid of a lot of stuff by smashing a ball as hard as you can, but who knows? You can't make generalizations about the human animal. And it gets worse. Take a man who's hungry: Christ, look at the things he'll do. He'll steal; he'll murder; he'll kill. Make him hungry enough, and he'll do almost anything that he would never do otherwise . . .

SON: Did you ever kill anybody?

FATHER: No . . . [*slowly*]

SON: . . . yourself?

FATHER: . . . no . . . no, no, I never did.

SON: Did you ever recommend a killing?

FATHER: No, no. I was never put into that kind of a box.

SON: How did you avoid it?

FATHER: The nature of my jobs. It never came into question.

SON: So what was it? You said at one point that working for the CIA was not for anyone with a weak stomach—because you had to do things that were against all . . .

FATHER: You persuade a guy to go out and do something and then he gets killed. It's hard.

SON: These must have been signal moments.

FATHER: I can remember the first one, which was really quite overwhelming. Dr. . . . Dr. Mologen, at the seminary, the theological seminary. The agency hired him, and he uh . . . dealt with people my age, people doing my work, to help them over the problem of—were they doing the right thing? Is this something I should be doing? A psychiatrist.

. . . and he veered off into a story about Dr. Mologen, who must have been his psychiatrist. He slowed down, deeply focused on his memory of this man whose name I'd never heard mentioned before, and brought me along; he took me into his confidence. I was warmed by him, flattered. My attention strayed. A personal detail turned into a small sidetrack, and by the time I realized that I was off the scent, if I did, we were too involved in some other subject, and I'd forgotten what it was I was asking him. He was off the hook again. Had this technique become habitual with him?

He once told me that he'd overheard a person say (it was General Amit, the Mossad chief), "Hadden sounds like he's really talking to you, telling you all sorts of interesting things, but he's not. On the contrary: you realize, as you walk off, that you're the one who's spilled all the beans." My father was very pleased; it was the ultimate compliment.

Yet there was something to be found there in his prevarications, had I been able to hear it. Looking it up on the CIA website, I find that the CIA regularly employs psychologists to try to keep its workers' psyches together, like shepherds herding their sheep. It says that members of CIA families, who are in unpredictable and often dangerous circumstances far away from home, often require counseling. Really?

I was too busy looking for signs of my father's inner life to recognize one when he put it right in front of me. Mologen. A psychiatrist. A great man. "It's like Brecht," he said a few days later; "Be careful what you look for, because it's right behind you!"

But like Bluebeard's wife, I wasn't paying attention to what he said. I wanted to see what was behind the locked door.

SON: What was the prevailing mood at Groton about the war?
FATHER: The focus was on Germany. I remember reading *Mein Kampf*. We had this wonderful teacher, the crew coach, who taught German. He had all kinds of excuses for the Nazis, saying that the Jews were running

the country, and that no musician could get a job because the Jews had all the jobs, etcetera . . . But we didn't really pay much attention to him. The sympathy at the school was so overwhelmingly against all that was going on in Germany, you know. . . .

SON: Was that partly because of Roosevelt?

FATHER: No. The school was anti-Roosevelt, of course.

SON: Despite the fact that all the Roosevelts went to Groton.

FATHER: My father was violently against Roosevelt, but that didn't mean much to me either. I sort of wondered why the hell he felt that way.

SON: Why did he feel that way?

FATHER: Oh Christ, everybody of his class thought Roosevelt would bring socialism. WPA, paying people not to work, feeding at the public trough, as he put it: "What kind of crap is that?" You know. Everybody like him was Republican and against Roosevelt. He'd betrayed his class.

SON: So there you are in your last year; it's 1941. Hitler's on the rampage . . .

FATHER: Yes, and that May, you see, in my sixth form year, was the breakthrough in France. The Germans brought the French to their knees and won the war there. But later that spring I went home to Connecticut, and I remember my father coming in and saying that the Germans had just crossed the Russian border and that there was war between the two. And my father said, "Well, that saves us all, they're going to kill each other off."

SON: He was right to a certain extent.

FATHER: Yes, he was.

SON: You were at that age, ready to enter the war . . .

FATHER: I remember a number of us discussing going to Canada and joining the Canadian Air Force. We came close to doing that, but I didn't have the get-up-and-go to do it.

SON: But you were interested in getting over there.

FATHER: One thing was the war, and the other was that I wanted to get away; I wanted out. I wanted to be free. I thought I'd go to West Point.

SON: How was going to West Point equivalent to being free?

FATHER: I wanted to get away from everybody I knew, or knew about. I didn't want anyone paying for me anymore. But my congressman died. You had to have your congressman recommend you for West Point. He died on Christmas Eve. That put me off a year. That's why I went to Harvard.

SON: The next congressman made you wait?

FATHER: Yeah, he wanted to see what signing cadets over to West Point would do to him politically.

SON: That must have been frustrating.

FATHER: Of course it was; it was an early lesson in the way congressmen work. Or don't work. What a bastard.

SON: And now you were going to Harvard. Were you on scholarship there?

FATHER: No, but my brother David and I worked. We spent fifteen dollars on a Model A Ford. We used to deliver card tables for ladies' bridge to different houses. We would get five dollars for moving them. And five dollars in 1941 was fabulous. Since we had the car, one of the bridge ladies wangled us into taking part in the big Thanksgiving parade in Boston, and we got two dollars for that, for just the afternoon, wandering up and down the streets of Boston, under these big balloons. I was a ballerina, or some damn thing. I got all dressed up as a girl, and I remember going through upper-crust Boston, and there was my brother Arthur's former roommate at Harvard up on a balcony with his family. I waved up gaily at him, and his mother thought this was some floozy he was sleeping with! My brother told me this later. But we made a lot of money with that car. My brother and I were nice to the lady who assigned the jobs for student employment, and we took anything that came along. One job was working as stagehands at the theater at Emerson, the girls' college. There was a mad Russian who taught dance there, and he was always chasing the girls up and down the aisles in the dark, and that was sort of fun. [*laughs*]

SON: So you and your brother David were friends.

FATHER: That year. That year we were very close. And then of course, we never saw each other again much. Because I went off to West Point and he went to work in Flint, Michigan, in a tank factory, and I never got home, and he never got home much, so . . . Harvard was a vacation, that's all Harvard was.

SON: What did you study?

FATHER: I was ROTC to start with. And I took Math. We were doing integral and differential calculus, and History . . . oh, I took a course from Hocking[20] in philosophy. That was a great course. I didn't learn much, but it was a great course. Hocking's lectures were marvelous, but all the teaching was done by graduate students and they weren't much good. Harvard was a waste of time in that respect. You had to be Walter Lippmann or somebody to get whatever Harvard had to offer. Go to tea with Santayana.[21] If you didn't do that, you didn't learn anything. I loved the football games. [*laughs*]

SON: Did you play?

FATHER: No, I was too small. I took up boxing and lost my nose.

SON: What happened to your nose?

FATHER: Oh Christ, I was just too slow, you see, for boxing, and I got murdered. That's why I can turn it in a circle, like a crank, see? [*He cranks his nose vigorously.*]

SON: When did you first think in any kind of political terms?

FATHER: I wonder if I ever did . . . It was really after West Point, going to Germany and seeing what the war had done. The worthlessness of the bombing. It began with Pearl Harbor. I'll never forget hearing it over the radio. That was an epiphany; that made you think.

SON: What were you doing at the time?

FATHER: I was reading history. The opera hour was on, for background noise so I could read peacefully. Midafternoon, two o'clock in the afternoon, the opera was interrupted and the announcement was made. We were at war. Japan had attacked Pearl Harbor and sunk all the battleships. . . .

SON: You went to West Point. How did it go?

FATHER: Very easy. For one thing, the discipline was totally impersonal. At Groton, the discipline had always been totally personal. *Pffft.* There was the tactical officer, who ran your company. There were about sixteen

---

20 William Ernest Hocking (1873–1966) was an antidogmatic philosopher of religion, an idealist who wrote about human rights and "negative pragmatism," in which an idea works if it is true, and doesn't if it is not.

21 George Santayana (1863–1952) was a Spanish American philosopher and writer who coined the phrase, "Those who cannot remember the past are condemned to repeat it."

companies. There were two brigades—A to H and I to P, eight companies in each brigade, arranged according to height. And I was in C-2, because I was very small when I went to West Point.

SON: You were grouped by size?

FATHER: Yeah, why not?

SON: And West Point was a breeze?

FATHER: For the most part. In my third year, a number of us were given the chance to go to Oklahoma to learn how to fly, and I leapt at it. I thought it was going to be fantastic—but the guy who ran it wanted to know if I'd ever been able to learn how to ride a bicycle. [*laughs*]

MOTHER: You shouldn't have been too bitter about that, because your eyes weren't good enough to make it.

FATHER: That's true, my eyes, my eyes . . .

My father said that he lost his good eyesight while he was at West Point. During the war, the Academy ran an accelerated course of training to produce more officers for the war. Tac officers, men assigned to keep the plebes in line, knew that he was tutoring his fellow cadets late at night to help them get through, in violation of the curfew. The officers would bang the doors when they made their rounds to give him a signal before they came around the corner, so everybody could put their books away and stay out of trouble. The faint light of these sessions and the effort of intense concentration weakened his eyes.

SON: You played lacrosse at West Point.

FATHER: That's how I was injured. It went into the bone. They operated in February, and in May—this was in my last year, three days before graduation—they told me I couldn't have a commission. That was another moment. You see, you don't really learn things until they happen to you.

SON: Who told you this?

FATHER: Nobody actually spoke to me about it. Orders were published at noon, and then they'd put them in a sort of box, for official mail. It was the middle of the day. They published general orders, you see, and they were numbered . . . and number 25 or something was cut off with a pair of scissors, and just left in the box, that Hadden was not going to get a commission, or words to that effect.

SON: You'd tutored your classmates to get them through, but . . . wasn't that unjust?

FATHER: It was totally uncalled for, because I was perfectly all right.

MOTHER: But you were walking with a limp.

FATHER: That's beside the point. Maybe I couldn't run thirty miles with a full pack but I was all right . . . It was a bitter moment.

[PAUSE]

FATHER: (cont'd): I started to get angry. Nobody ever came and said anything to me; nobody said a word, not one. I went to the hospital to talk with the doctors and that didn't get me anywhere. Then I called my father and he got hold of General Groves. I knew General Groves by then, because his son was in my class. Groves and my father would come up to see us from time to time. They'd been working together on the Manhattan Project for several years now, and he really moved heaven and earth to help me. He got hold of the former surgeon general, who was a close friend. But the former surgeon general and the new surgeon general didn't get along well, so that fizzled out. But he was able to get me what they called an AUS commission, a limited service commission that would end with the end of the emergency. It wasn't much of a commission—I wasn't supposed to go overseas. But I joined my classmates in branch school and I was sent to Germany. Against all rules and regulations.

MOTHER: After you called the Pentagon.

FATHER: My name was at the bottom of the list, because of my . . . my number. What do you call those numbers?

MOTHER: Serial.

FATHER: My serial number was out of whack with all these regular army officer numbers, so I ended up in Bowling Green, Kentucky, building log roads in the swamp. [*laughs*] Corduroy roads, they call 'em. I went to a pay phone with a whole bag of quarters. I started punching them into the machine and I got the Pentagon. I asked for the G-3, because I knew that the G-3 was responsible for all appointments, you see, and I asked to speak to the commanding general in G-3. I got this colonel. "What do you want to talk to the general about?" So I told him the whole story. He said, "I really don't think you ought to talk to the general—let me see what I can do." So I got moved up the list and went to Germany. [*laughs*]

He had more sense than I did. That's what taught me the lesson, always start at the top. And never take no for an answer.

SON: You said that you'd expected to get to the war after graduation, but by now the war was over.

FATHER: It never occurred to me that we would be at West Point for more than a year. We would be off in the war.

SON: Do you think they should have sent you?

FATHER: That's what they'd done in the first war. They sent them all off early, and we thought, well of course they'll do the same thing this time, but of course they never got around to it.

SON: Why not?

FATHER: They didn't think the guys who'd been to West Point for a year or less had done them much good in the first war. I shouldn't have gone to West Point at all. I would have had a much better career in anything I might have done had I signed up and had a war career, rather than sitting there . . .

SON: . . . in officer's training. You think you should have joined up as an infantryman?

FATHER: I would have learned more in three minutes of combat than in five years at West Point. That's obvious.

MOTHER: When we were over there, he kept saying, "I should have been here, I should have been here." At one point he had tears in his eyes.

FATHER: Yeah, that's been with me all my life, that I sat out the war. Hey, turn it off a minute, I'll show you something. [*He retrieves a paper from a nearby pile*] Here's a letter I wrote to West Point. I wrote to them saying I thought it was high time that West Point had an ROTC program for those cadets who wanted to make the military a career. They didn't answer. [*chuckling*]

SON: Maybe they didn't understand the joke.

FATHER: In general, the army is not big on irony. In any case, I was in the Engineers. And then I met this guy in G-2 and he switched me over to, uh . . . to OSS.

SON: Before that you were rebuilding bridges?

FATHER: Autobahn bridges. Not in the construction end so much. I was in transport. I would go get liquor rations in Nuremberg and take trucks on the Autobahn to Berlin, stuff for the whole battalion.

SON: Why were you chosen for that?

FATHER: I was in Headquarters Company, and being a West Pointer, they didn't think that I would sell the whole goddamn thing to some black marketeer.

MOTHER: Then you had an experience driving to Berlin, that . . .

FATHER: They tried to hijack my truck. The liquor ration for the battalion was in that semi along with a lot of other stuff.

SON: So you . . .

FATHER: At the time Berlin was isolated deep in the Soviet zone, surrounded by Soviet troops, and the Autobahn was the only way in except by air. So I was driving along and all of a sudden there were trucks blocking the road, and Mongols sitting there with their submachine guns, all standing there in a line with those funny fur hats that they had. And my driver had gotten tired, so I had taken over and I was driving for him, and so I just took the thing and swerved over, *pfffffhphph* . . . and the whole thing went way up in the air, cause there was a concrete strip down the middle, and thank God the strip was level, 'cause God knows what would have happened if there'd been a dip. I never would have come back. And then I just went down the other side of the Autobahn, head-on into traffic. Of course there was no traffic for forty-five miles. We were alone.

SON: You were driving down the wrong side of the road . . .

FATHER: Until I got past this roadblock, and then I waited until I got to a crossover. And the other guy slept through the whole thing.

SON: So they would have stopped you . . .

FATHER: They would have taken everything and they would have shipped the two of us back on a train or something, to Berlin, and I thought that was pretty low, no way to behave. I didn't see any point in giving up the regimental liquor ration. I mean, good grief, first things first!

SON: That was mainly what it was, liquor?

FATHER: Well . . .

SON: What was the rest of it?

FATHER: Engineering tools and gear. Stuff, you know. War is not a serious line of work. Except for somebody like Patton.

SON: Who was the general who kept wanting to push the button?

FATHER: Oh yeah, Strangelove. [*laughs*] Curtis LeMay.

SON: LeMay.

FATHER: I worked for Curtis LeMay. He was an interesting man. My engineer regiment was transferred to the Air Force, 'cause they didn't have any engineers. We were rebuilding the Army-Air Force headquarters in Wiesbaden for the NATO–American Air Force headquarters. LeMay was shifted from the Pacific to Germany to take over as chief in Europe. He lost his temper the day he arrived, asking why the airfield lighting had not been put in place. Our regimental commander said, "General, if you'll give me fifteen minutes I think I can answer your question. I'll be back in fifteen minutes." And he went out and he came back, and he had a pile of requisitions three feet high that he had given to the Air Force chiefs, asking for the equipment. Wire and lights, and you know, all the stuff that it takes to do something like that. And none of them had ever been filled, not one of them. [*My dog, Leo, groans.*]

And LeMay! Hah! He collected every lieutenant-colonel in the headquarters, and there were a hell of a lot of them, 'cause that's the way the Air Corps worked, you know, they promoted every putz beyond their . . . they were all a bunch of bus drivers;[22] they didn't know anything. Fill out a requisition? They didn't even know what a requisition was. They were sort of like Bush. Requi-what? And he had all these Air

---

22 Bus driver is my father's word for pilot.

Corps officers out there, under our supervision, with spades, digging the trenches by hand, to lay the wire . . . LeMay. Crazy. Later became SAC Chief. Wanted to atom-bomb everybody, but that was his business: professional bomber. [*chuckles*]

How do I reconcile this kind of gallows humor with his passionate career-long effort to decry and prevent bombing? I don't try to anymore. I'm grateful he was unguarded enough to let me see the contradiction. He was kind of a cowboy himself, and maybe that's why he hated them so. Jung's shadow principle at play.

Next, another contradiction—his friendliness with Nazis:

SON: You had German doctors and professionals on your crew.
FATHER: I was in charge of building a railroad line into a concrete plant. I would get prisoners every morning from the POW cage, and take 'em to the job. You knew they weren't going to run away, because where would they get lunch? At the end of the day they'd all pile back into the truck and I'd drive them back to the cage.
SON: These were ex-Nazis . . .
FATHER: . . . waiting to be de-Nazified or something. And they worked pretty hard, 'cause they liked lunch. What else was there to do?
SON: Did you get to know them pretty well?
FATHER: There was a Luftwaffe colonel, SS colonel, really nice guy, and we'd chat while he was knocking spikes into the ties. [*high laughter*] Crazy, huh?
SON: So everything was going fine until this doctor finally caught up with you and sent you back?
FATHER: You had a physical each year. In '45 I had a physical, in '46 I had a physical, in '47 I had a physical, and each time they wanted to send me home. And I would say, why not just put my file back in the cabinet and forget about it? And they'd think for a moment, and then do it. It didn't make any difference to them. But in '48 my commission had run out. . . .
SON: The emergency was over . . .
FATHER: The emergency had been over six months, so they came to me and said you have to sign a statement saying you want to go home. Or you have to apply for a reserve or a regular commission. And I said, "Look,

I've been trying to get a reserve or a regular commission for three years and I refuse to sign a statement that says I want to go home, 'cause I don't want to go home. This is your problem, not my problem," and then I took a month's leave. I just left. I went to the Olympics in Switzerland and I went to Holland to visit some friends of the family, and I came back at the end of a month, and there was a note, on Friday, saying I was to report to headquarters on Saturday. And on Monday I was on an airplane, and on Wednesday I was on Westover Field, out of a job. *Ppphhphph.* [*laughs*]

SON: Westover, Massachusetts? Funny, I pass there all the time. They have these huge military transport planes that look like they're from the forties droning over the highway.

FATHER: That was my last day in uniform.

SON: And then what?

FATHER: Then my father said a guy—so many of these guys in his office were engineer generals—wanted to talk to me. He had a job that would interest me. He wouldn't tell me what it was, but I gathered that it was intelligence aimed at atomic energy research. What the Soviets were doing, that kind of thing. So I said, "What would that entail?" "Well, you have to go back to school to get a graduate degree in nuclear physics." I should have done that. I was too dumb. I said, "Look, from what you say it seems to me that you have a worldwide activity going on. Why don't I go back to Germany, and work for whatever it is you're doing there?"

And he said, "Go home and think about it," and I went home and I thought about it. I came back the next day and gave him the same answer. Then he called the major in and the major took me over to OSS, and there I met the same guy that I'd already been working for in Germany. And he said "What are you doing here?" I told him and he said "We'll hire you. But you'll have to get cleared now." Clearance, what was that? I'd already worked for them. But everything was new. I said "Okay, how long will that take?" Well, it would take three months. Oh, Christ.

Then instead of doing something useful, I bought a car in New York, a Buick Roadster. It had been used by a doctor who had taken the wall out of the trunk so he could put a body into the back of the car, and I thought that was pretty neat. So I got a mattress and put it in the back, and a sleeping bag, and I spent the three months driving thirty or forty thousand miles around the country.

SON: Where'd you go?

FATHER: I started by heading south. I went through the Smokies and all the way down, and slept along the beaches in Florida, and then went out to Key West, and then back up. I had friends in the army all the way across, and there was one in that airfield, Pensacola, so I stopped in Pensacola, and I went and saw my brother, and he was in Oklahoma, and I saw him in Oklahoma. I went down to Houston, and had a wonderful evening fishing there in Galveston Bay, then across the Panhandle, the Grand Canyon, and went into Southern California, where the Gestapo tried to stop me. The highway patrol. They thought I was an army deserter or something because I was wearing an army jacket, that I had a . . . *ddwhhwppp* . . .

MOTHER: He's never gotten over this.

FATHER: They kept me there for hours, while they put the car over a ditch, tore everything out. Stuck knives into the mattress. Crazy. So I said, "You know, I've spent three years over in Germany trying to take care of storm troopers like you, and now look at this." They didn't take very kindly to that.

I went to see the old lieutenant colonel of the regiment in Utah. He was a lush, and we used to carry him home and put him to bed in Germany every night. He was a Mormon, I guess that was his trouble, and he came home and died of cirrhosis of the liver, in Salt Lake City. But I didn't know that. So I turned up in Salt Lake City and called him, and his wife answered the phone. I asked for him, and she said, "Oh, didn't you know, he died." I said, "My God, I'm sorry." She invited me over and I spent a number of days with her. She had two daughters, and they showed me all over Salt Lake City. They drank nothing but Coca-Cola, which was sort of boring, but . . . They never knew what he'd died of, that he'd died of drink. Denial or something.

And then I went to see my old battalion chief who was living in southern California. Twentynine Palms. Then I went up the West Coast. One of the lieutenants in my company—he was D Company commander—his father was a contractor in Sacramento. I stopped off there to see him, a really nice guy, and he said, "We're farming." I said, "Let me help." And he said, "It's pretty dusty and hot," but I said, "Great, I've never seen anything like this."

This contractor had sold his business and bought three farms, a thousand acres each, and he had these big machines, tractors and whatnot, and he'd plow a field. Then he'd pay a guy fifty dollars to seed it from an airplane, and he'd take the tractor and harrow it or whatever one does. And then he'd go off to the beach for a month. By that time the whatever-it-was—barley, rye, and rice were the crops—was ready to harvest. We'd go down before dawn, to downtown Sacramento, and we'd pick up a wino. Kick a few of them to see which one was which, and we'd pick one of them up and dump him in the back of the jeep. And the bouncy jeep on this rough road out to the field would wake the guy up.

Then we'd stick him on the back of the harvester and one of us would drive. The harvester would cut, thresh, and suck the grain up to the funnel and the guy in the back would tie the sack to a pipe, open it up, and *ppthddrw!* When it was full he would close it and take the sack off. These guys were so good. In about three movements of their hand they'd have this thing sewed up at the top and dump the bag down a chute, and then it would be sitting there in the field. And you'd be driving this harvester. The first day you'd go around about once, maybe a little more than once. It would take a week to do a whole field. And then he'd pay another guy fifty dollars to come and pick up the sacks and sell them. He just sat there, he earned thirty-five thousand dollars a field from each crop, three crops a year. In 1948 that was a hell of a lot of money. He and his sons were sitting pretty and spending most of the time at the beach. It was a real eye-opener about American farming.

I went on up to Crater Lake, and Tahoe, and the Columbia River. I wanted to see all the dams, Hoover Dam, and up to Vancouver, and Banff and back, and I came back across the northern states. The Dakotas. I saw my brother in Detroit then, and finally made my way up through New England and back down to Washington.

My clearance went through and I was back in—by then it was CIA. They put me in training for a short time and off I went to Berlin.

CHAPTER 3

Changing Partners

"In times like these, I would take the hand of the devil himself."
—Winston Churchill

I was born in Berlin, during a week in June 1953 when it looked like riots in the eastern sector and the subsequent massacre might trigger another world war. My father was supposed to pick up my mother and me from the army hospital on the day of the crackdown, but it was a bad week at the office, and he did not appear. My mother hadn't heard a word from him for some time, and didn't know what to do. She didn't know if he was still alive.

I made my way back to Berlin forty years later, not long after the wall came down. I was rudderless, looking for answers—my little family had fallen apart and I was broke. My son Reilly, ten years old, was without his father on Christmas, and I missed him badly. Out of the blue, a friend gave me an envelope with a plane ticket and a key to an artists' loft in Kreuzberg, a Berlin neighborhood full of artists and Turkish immigrants near the old Wall and the River Spree. I went. I found some work at the old Babelsberg film studios playing the ambassador from a coalition of evil planets, worked with a wonderful troupe at the Chameleon Varieté developing late-night acts, and did a bit of cabinetry for a wealthy businesswoman. Berlin had become a gathering spot for artists from all corners of the world. I got to know people, heard a lot of jazz, and was tremendously revitalized by the overall scene. There was a lot of life in the dark hours. I saw very little daylight.

Without my usual routines, I became aware that loneliness was a constant state for me, not an occasional response to being alone, but a

weakness in my bones. I was prone to despair if I let it spread through me. One way to keep it at bay was to make friends with solitude; the other was to be never without a project, or several projects.

My project on the night before Christmas 1993 was to explore Prenzlauer Berg, a neighborhood in old East Berlin where I would be moving in a few weeks. It was raining slightly, perfect weather for my mood, riding an old bicycle around East Berlin at three in the morning. I came upon a thousand rats sweeping across the road, back and forth, scavenging the remains of an open-air market. I held my feet up off the pedals as I rode through them, hoping the wheels would miss them. I gradually lost my way and came upon a city square with a series of black-and-white murals painted on the walls of the buildings. They were copies of photographs I knew well but had never quite understood, taken the day I was waiting for my father at the hospital, five days old. One mural shows a young student throwing a Molotov cocktail at a Soviet tank. A young policeman, an ex-Stasi officer, the only other person there, posted no doubt by his new Western bosses to do penance on Christmas Eve, came over to me. We struck up a conversation, found we had much in common, fell silent, and stood there looking up at the images on the sides of the buildings. This is where I'm from, I thought.

* * * *

SON: What did you do when you got to Berlin?

FATHER: All I had when I got there was a telephone number. So I called this number. And this goddamn German answered the phone. I told him who I was—what was I supposed to do next? He told me where to go. I went there, went in the door and of course, I was really quite exercised. Here I was in the most supersecret agency of the United States government, and they had some goddamn German answering the phone, as watch officer? Well, he turned out to be the number two guy in the group, under Peter Sichel.[23]

MOTHER: He arrived at Peter's house, and I was there having dinner with him and Brian Weller. And in came this character, his hair standing up on end. He was furious because of this German. And all I could think of when I saw him was, Who in the world is this?

FATHER: And why?

MOTHER: That was our introduction.

FATHER: Who else was in the group in Berlin?

MOTHER: Walton . . .

FATHER: Walton was there.

MOTHER: And Daddy Bob Smith.

FATHER: And Daddy Bob Smith, he came with me. And Tom Polgar[24] was there, and Bibo Kraczlic. Hoffman was there. And the German . . .

MOTHER: Henry.

---

23 Peter Sichel, chief of station, Base of Berlin at the time. He is my parents' oldest and dearest friend. He came from a distinguished German Jewish wine family and after his career in the CIA he became a well-known wine merchant, taster, and writer in New York.

24 Thomas Polgar was a CIA founding member who was sent as station chief to Saigon in 1972 to pick up the pieces and destroy the files. His last telegram from Saigon, under siege in April 1975, said, "It has been a long fight and we have lost . . . Those who fail to learn from history are forced to repeat it. Let us hope that we will not have another Viet Nam experience and that we have learned our lesson." He then destroyed the telegraph machine and boarded the helicopter.

FATHER: Henry Hecksher.[25] Oh, and uh, what's his name, the one, you know, with the wife, and they were very serious-minded. Baker. Len Baker, yeah.

SON: Who was in charge?

FATHER: Peter.

MOTHER: Peter was in charge. And he'd come via . . .

FATHER: He'd been a captain in OSS, running agents behind the army into Germany, as the war was finishing up.

SON: He'd been through the war?

FATHER: He started in London . . .

MOTHER: He must have been the youngest one there.

FATHER: Just about. He was a German too, originally. As a teenager he'd made his way across Europe, black,[26] down to Lisbon—his family was being wiped out by the Nazis, you see—and had made it across to the States. Where he turned right around and went back to fight. Then he joined OSS. The day he arrived in Berlin, one of his higher-ranking case officers came up to him and said, "I'll give you six hundred dollars for your watch." And Peter said, "I want you to submit a complete accounting of your financial affairs, tomorrow, and should there be any discrepancy between what you hand me and what we find out about you, you will be dismissed for cause. Or you can simply resign right now." And the guy resigned. He was up to here in black market activity. But that was the atmosphere of the time.

SON: What was your job?

FATHER: You sent people out to look for people. Polgar used to say that the thing to do was to sit in a Berlin bar and listen. And when you heard something of interest, follow it up. But there were other ways of doing things. For instance, we had a wonderfully simple operation—we put an ad in the German press, looking for scientists. And when these guys turned up for the job, we'd touch on their political beliefs and see

---

25 Henry Hecksher, born in Hamburg, another founding member of the CIA, was involved in the Guatemala coup, assassination attempts on Castro, covert operations in Laos, and was the station chief in Chile, instrumental in the 9/11/1973 coup of the democratically elected government of Salvador Allende.

26 When my father says "black," he means "with false papers." Peter Sichel tells a very different story about his own life, and it is surely more accurate than this one.

how motivated they were, and if they weren't—next! And we got a nice corps of guys. East Germans would come over there—this was before the Wall—and some of them were very well placed. And having a scientific background, they had all kinds of great technical know-how. It was a great operation, dead simple.

SON: And where did you get the training?

FATHER: You just do it.

SON: So far you'd been building bridges and driving trucks . . .

FATHER: Well, they teach you the lingo—what a dead drop is and what a letter drop is and what a courier is, but how do you persuade somebody to do something? It's a little bit like running a company in the army, you have to do it your own way; you can't do it somebody else's way, so you just do it.

SON: How did you go about it?

FATHER: We'd get leads, for example, from the stream of refugees passing through Berlin every day. You'd never approach somebody cold. That'd be idiotic, you wouldn't know what you had.

SON: And then you'd work on an exchange, some kind of contract—money for information?

FATHER: Each case was different. Some would be asked to sign a voucher—the people in Washington were very sticky about expenditures. You say, "Well I gave it to XYZ," and of course you can't tell them his real name, and they say, "Oh did you, well what evidence do you have that they ever got it?" You had to have a receipt. It was so silly, because it was just as easy for me to dummy up a receipt as it was to lie about giving to some guy. But they love paper in Washington. There's no rhyme or reason to it. It's not like learning a profession; it's a trade. How does a shoemaker learn to make shoes? He watches somebody else make shoes, and once he's made his first pair, he's way ahead. Then he makes his second pair.

SON: Did somebody break you in, show you the ropes?

FATHER: Oh yes, I went with Len Baker to see what he would do, and read his contact reports, and then I would do it in roughly the same way. Len Baker was very security-minded; he placed himself in an office away from all the rest of us. We had Allen Dulles's old office in Berlin, on a place called Föhrenweg. I think it had been a Luftwaffe building. We were a little crowded but it was a nice place. But Baker said that's bad security for you guys, to be all working in the same building. He turned out to be right.

All espionage is about calculating risk. When you recruit an agent to betray his or her entire milieu, her people, you risk exposing yourself to those people too, if she turns, so you have to be very careful how you treat her. We had a crazy case officer who started sleeping with one of his agents and then he decided to drop her. So she got mad, and she started to go after him. Each morning she would follow him to the corner, and the next morning, to the next corner, until she got to Föhrenweg—where she watched him drive in to work. Then she sat there and noted all the license plates that went in and out. All of them! And started following them. All she had to do was see where someone parked at night and she was able to find out who it was. She was very clever. I think she must have gotten a list from Army Housing. So she rolled up the entire office, the whole Berlin base. Every name, every license plate, every car, every address, every telephone number. She had everything.

She even had Len Baker, because he would visit the office and she picked him up and knew that he was working in a separate place, and knew where it was, and knew who he was, and what his name was . . . So she called him and said that she wanted compensation—she had a list of demands. And Baker said, "I don't know what you're talking about, is there anyone there with you?" And she said "Yes, my Catholic priest is with me." "Let me talk to him," says Baker. And the priest said, "If I were you, I'd go easy on this woman, because I think she can do you a lot of damage. She has stories and she'll call the press. She's got you all wrapped up; she's got a card file and she's got a copy of the card file hidden somewhere else . . ." So Len Baker said to her, "You just stay where you are, and we'll see what we can do."

He called the Counterintelligence Corps (CIC) and turned her in, and CIC went to pick her up by following her telephone number. They were going to lock her up—and she realized this. When the car came to a stop at a street corner—these clowns—she jumped out and ran, and they lost her. She then called up and said "You better not try that again." So Len Baker went to pick her up and they put her on an airplane to West Germany with x-thousands of marks, to start a new life and all the

rest of it. [*laughs*] This was during the airlift. You had to fly out. Germans couldn't get out.

MOTHER: She came out pretty well.

FATHER: She did. She did very well. She was . . . Well, it was dumb to drop her in the first place. She was a good agent. It was Clouseau who did that. The great dancer.

MOTHER: He's the one flinging me around, in our wedding pictures.

The wedding pictures. I knew the wedding pictures, but only then, listening to my parents recall the old days, did I realize that I could look at them again and see a room full of spies. I suppose the same thing would be true of many of the old family pictures.

My mother loved to dance but my father proudly considered himself a lousy dancer. They laughed at the irony of it.

FATHER: He was flinging everyone around, is what he was doing.

MOTHER: He was a good dancer.

FATHER: A group of us used to have lunch together in Berlin. We would read the *Stars and Stripes* . . .

MOTHER: They wouldn't let me read the paper. You and Walton, and . . .

FATHER: No, there were things that . . . that weren't fit for female ears, like the story about the minister who got ants in his pants at a picnic and he had to drop his pants and they arrested him as a sexual offender. The *Stars and Stripes* had an ear for the news. They tried to have a story like that every day, so we would look for it and of course we'd find it. "Ho, ho, ho, look on page four, column three!" But we couldn't tell her what it was. Then there'd be roars of laughter.

MOTHER: I didn't want to go eat lunch by myself. I was relatively new then and I was the only decent . . . I mean, all the other girls there were really . . .

FATHER: . . . viable female . . .

MOTHER: I was the only sort of normal one. The men were very friendly, and I would say, "Who's going for lunch?" and we all went together.

SON: Was Hal Turner in that group? He was one of your closest friends at the time, wasn't he?

FATHER: Yes. I lived a couple of years with Hal Turner, and when I saw what sort of a life he had to lead—I thought holy Christ, what is society doing? He was gay, really the first gay man I ever knew—and I got to know him well. Interesting. I knew a psychiatrist in Berlin. We had recruited him to go through our agents. He'd worked as a psychiatrist for Zeiss Jena.[27] His job was to find out what kind of person would be good at grinding lenses. What kind of mentality, what kind of personality . . . ? The training was so long and arduous that to get to the end and find that the guy either didn't like the work or was unsuited for the work would have been a terrible waste.

They set up this program so they could weed people out. It was extremely successful—he never missed. All the guys who were recruited through this program did well and became permanent employees. Earlier, when Hitler came along, our friend was recruited into the German defense mechanism to set up a program to find people that would make good officers. Which he did. And it was extremely successful.

---

27 Zeiss is one of the oldest and finest manufacturer of optical instruments since the mid-nineteenth century. During World War II Zeiss used forced labor, and after the war a part of the company remained in Jena, East Germany, and made military optics, cameras, and microscopes for the Soviet Union.

And so we hired him to do the same thing for our agents. Who would make a good espionage agent? Is this man suited for it or is he somebody we should be careful of, stay away from? There were two things. One was being a good agent and the other was, is he honest? Is he going to be a double agent, is he going to compromise us? So he set up this program for us—and I was his case officer. I would pick up the prospective agent and bring him to a safe house and we would dummy up the guy's whole background, to protect him. But invariably in working these guys over this man would find out who they were, where they were from, what they were doing in life; he could identify them all with no trouble—he was that good.

One of his tricks was to have me play war games with the prospective agent—you know, board games with materiel and reconnaissance and battleships and so on, just like chess—and he would watch. It was all in fun, on the surface, but he got a good view of the person's strengths and weaknesses that way. Of course he got a good view into me too, but what the hell, we didn't give a damn about that. But he would analyze what kind of person the agent was by how he reacted to the moves.

He met Hal Turner. And this corporate psychologist said later, "You know, your friend, he's in a deep, dark pit. He's a very troubled man. Did you know that?" and I said no! He didn't pick up what it was, but he saw at once that life was very hard for him, in a way that I never imagined. And he was absolutely right. He had Hal pegged in a way I had never even seen.

Son: Why? Because he was a breezy . . . ?

Father: Yeah, he was a very witty, bright guy, wonderful company. Of course, he drank a lot, which was part of the darkness.

Son: Hal killed himself eventually, didn't he?

Father: Yes, he did.[28]

Son: But you drank quite a lot too, didn't you?

Father: Oh, much too much.

Son: For fun?

---

28 Hal (not his real name) left the Agency soon after this period in Berlin, and later developed AIDS before there was much help for it, and probably died of it.

FATHER: I was becoming an alcoholic probably, until I got hurt. Had to knock off the sauce.

SON: How so?

FATHER: I was chopping ice in '49 and the top of the ice pick came off in my hand. Came down and the spike went quite deep into my hand. It got infected and my whole hand turned red and I went to the hospital, where they gave me a couple of shots of tetanus. And of course I'd been filled up with all kinds of inoculations at every turn since I'd been a cadet, you know. This pushed me over the edge, and that's why I got this terrible reaction and got sick.

SON: The tetanus injection triggered the actual tetanus?

FATHER: Yeah. Lockjaw. But I didn't know what was wrong with me except that I was sick. I was twisting up in bed at night and I couldn't sleep; the sheets were soaked with sweat. I remember being on a trip to Brussels on a job from Berlin hoping that the airplane would crash.

SON: God, I had no idea. I never heard this.

FATHER: When I came home—we all had guns, pistols, you know, for whatever. I never used one but it was always there; you had it.

SON: I remember finding them, a bunch of them, in your bureau.

FATHER: I collected them when I was in the military, brought them home in a big satchel. I was so scared . . . this business of wanting the airplane to crash made me scared of the gun, so I turned it in. I finally went to Peter Sichel and said "I don't know what's wrong with me but I'm unable to work. I'm incapacitated." I was just like a piano wire, stretched too tight. I could feel myself under my coat, just . . . I was hallucinating and I had all this nuttiness in my head. It was a very good experience for me because it taught me what mad people go through, and people who have nervous breakdowns, what strain they're under—and why they commit suicide. That became very clear to me. And I said, "Peter, maybe I'm having a nervous breakdown. I'm no good any more. He said, "In the first place, you're not going crazy as you suggest because crazy people don't know that they're crazy. You'd better go see my friend Dr. Schaeffer."

Schaeffer was a heart specialist, but he was an all-around doctor too. "You've got *Starrkrampf.* You've got a light case of lockjaw. That's the biggest symptom of lockjaw—it strikes the circulation. You can't

smoke anymore. And you can't drink hard liquor anymore. You've had
it. You're spiraling in, your circulation is getting worse and worse and
worse because of those two things. You're a very young man." And I was,
I was twenty-six. "You're a very young man. I can give you chemicals,
you know, medicines, but these medicines are so harsh that you'll probably be worse off with the medicines than you are with what you've
got. For an old man I would prescribe them at once because an old
man is going to die soon; the medicines wouldn't be so bad. But for
you, I advise you not to do that." So I said, "What's going to happen to
me?" He said, "Well you knock off the hard liquor and you knock off
the cigarettes; don't smoke." I said, "Well, the cigarettes I can handle. I
can do that; that I can stop"—I didn't know whether I could or not,
but I thought I could—but for the liquor! I said, "I can't knock off the
liquor." I was that far gone. He said, "Wine and beer will be all right. It's
the whiskey and gin and that kind of thing that's hitting you." I didn't
know anything about wine. But he said, "I'll teach you." He was a great
wine connoisseur, Dr. Schaeffer.

SON: What was his interest in you?

FATHER: He was a very friendly guy and he was interested in people. He
would order about two or three hundred cases of wine from West Germany. He didn't have any room for them in his apartment, but he was a
very good friend of a guy named Neumann who had a Wein Keller not
too far from his apartment. A *Weinstube.* And he had a *Stammtisch* there
for himself and his friends. And every Tuesday night I would turn up at
Neumann's and we'd open about six bottles of wine for wine tasting. He
taught me the difference between German wines and French wines—
Ruhr wines and Alsace wines and Rhine wines and the whole schmear
and what all this stuff meant on the labels and so on. It was quite an
education.

Schaeffer was the top in his profession. That's why Peter knew him.
The very topmost officials in West Germany were his patients. The top
officials in East Germany were his patients too. So the connection between
Peter and Dr. Schaeffer was a very interesting one. I think that partly
explains why he was so good to me. He wanted to find out what kind of
person I was. There were some really interesting evenings—because the
top artistes in Berlin were his patients as well.

He took me to a place called Eldorado, a gay bar.[29] Sort of. And
there at the table were transvestites who made money servicing gay men.
Men dressed up as women, lipstick and so on. And the only way you
could tell was—they had busts, wore dresses, were filled out—was by
looking at the hand. The hand of a man is so different from the hand of
a woman—I had never realized the incredible difference. Until Schaeffer
took me to these bars and introduced me to these people. I didn't know
what to make of it at first. Transvestites! He said, you don't understand.
These are workmen. They've got wives and children and families and
live in an apartment and they live as normal a life as you or I. This just
happens to be their job!

"What do I do about this *Starrkrampf?*" I asked Schaeffer. "There's
nothing for you to do. It's going to take ten years for this to work out of
your system. You have to wait until your whole body changes and your
complete blood changes and only then . . . It'll take ten years." So I waited.
It took ten years to the day. And it was gone. The symptoms were sort of
nutty. I still have some of it. I still have circulation problems, I still get cold,
but nothing like it was. The slightest change in temperature if I washed

---

29 The Eldorado was an enormously popular bar/cabaret/movement in Weimar
Berlin, shut down by the Nazis, reopened after the war.

my hands—my hands would cramp from the wrist. The end of the fingers would turn blue. So I'd go like this to get the blood back into my hands. [*He whirls his arm around in a big circle.*]

SON: I remember you doing that.

FATHER: Ten years, and then I was all right. That was in '49. I married in '52. You were born in '53. You were six years old when it finally let go.

SON: Usually you don't like people, but now you're talking about guys you really appreciate.

FATHER: That's true. Peter Sichel was one. Think of how fortunate I was. If I'd gone to Bill Harvey[30] I'd have been sent home the next day, because he wouldn't have understood. Harvey didn't understand anything; Peter understood everything. I owe my life—and my career—to him.

SON: Wow, I've never heard you talk so positively about anyone.

FATHER: There are exceptions, aren't there? There are raisins in the cake to which my usual view of these people doesn't apply. [*laughs*] The nuts are on top.

SON: Was there a specific mission in Berlin, or was it all about the airlift?

FATHER: Everybody, right through '52, was convinced that World War III was going to happen. So you busied yourself trying to figure out when and how the Soviets were going to make a move, by watching their trains, and by watching the troop movements across the Oder,[31] to see if there was a buildup. There never was a buildup.

SON: But the surrounding area was filled with Soviet troops.

FATHER: Oh, yeah, swamped with them. But that was just how they did things. How they ran the zone. That was one of Eisenhower's big mistakes. It's like that lady talking to Samuel Johnson—Dr. Johnson, how could you make such a mistake in your dictionary? Stupidity, madam, sheer stupidity! Eisenhower held American troops back so they wouldn't run into the Russians—and gave up Berlin! He was incapable of seeing the political implications. We could have gotten to Berlin first—or at least the very

30 William K. Harvey, famously alcoholic, was Sichel's replacement as chief of Base of Berlin. He ran the tunnel project, digging under Berlin to intercept Soviet communications, and operations against Castro, becoming deeply involved with the Mafia.

31 The Oder is a river in Poland that runs along the border between Germany and Poland in the north before is empties into the Baltic Sea.

least simultaneously, so Berlin wouldn't have been isolated out there. But he just didn't have the wit to understand it, just as he didn't understand why we had to drop the atom bomb. He told Truman when he first heard about it, that's a dumb thing to do, don't do it. We all make mistakes.

SON: He wasn't alone on that one.

FATHER: He was pretty much alone.

SON: Not from what I've been reading.

FATHER: Never mind what you've been reading. Every single one of Truman's advisors told him to drop it. Only a few scientists in Los Alamos didn't like it.

SON: And a general . . .

FATHER: General Eisenhower.

SON: But another one, and . . .

FATHER: President Truman's principal advisor was General Marshall. Among the military. He certainly didn't listen to Eisenhower on anything to do with Japan—he was making enough mistakes in Europe as it was. There was Acheson . . .

SON: Back to Berlin—what kind of stuff was happening?

FATHER: Well, the airlift was interesting.

SON: In '48.

FATHER: I arrived in the middle of it. It started after I had left.

MOTHER: I'd been working in Rome, in the embassy there, but I'd quit and gone to Berlin to meet my parents there on my way home—they were heading back too, and I was supposed to go with them. The airlift was on.[32] I had no reason to stay in Berlin, since I'd quit, but I thought, this is a great place. The airlift was kind of exciting, and I didn't much want to be back to Washington. Angleton had said . . .

Angleton makes his first appearance! James Jesus Angleton was Washington's brilliant and paranoid counterintelligence chief for twenty years, famous for controlling his DCIs[33] and hunting for moles

---

32 The Soviets cut off all land access from the West to Berlin in the middle of June 1948. They lifted the blockade in May 1949, but the airlift continued until September.

33 Directors of Central Intelligence. Angleton was counterintelligence chief from 1954–1975.

among his own men. He was a poet at Yale, he knew Ezra Pound and T. S. Eliot, and was best friends and protégé of Kim Philby. Philby, one of the top MI6 officers, was a Soviet spy who passed along troves of juicy information Angleton handed to him, over countless martini lunches at Harvey's Oyster Bar in Washington, as well as boozy parties at Philby's house, that resulted in massive operation failures and the deaths of agents—all over Eastern Europe and, most gruesomely, in Albania.

Angleton was my father's nemesis. It was principally because of Angleton that my father ended his career twenty-five years later. Angleton had been my mother's boss in Rome and here he was enticing her to come to Washington. But she thought Berlin was more interesting. Mailer's novel *Harlot's Ghost*, which is weighty in high-stakes global and personal complexity, as well as pure heft, is driven by similar dramatic elements, and thinly veiled allusions to Angleton, Philby, et al, involving a retired CIA officer and his wife who live in Maine. My father hated Norman Mailer.

MOTHER (CONT'D): Angleton had said, "Just tell her to come back to Washington, don't let her quit," and I didn't want to go, because then I would have to get cleared all over again. But it was that same general who knew my father . . . my parents were literally waiting for me on the boat to go home, but I got word at the last minute that I didn't have to go because this general said, "Is that old Wally Falck's[34] daughter you're talking about? Yes! Oh for heaven's sake, let her stay."

A few years ago my father was asked to give a lecture on the airlift at Bowdoin College, across the street from their house. I drove over to Maine the night before. We went out and saw Imogen Stubbs' *Twelfth Night* film. I've spent enough time over the years in the world of *Twelfth Night* that it's like home to me. I found the film version lacking, though Stubbs is always terrific, but I didn't want to

---

34 Colonel Waldemar A. Falck, my mother's father, was the last mounted colonel of the 10th Cavalry, of the famous "Buffalo Soldiers," dismounted in January 1944.

dampen other people's enjoyment. I felt a bit isolated, as I imagine Pop must have felt in countless parallel situations, smiling and nodding.

I arrived at the hall the next day, early enough to help him with his wireless mike. He liked the screeches of feedback and kept setting them off. Like a little kid, he drew a picture of Snuffy Smith on the blackboard to see if it worked (the blackboard). "Does it work?" he shouted to the back of the hall. The speakers thundered and screeched.

The professor walked in. He was plump and prosperous, a full professor in his thirties. We exchanged pleasantries. We'd met him by chance after the movie the night before and he'd talked with great authority about the role of the Fool, a role that has become practically an alter ego for me. I smiled and nodded.

The hall filled up with students, the professor gave an introduction, and my father mounted the stage, fingering his lapel where the mike was clipped. It made a rasping sound. He looked out, shifted his weight back and forth, and smiled. I'd never seen him teach. I'd seen him declaim at the dinner table, make toys or furniture, or whimsical carvings, in the basement, and read books. This was a chance to see him in a whole different light. He looked old but young: elfish, as though he would suddenly steal the microphone and hop into the next world. He has always reminded me of Burgess Meredith. There was a long silence. I wondered if he would speak at all.

"I'll begin by saying that there never was a Cold War."

He looked out. The course was entitled "The Cold War." Nobody got the joke. Maybe it was not a joke. He began to speak, slowly and deliberately. I thought he'd never finish in the allotted time.

"It was a steady conflict that had begun a long time before."

He had prepared meticulously for the lecture, reading a stack of books and making careful notes. That was characteristic of him— overly thorough, my mother thought.

He began with the Stalin–Hitler Non-Aggression Pact,[35] separating all of Europe into their two spheres of influence. The pact did not

---

35 Signed August 23, 1939, only a few days before the outbreak of WWII.

last long. The Soviets had been bitterly surprised when the Germans struck. Six hundred thousand Russian soldiers were taken prisoner; many were killed. Stalin himself had just killed twenty million of his own people, including most of his officers, to establish his iron fist and get rid of White Russians, the old aristocracy, leaving his own army without a backbone. It was an easy slaughter. Before the war was over the Soviets lost ten million men. As with Napoleon, Russia's best strategy was to retreat. No European army had ever chased an army into Mother Russia in wintertime and survived.

Churchill saw early on that Hitler was a menace. (Many in England did not: Chamberlain's appeasement policy was not much different from Stalin's pact.) Western Europe could not stand alone against Hitler, and America was nowhere in sight. Churchill pressed for the alliance with Stalin. As Trinculo says, wrapping himself in Caliban's smelly hide for shelter from the storm, "Misery acquaints a man with strange bedfellows."[36]

The US finally joined in after the Japanese struck Pearl Harbor in late 1941, and the Allies narrowly won the war. Germany was divided into four zones at the Yalta Conference[37]—one for each of the three allies and one for France. Leaders in the west, General George Marshall in particular, remembered the effect of humiliation on the Germans after the first war, and pursued a policy of reconstruction. But Stalin wanted Germany utterly destroyed. Poland was essentially thrown under a bus, but that's another story.

In the German countryside the Soviets routinely blew up any rebuilt roads or bridges. Rape and pillage was one effective policy; destabilizing the economy was another. The Soviets obtained the plates for printing currency through the influence of Harry Dexter White,[38] the assistant head of the US Treasury—who was, it turned out, a Soviet agent. With the means to print money, they flooded the

---

36 *The Tempest*, Act II, scene ii.

37 February 4–11, 1945.

38 Harry Dexter White was under-secretary of the Treasury under Henry Morgenthau Jr., and was one of the founders of the IMF and the World Bank. He was exposed as a Soviet spy in 1948.

country with worthless Deutschmarks. American cigarettes became the unit of exchange, and GIs got rich quick.

But a general collapse was not enough for Stalin. He set about suffocating Berlin, which had been left buried deep in the Soviet Zone, a hundred miles from the western border. Lack of foresight and excessive caution when the final push came, mostly on the part of General Eisenhower, had left Berlin isolated. Berlin was and remains the heart of Germany and, arguably, of Europe.

American and British groups began working closely with the Nazi anti-Soviet intelligence network, betraying in short order the alliance with Stalin. No matter that the Soviets were much better at the game and knew every move the Americans made with their new ex-Nazi friends. The eye-to-eye contest that had begun when the Americans had supported the Kerensky government, fighting the Bolsheviks during the October revolution in 1917, resumed. The epicenter of tension was Berlin.

Berlin was given no access to the West, except by Autobahn, rail, and air. To illustrate the tightening of the noose, my father told his story about evading the roadblock with his truckload of liquor.

The Soviets cut off the supply route altogether a few weeks later and waited for Berlin to fall. Surrounding the city with 1.5 million troops, the Soviets expected no resistance and celebrated the fall of Berlin.

Curtis LeMay, commander of the US Air Forces in Europe, wanted to bomb Soviet installations to support a massive troop movement into Berlin. The stage was set.

There are few men in history that my father truly respected. New York Mayor LaGuardia, Truman, certain astronomer-mathematicians, Admiral Nelson, and a handful of little-known military men who had the knack of creating a band of soldiers out of a bunch of lousy men. General Lucius D. Clay, who was in charge of the American forces in Germany at the time, was one. If the Soviets were willing to go to war over Berlin, it would be just as well to find out now as later, but he thought they were bluffing. Clay vetoed LeMay's plans and decided to resist the Soviet pressure in a different way. He organized the airlift: a system for supplying Berlin by air, flying cargo planes in and out and unloading them at a rate that was impossible but for the most heroic commitment on the part of Americans and Germans alike. For about a year, once the incredible logistics had been worked out, planes flew into Berlin at a rate of one per minute.

It took hundreds of men on the ground unloading planes around the clock as well as airmen who put in brutal amounts of flying time, often in foul weather. The constant din of the aircraft became the noise of resistance, of hope. The US General in Berlin, Frank L. Howley, drove about in an open car to every corner of the city, personally encouraging civilians and soldiers in high theatrical style. The airlift had the unintended result of bringing Americans and Germans closer than ever.

The Soviets blinked—and lifted the blockade. On the last day of the airlift, around noon, the Soviet officer in the tower at Tempelhof Airport, whose job it was to keep records of all planes and cargo, threw his logbook into the air. He couldn't keep up. The planes were coming in every thirty seconds, as if to flip one last, grand, obscene gesture across the delicate borders. There must have been some on the other side who quietly appreciated the joke.

What a time! It was a world on the edge of ultimate disaster and yet one that withstood the bravura antics of a schoolyard. After the airlift a party atmosphere prevailed in Berlin, a city of Germans, a few thousand American soldiers, and a handful of spies, surrounded by

millions of hostile Soviet troops. Berlin was like a rat terrier that has outfaced a pack of Dobermans, and acts like it.

My father concluded his speech with a laugh of delight.

After his talk, as we were ambling down the hall from the lecture room, a Hungarian student said to him, "Why did the Americans not start a war then? It would have been much easier for us." We both stared at her in amazement. What hell she and her people must have gone through to prefer a conflagration to life behind the Iron Curtain.

SON: The Germans must have loved you guys after that.

FATHER: The Americans in Berlin were much closer to the Berliners than they were to the Americans in Bonn. They were attached to us. They were terribly worried that we'd leave. Condoleezza Rice doesn't get it when she compares the disaster in Iraq to the Marshall Plan—but that's another story, we don't have to talk about it.

SON: Let's talk about it.

FATHER: We'll talk about it later. Next question.

SON: You mentioned the currency problem in Berlin.

FATHER: During the occupation in Berlin, you could get $120 for a carton of cigarettes. And from the PX you got a ration of two cartons of cigarettes a week, and you got a carton for fifty cents. So for a dollar you could send a money order for $120 to your bank. If you did that twice a week it mounted up. It was a totally amoral society. It was very interesting; there were people in the occupation that became totally corrupt and wouldn't go home. Those who had a shred of decency, and couldn't stand it, left. Then came the currency reform in '48, which turned the whole situation into a legal economic base overnight, and all the amoral guys couldn't take it.

SON: How did you deal with it?

FATHER: I was just watching. Actually, we put our pay in a bank in Switzerland.

SON: What did you do with all your cigarettes?

FATHER: Smoked 'em. I smoked three packs a day. That's twenty packs a week. Two cartons.

SON: That was when you started drinking?

FATHER: It was.

SON: Was drinking a part of the work?

FATHER: Well, that was the justification. The idea was that you couldn't be a case officer unless you drank with the agent. It was a part of the mythology. Crazy. I should have resisted but I didn't. Knocked it back with the rest of them. It was lucky that I had to quit. The cigarettes were hard—harder than I thought. I thought I'd cut back. But when I got down to one a day I spent the whole damned day thinking about that one cigarette—and that seemed dumb, so I quit altogether.

SON: It's a tough addiction. Reilly's got it.

At the time of these interviews my son Reilly was about twenty, a little younger than my father was during the airlift. When Reilly was very young, my father made him a collection of amazing toys—an airplane, a gypsy wagon, a small green wheelbarrow that I now use to hold kindling, a marionette of Don Quixote, an enormous castle made of a series of crenellated gray PVC tubes and lauan, and a big square-rigged brigantine with cannons, powder kegs, scuppers and stays, topgallants, blocks and tackle. By the time he was done, the ship had to be put into a glass case because it had become a full-scale model, not a toy. We kept it for a couple of months and admired it in its caged glory before I took it back to Maine. Pop gave it to the library, which placed it on display with a small plaque crediting the builder. Then he made Reilly a wonderful toy ship that came apart at the waterline so it could sail flat on the floor. This one also had cannons and rigging, but they were meant to be moved around and exploded if an armada happened by.

With the world spinning out of control, I used to worry about my boy, and once suggested that he move to Ireland and marry an Irish lass and live in a real community. Get out of this mess, I said. Of course there's no way out; we're all connected.

As he was growing up, I enjoyed a completely open dialogue with Reilly. I reveled in it. I answered any question he asked me as truthfully and completely as I could. The first time I evaded a question of his was when he asked me what "apocalypse" meant. The second time, I see by a note I jotted down while transcribing these interviews, was when he called asking me what I thought about the second election of George W. Bush.

FATHER: Reilly smokes? Make him stop. It's a killer. I feel like going up to people—'cause they all smoke, outside the office buildings and the supermarkets—and saying *Stop!* . . . I still want to smoke. My fingers still want to . . . you know, it's a tea ceremony. You tap the cigarette . . .

SON: I think there's a whole Promethean thing about it.

FATHER: Well, I don't know. I think it's more like oral sex.

SON: To be in control of the fire.

FATHER: Freud had some interesting ideas. No, I think it's more a tea ceremony thing where it gets to be a ritual—you tap it and you stick it in your mouth and you light it up and *sssss* . . . and you drop the ash on the floor . . . I enjoyed every bit of it. I tried to switch to a pipe but I got sores on my tongue so I had to give that up, because by that time I was over the edge. Having smoked three or four packs a day.

SON: How long had you smoked?

FATHER: Let's see . . . I was in the hospital in West Point and one of the nurses gave me my first pack of cigarettes. And we'd smoke together. And then I'd go across the hall to an old colonel who was in such pain that he didn't sleep all night so I'd roll my wheelchair into his room and we'd sit there smoking until three or four in the morning. I started in '45 and then I had to quit in '49—four years. But when Jumper[39] opened me up, you know, for my operation, and he said, "You know, I took a look at your lungs while I was in there and boy, you're in great shape." I said, "I am?" I was so clean that he couldn't believe that I'd ever smoked at all.

SON: Okay, back to Berlin. You arrived in 1948 . . .

FATHER: It was 1945.

SON: But after you'd been ousted and found your way back.

FATHER: The second time, in 1948.

SON: You arrived at Peter Sichel's safe house where you met Betty Falck for the first time. . . .

FATHER: I began to run cases. That went nicely for a few years but then the tunnel project started and I wasn't brought in on that, so . . .

SON: And the tunnel was . . . ?

FATHER: The tunnel was . . . you know, digging from the British Sector under the border with East Berlin to tap the main phone lines to Moscow.

---

39 Dr. Brian Jumper, my father's doctor in Maine.

It was Harvey's idea. It was a dandy project—the problem was the Soviets knew all about it. There was a man named Blake,[40] a British Foreign Service officer who'd been captured in Korea during the Korean War. The Koreans passed him on to the Soviets and the Soviets recruited him. He was spying for the Soviets when he was released at the end of the war—traded off. He was trained by the Soviets, and with Soviet assistance, transferred to MI6. He was one of their senior guys. So the Soviets knew all about the tunnel; they knew exactly what was going on before the first spade struck ground. They let it go on because they didn't want to compromise Blake, and it amused them to see the Americans and the British, Dulles and his crowd, digging like busy beavers, getting all excited about it. When they decided that it had gone on long enough, they—accidentally—discovered it. Blew it. And I suppose at the end it was so obvious. Harvey banging around under there himself, in the flesh, playing spy, caught red-handed by the Soviets. It would make a great comedy routine.[41]

SON: And Blake remained untouched?

FATHER: Yeah. At that point. He was later betrayed by an agent and put away.

SON: Who was Harvey?

FATHER: Bill Harvey was an FBI guy who'd gotten thrown out of the FBI for cause. He became chief of base Berlin, and got all the credit for the tunnel . . .

SON: I thought Sichel was chief.

FATHER: Yes, he was. But there were people who didn't like Peter or were ambitious for his job or whatever, and got rid of him.

SON: Who was that?

FATHER: Oh, Dulles, those guys.

SON: Why did they do that?

---

40 George Blake, who volunteered for service to the Soviets after witnessing the American bombing of North Korean villages as a POW and was sentenced to forty-two years in prison in England for passing secrets during peacetime, escaped, fled, and continued his communist career in Moscow.

41 According to Peter Sichel, the tunnel was a legitimate project, though he acknowledges that the Blake factor is true. But Sichel had a much better opinion of Harvey than Pop did, and presents a more genteel version of this entire period.

FATHER: Well, Peter was the last man to see a man named Otto John. Otto John was the head of the BND, the West German Intelligence Service. One day he went over to East Berlin and—God, nobody has ever to this day understood exactly why he did that—when they snapped him up and put him away and had him say things about the West. In other words, as far as the outside world was concerned, Otto John was a defector to the East.

SON: This occurred on Peter's watch? He was considered responsible?

FATHER: Nobody knows what really happened. The real story is that Peter Sichel was Jewish, and they were getting rid of all Jewish officers in the East. But Peter said, I'll be goddamned if I leave under a cloud. I'll wait till I'm cleared of all this. And so they sent him to Hong Kong to be chief of base there. As far away as he possibly . . . And he was completely cleared. And then he said fuck you, and left. He had a very successful career in the wine business in New York. Very successful and lucrative.

SON: So Harvey moved into his spot?

FATHER: Yes, Harvey took Peter's place in Berlin.

SON: Was Harvey there, working his way up?

FATHER: No, no, this was Harvey's first overseas post of any sort. He was no operator. He was an FBI officer. Policeman. They found him drunk in the morning asleep in a car in Rock Creek Park and was fired out of hand by J. Edgar Hoover. And so of course we picked him up as if he was the jewel of the crown.

SON: Why?

FATHER: Why does the sun come up? I mean, you know, who knows? The earth turns. I have no idea—no idea—whether he had a special friend or some information that he could hold over people's heads, I have no idea how he managed that.

SON: Is it possible CIA thought they might get some FBI stuff out of him?

FATHER: No. That's a dumb idea. I can't imagine. Maybe. I have no idea. The answer is, I don't know.

SON: So he was with the Agency in Washington.

FATHER: Yeah, he was in charge of whatever NSA stuff was done in the Agency. It was a thing called Staff D. The closest he ever got to operations was cryptography and the use of interceptive material. When he got to Berlin he'd had no experience, no background at all. And he had no imagination at all. He was not an idea man; that was beyond him. He came from a very limited background. He was a very limited man, period. But he was good at running a meeting. Sitting people around a table and asking them questions. And then, almost without pause, wrapping up a consensus of everything he had heard and making a presentation of where to go from here that made sense. He was good at that. But it wasn't him that was so great, it was the input.

Then of course he screwed up royally over Cuba, which was his next posting. He was leaning over a table with a map of Cuba with Bobby Kennedy, who was running the Agency's Cuban operation at the time, God knows why. And in leaning across the table, Harvey's pistols fell out onto the table—out of his holsters. 'Cause he was such a fat man that he couldn't control the guns when he leaned over. And Kennedy was so appalled that he was fired out of hand. And he was drinking too much so he died pretty quickly thereafter, of the drink. Hopeless man. And so full of himself—such a pompous ass, you can't imagine. It's hard to know with people like that how much of it is insecurity.

Not long ago I read an account of the antagonism between Bill Harvey and Kim Philby. This caught my eye because Philby was the mysterious name carved in my memory from the time I was ten years old in Israel and saw the file with Philby's name on it in my father's office.

Apparently Harvey and Philby knew each other well, when Philby was the British station chief in Washington. At one of the hard-drinking parties, Philby passed around an obscene cartoon of Harvey's wife, and Harvey went after him. I don't remember whether there was a brawl or not, but Harvey began a vendetta against Philby. He clung to the idea that Philby was a Soviet agent, and dogged him for years. He happened to be right; Philby was a spy and was finally caught years later, when he was very close to the top of MI6 in London. It was the perfect revenge for Harvey.

Harvey was out of his element in the Berlin social scene, disliked by the urbane crowd there, Americans, British, Germans and all. The feeling was mutual. My father must have hated him anyway, as Harvey had displaced his best friend. It is unlikely that he would have hidden his contempt from Harvey. Contempt is something I've never seen my father hide successfully.

I wonder if my father ever knew Kim Philby. He said he didn't. In Washington in the early 1950s, Philby was cozy with Angleton. That would have put my father off. But I never found out what his innermost thoughts were about Philby. I can't imagine that my father wanting to take part in the jackal-eat-jackal cocktail scene in Washington. He probably avoided it altogether and had the sense to keep a low profile.

In any case, Harvey's Berlin tunnel operation ("Operation Gold") got into full swing just as I was born, and that coincided with the downward turn my father experienced in his early career in Berlin.

SON: Did you know each other's agents in Berlin?
FATHER: No, no, didn't want to. [coughs violently] Except the chief, who knew everybody's.
SON: So what was the prevailing tone at the office? Collegial? Mistrustful?
FATHER: Well, that differed, that was a . . . It depended . . . For instance, I wanted nothing to do with the tunnel so I was made the head of the Polish section, and there was a guy who thought that he should have been made the head of the Polish section, so he organized a mutiny against me. He finally got everybody—all but one—to join him, and go in to Bill Harvey, and say, "Harvey, he's got to go. It's either us or him." And Harvey, being a wimp, you know, he passed it all off to Frankfurt, and . . . [calling to the kitchen] What was the general's name? Oh hell, wonderful man, a friend of your grandfather's, a big friend of Colonel Falck. He was an old cavalry man, and he'd been a division commander in Germany and was now chief of station in Frankfurt. Polgar, whom I knew from the early days, was the one who told him what to do about espionage, 'cause he didn't know anything about espionage. A great guy, knowing he didn't know anything, which put him light-years ahead most of these other people. So he and Polgar came up to see what was going on, and he talked to me for about fifteen minutes, and he turned to Polgar and said, "Well I guess that about does it," and they kicked those guys right out of Berlin. Within a week or two they were gone.
SON: The whole group?
FATHER: Every last one of them. Except for one guy. And he was [laughs] he was the big Pole who'd held that woman in her chair. I didn't tell you?

Oh, I had an agent who was a nymphomaniac. I had to take this big Polish case officer with me to keep her on her side of the room. She was crazy. But she was very useful, because she was sleeping with the chauffeur of one of the big East German bigwigs in Karlshorst. When you were the chauffeur, you heard everything. He was great. And we recruited him through this woman. That's the only woman I ever dealt with. He was a great guy, the Pole. He was very loyal to me. He was very good.

SON: So there you were in the aftermath of this bureaucratic bloodbath, face to face with Harvey. Then what?

FATHER: Well, I knew what I wanted to do. I'd been offered a job as chief of base Hamburg. And I wanted that. I wouldn't have wanted to leave Berlin except this was a . . .

SON: Hamburg opened up.

FATHER: Hamburg opened up. For me.

SON: Uncharted territory.

FATHER: For me. Yeah, nobody had ever been there before.

SON: Except the British.

FATHER: Except the British.

SON: But Harvey didn't want you there.

FATHER: No. If I wanted to go, he wanted me to stay. He wanted everybody up there under his thumb so that he could move them around in his tunnel project.

SON: So he kept you in Berlin?

FATHER: Well, he tried to, but then I went home on leave and I saw [an old friend[42]]. I said, "Jesus, what do I do now?" I don't want to have anything to do with Harvey. He said, "Well, if I were you, I'd just accept the job and leave. Don't ask Harvey. Don't ask headquarters." I said, "How can I . . . ?" He said, "Just do it. Just get out."

SON: Who had offered you the job?

FATHER: Frankfurt. I think it was Tracy Barnes. Who then got mixed in the Bay of Pigs and was fired along with Bissell.[43] Ruined his career. Gone.

---

42 This was one of the names Pop's red pencil went through.

43 Tracy Barnes (Groton/Yale) was decorated for courageous service in WWII, joined OSS, and was part of the Guatemala coup before he became involved with the Bay of Pigs. Richard Bissell (also Groton/Yale, with Joseph Alsop), Barnes's longtime classmate and law partner, attended the Yalta Conference as a young

SON: Is there any one incident that happened, to put you off, to make you question the whole thing?

FATHER: Well . . .

SON: . . . any *Eureka* moment?

FATHER: No. No, it was all about watching, watching the way it works. When Peter was there, it was all gung-ho, because he was so competent, and everything was really interesting and it went well. Then Bill Harvey came in. It was things like that that triggered the mind.

My own memories of Berlin as a one- and two-year-old are entirely fabricated. For instance, I remember sleeping in a chest of drawers. The blanket made a cozy little nest but there was something shaky about the position of the drawer itself. What if it slipped out of its cabinet in the middle of the night? Or somebody came by and closed it while they were tidying up? Or mistook it for a package and sent it to some other address?

A Polish woman named Fräulein T had worked for my parents as their housekeeper. When I was on the way, they asked her to become a full-time nanny. She declined at first but then gave in and became my primary adult contact for my first seven years. She was very good to me. She was often in conflict with my mother about the duties of motherhood and housewifery. She used to carve the butter into elaborate floral sculptures for dinner with special butter-carving tools she had. I think she was careful and deliberate about everything she did. She had given her life to be with us. She died not long after we moved away for good.

My ex-wife used to look at the old photographs and say, "My God, even as a little one you had a demonic gleam in your eye; no wonder they had so much trouble with you." It's true, I was always getting into trouble. I remember feeling unwilling to obey almost any order. Once we went to visit another foreign service officer who treated his children like prisoners of war. They had to line up and bark

---

economist. He became overseer of the CIA budget and was in charge of black ops (overthrows and assassinations), in service of which he became entangled, without any profit to CIA interests, with the Mafia. He presided over the Bay of Pigs operation.

answers to his questions and so on. Pop took us there, he explained, so we could see how easy we had it. I idolized my father and I wanted more of him. In a pinch, getting on his bad side did the trick. But why was such an interesting and lively man so remote to me? I thought it must have been my fault. There must have been something about me even as a baby that threw him off.

But the picture is shifting. It now seems likely that the idea of having a baby came at an optimistic time, as it did when a baby came into my life. My arrival didn't throw everything off, but the times did. Before I appeared, things had been exciting and romantic. Pop had returned to Berlin in '48 during the airlift. It was a promising time. He met Betty, he enjoyed several deep friendships, and everybody was fighting the good fight. They were a disparate, irreverent crew. In my mind's eye I see comic book tough guys, mostly young, smoking and drinking hard, funny and cynical, with nothing to lose but the free world, nutty existentialists making outrageous passes at good Catholic Lauren Bacall types like my mother. The Germans adored the Americans in Berlin and gave them the best nightlife the world had to offer. Friends at CIA headquarters ran their own show, far away from Washington—far away from Frankfurt, for that matter. Danger lurked in the air, but in this phase a lot of blood had not yet been spilled.

John and Betty were married on June 8, 1952. He made her a beautiful bracelet—three twisted bands of burnished silver inscribed on the inside, *What is so beautiful as a day in June?* Then my father's old friend and patron Peter Sichel was smeared, Bill Harvey came in as the new chief, and things changed. A year passed, and June 1953 rolled around. The East German state had materialized as an all-out Soviet puppet, and the machinery stiffened. Barbed-wire borders between East and West Germany went up, and Berlin, which did not yet have a physical barrier down the middle, became the funnel for people who wanted to get through. Sizable portions of the East German population defected through Berlin before the wall went up in 1961. That made things very tense in Berlin. A cold, gray vein of reality took hold of Pop's life, one that would not let go for some time.

Stalin had died in March, and yet Soviet imperatives in East Germany tightened in every way. The state forced farmers to give up their independence, lowered wages, cut utilities to benefit factories and pinch households, and sacrificed human needs in order to boost industrial production. In early June, when higher production quotas were decreed, it was too much for the everyman to bear.

On June 16, a few hundred construction workers went on strike and marched down Stalinallee toward government buildings. By the next day, forty thousand people were in the streets. Strikes also occurred in outlying towns, and eventually over a million people were involved in the protests. There were calls not only for better conditions but to oust the government. Twenty thousand Soviet soldiers with tanks and guns came into the streets to quell the uprising. Of course, Western radio broadcasts had egged everyone on, but as often happens in these cases, the West didn't show up when things got rough.

On the seventeenth, we were at the army hospital, my mother and I, waiting for my father to pick us up and take us home. There'd been some problem with my birth that required us to stay at the hospital for an extra week. But he was running around East Berlin watching the riots. Playing the game!

One of my father's weirdest stories, repeated often enough to sound ordinary to me, involved traveling in a coffin: If the Soviets moved in (they outnumbered us in troops, a thousand to one), the official evacuation system would never work for him, so he had a secret plan that involved a doctor (Schaeffer?) who was going to stamp a death certificate on the lid of the the pine box where he was hiding, to be shipped out with all the other corpses, back to the West. I think he calculated that there would be too many pine boxes for the Soviets to check each one.

The story always appealed to me, but only now did I stop to think about what my mother and I, who could be used as hostages if we were caught, were supposed to do.

SON: You said something about how we were supposed to wait in a farmer's hayloft outside the city, in the Soviet Zone, some farmer that you knew, that you trusted?—bombs falling—and you would come pick us up sometime . . . later . . .

FATHER: Never trust anybody! [*mock-serious, then laughing*] Those were good years, in Berlin, there was the airlift—of course that was before you were born. You remember that Hungarian student who asked me, why didn't we just drop the bomb when we had the chance? Different perspectives, huh?

Once, on a visit while I was doing my theater training, he talked about how the great playwright Bertolt Brecht, one of the real giants of the theater, had betrayed the workers. I looked it up myself and was shocked to learn about it. Brecht had always been the working-class hero. On this occasion his support for the downtrodden, vocal at first, went notably quiet. His diaries turn vague and evasive during these months. After the massacre, Brecht was awarded an enormous building to house his beloved Berliner Ensemble. His career went very well from then on.

Günter Grass's 1966 play, *The Plebians Rehearse the Uprising*, posits a scene in which the protesters interrupt rehearsals (Brecht is rehearsing *Coriolanus*, the scene of the plebians' revolt) to ask him and his actors to join the protests, but he is too busy with important work to walk in the streets.

In any case, halcyon days for my father came and went. Harvey had arrived with his own gang, ending the one period in my father's life when he was part of something that felt right. From now on he would be on his own, sometimes winning, sometimes not, but never again would he be with a band of brothers.

CHAPTER 4

Hop Scotch

"Kathy, I'm lost, I said, though I knew she was sleeping . . ."
—Paul Simon

Paul Simon would have told Kathy he was lost even if she was awake. I would have told her only if I knew she was asleep. My father ("the man in the gabardine suit") would have said nothing at all. To start with, he would have assumed she was feigning sleep. He never would have said that he was lost unless it was to soften her up, to get her to betray some weakness of her own.

I begin to imagine, while going over these stories, what it must have been like to be at odds with my father at the office. He must have been a pain in the ass. His near-demise in Berlin at the hands of the Harvey boys must have taught him to operate more carefully. He became circumspect; he did not let people know what he was thinking unless it was useful. What he was thinking, for the most part, was that they were idiots. He started playing a number of roles, playing deadpan or zany, affectionate or respectful, while collecting impressions, keeping files on people, taking it all in, giving the impression of sympathy and willingness to help in any way he could, but playing his moves slowly, waiting until he was certain he'd thought of every possible outcome before moving in for the checkmate. Peter Sichel told me after Pop died that whenever he really told the truth it made him laugh. If he was playing earnest, chances were he was shaping it or holding something back.

I think the chiefs in Washington thought of him as troublesome and saw that he might be more useful on his own—and more disposable. They sent him on a dicey mission to Hamburg to develop the first

CIA presence there because if he blew it, they could get rid of him without looking bad themselves. If he did make something if it, they could replace him with somebody they could control and put him somewhere else, by himself, and keep a close eye on him.

Hamburg was the first of four quick postings. Hamburg for two years; DC (we lived in Falls Church, Virginia—my first glimpse of the US—for a little over a year); then Salzburg, Austria, for three years; DC again (49th Street this time, NW) for under two; and then off to Israel. Israel became something to really settle into, but before that his life and career were a bit helter-skelter. He was looking for a niche, and they were experimenting with ways he might fit into their Byzantine goals and structures.

*   *   *   *

SON: You arrived in Hamburg in . . . '54?
FATHER: Fifty-four. It was before Thanksgiving, 1954. It was brand-new. I could do everything from scratch. Set up a base and operate it. But there were two obstacles. There was my liaison in Frankfurt who thought he should have had the job. His nose was out of joint, so he was out to scuttle anything I did. And then there were the British, who thought the British Zone was part of the British Empire, so they were going to destroy any American who came in.

The minute I arrived I went to Timberlake[44] who was the American consul general and my supposed boss, and asked him for his help. He knew who I was and what I was supposed to do. I said, "I don't want to pretend to be something I'm not—I want you to bring your whole staff in here and tell them all that I'm CIA, and to please cooperate with me. Tell them you've got my hand in the fire and that I will do everything to help them if I possibly can." I didn't know if I could or what it might be, but . . . I knew that they could be extremely helpful to me in pointing things out and answering questions. I was not arriving as a deus ex machina, for Christ's sake.

---

44 Clare T. Timberlake later served as the first US Ambassador to the Congo (Zaire).

And Timberlake did that, and he asked me was there anything else he could do? And I said, "Yes there is. You can invite the chief of police to come in and the local BND, the local *Nachrichtendienst*, and one or two others, and introduce me to the local Germans. Which he did. He was very good to me. Some of the State Department people appreciated the Agency, for reasons that were a little unclear to me. The rest of the State Department hated us, of course. But some of them, like Timberlake, enjoyed having CIA people around.

So I made myself pleasant and accommodating and pointed out to them that I could be a channel for them to get information that they could get in no other way, and certainly in no other secure way, which would be—*puwhhht!*[45] I had ways of communicating that were totally secure. Nobody would ever see anything that I wrote. And I could be persuasive. They all nodded their heads like typical German bureaucrats—all good men, but bureaucrats. Like me! I mean what the hell, let's face it, that's all I ever was. And they tottered off. . . .

Meanwhile the British came to me and said, "We've been here now for six years, we're iron solid, and we've set the whole thing up, and we know things that you don't. If you agree to cooperate 100 percent, we'll make sure that you look good. But we'll be in charge. If you don't, we'll go to all the Germans and tell them not to cooperate with you."

When the British finished making this pitch, I said, "Gentlemen, there is nothing I would like better than to make my stay here successful. I would really like to get your help. Unfortunately my orders are such that I am unable to accept your offer. If you feel that you must go to the Germans, as you have threatened, so be it. That's the cross I have to bear and I'm sorry." And I left.

Of course they went to the Germans and told them not to cooperate with me. And then all the Germans, to a man, because they knew this was going to happen—they knew the fucking British; they hated them—and because the Americans had never been around, they didn't know enough to hate the Americans. They hated the British for being such pompous,

---

45 These are scatological noises my father made, usually by sticking his tongue out through pursed lips and playing variations on a Bronx cheer. Though he was unmusical in most other ways, he perfected a good upward inflection with a sharp finish.

upper-class snots. I think they'd gotten together on this, 'cause to a man they all said to the British, "We're very interested in what you have to say and we would certainly follow your advice, but Mr. Timberlake has called us in and introduced Mr. Hadden to us as his Intelligence representative. If you have a problem with Mr. Hadden, we suggest you take it up with Mr. Timberlake." It blew up right in their face. They had royally screwed themselves. 'Cause then the Germans had them by the throat. And the Germans all came to me later and said that the British had come to them, each one of them chortling and chuckling, and I chuckled right back. What a marvelous joke this is to play on those bastards!

SON: Did this haunt you afterward, with the British, in the years following?

FATHER: There was nothing they could do. . . . So I then began to get out and look around. The Consular area was huge. It included Bremen and Bremerhaven and other *Länder* up there in the British Zone—I was responsible for the entire British Zone. So I went to each of these offices in the British Zone, the BND office over in Kuckshafen, all of them, paid my respects, said I'm here to help you guys. And one of these British proconsuls in one of the other *Länder* just went right through the goddamned roof and made an all-out pitch against me in Bonn. But the Germans in Bonn told him that it was the year 1955 and Germany was now a sovereign state. If he had a problem he should take it up with Chancellor Adenauer [*high laughter*]. A German friend told me all this later.

SON: So you had a good time over there.

FATHER: Oh Jesus, it was the high point of my whole career. In my eyes. I had a lot of fun. I learned a lot. I was lucky.

I did something else that got me even deeper in bed with the Germans. The chief of police, a man called Brauer, was a Socialist, and the Hamburg people were not Socialists. They were all shipowners, see, the upper crust—like Buddenbrooks, these upper-crust Germans in Hamburg. But Brauer had this Socialist base, a big political base. Underneath this crust.

I went on home leave—my father died. I was gone for a few weeks; I came back. Jesus, I picked up the paper and there was Brauer, fired out of hand. Brauerei everywhere. Brauer this, Brauer that. And you know, I'd gotten to know this guy right from the beginning, right in Timberlake's office—and I felt very close to him. Besides, I liked him. Very *burschikos* guy, exactly what Hamburg needed.

I went straight to his house, the very day I got back. And I said, "What's going on here?" And his wife started weeping. I asked again. He had a tear in his eye. He said, "Don't you know? They've cooked this case up against me, that I've misused municipal funds for my own private business." He had sent guys out with an expense account. It wasn't exactly by the book, but it was more expeditious, more efficient. His wife turned to me (welling up) and said, "You know, you are the first person that has come to see us since this has happened." It was a touching moment.

Brauer was a very powerful fellow—chief of police in Hamburg and outlying sectors. Not a single Britisher had come in to see him, not a single senior German. They'd all dumped him, thinking he was *finito*. Thinking it would be death to be seen with him or to deal with him or anything else. But then I had the good luck—boy!—he was completely cleared. He came back to his job and to his office; he got it all back.

Unbelievable. Can you imagine, how people behave? And the closer you get to the top, the worse it gets. The meaner, the more vicious. Awful, the way they go after people. Like Bush when he went after that ambassador they sent to Nigeria, Wilson. And outed his wife who was a CIA officer. Holy shit . . .

SON: Valerie Plame, who was working undercover to track contraband nuclear material, to keep it out of the hands of terrorists. They blew that whole operation, right?[46]

FATHER: Yeah, probably killed a few people, made sure nobody would ever trust an American again. So much for antiterrorism, huh?

SON: Back to Hamburg.

FATHER: So many funny things happened on the way. Bribery cases, a rogue American colonel who was running his own espionage outfit through Ham-

46 Personally, I think Plame's group was getting too close to Cheney and Rumsfeld's own dirty business in the Middle East, and that was the main reason to blow her cover. I have no evidence for this belief—and my father pooh-poohed this idea, saying I had much too high an opinion of the Cheney-Bush people.

burg, out of Wiesbaden, what a nutcase! We had to shut that down. Most of this work is just sorting out the nuts. So things worked out very well. I was there two years, and then Tom Polgar took my place.

SON: It seems like a very short time.

FATHER: It was a short time.

SON: Wouldn't you have liked to stay a little longer?

FATHER: Yeah, well, I was the guinea pig. CIA didn't know anything could come of it, but when they saw that there was a real post there, they put in Polgar, who was very senior by then. He later became chief of station Saigon. He was very good. I was a junior case officer, more or less, and they wanted a dispensable, disposable body up there. So that if it blew, they could get rid of me and nothing would besmirch them. It was very satisfying to set the whole thing up.

I'd spent the entire two years casing the joint. Building files and coming up with personalities. There was one magnificent opportunity that Frankfurt wouldn't let me go ahead with. This liaison Tracy Barnes had given me was doing everything he could to make sure that I failed. I complained bitterly to Barnes—I'm chief of base, why don't I deal with you directly? But I got nowhere. This guy wormed his way against me and that was that.

I turned over to Polgar a thing that was running with very good contacts, good liaison with all the Germans in the area. For which Polgar was very appreciative and he later said, "Nobody knows what Hadden has done up there. He had a two-year head start up there." He had a two-year head start. Later I picked up his number two in Washington, brought him over to Hamburg, and spent three weeks plugging him into everybody there.

SON: That was nice of you.

FATHER: I thought it was crazy to put someone up there for two years and then just throw it away. Idiotic.

As for me, all I really know about Hamburg is that it's a port city, the jazz scene is great, the Beatles started off there, and that my father once sailed with a friend to England through the fickle waters of the North Sea. My sister, Barbara, was born in Hamburg. I was not yet two years old when I went to the hospital to see her. I was, so the story goes, entirely puzzled about the whole thing until I saw her nose. "Nose!" I said happily, pointing to her face, recognizing something like myself. Another creature was going to accompany me in this strange life. I had good reason to be happy, and still do. I owe a lot to Hamburg.

We spent two years after Hamburg in Falls Church, Virginia, a suburb of Washington. It was a drab existence for Barbara and me. We didn't know anyone. We spent time watching American cars go by. They were much lower and sleeker than the cars we'd seen before. We called them "fancycars."

SON: What did you do in Washington?
FATHER: I learned Polish, to go to Poland. But instead of sending me to Poland they sent me to Austria.
SON: The only thing you did in Washington was learn Polish?
FATHER: Yeah, in effect.

This lackluster answer demonstrates how his ordinarily avid interest in things slumped during his postings in DC. This was 1956–1958, a time that saw Sputnik 1, the Suez Canal crisis, Viet Cong incursions in the south, Elvis topping the charts, *From Russia with Love*, and HUAC in full swing, sending writers and actors to jail.

SON: What did you do in Austria?
FATHER: Austria was a "stay-behind" operation. The idea was to hide stashes of gold and weapons, explosives and stuff, and recruit people to be insurgents, underground armies in all NATO countries and beyond, to literally stay behind when the Soviets rolled over Europe . . . and it was all supposed to work. And no one was supposed to know about it.
SON: This was a contingency plan for when the Russians rolled in.
FATHER: They picked me because I'd gone to West Point.
SON: You expected the Russians to attack?
FATHER: We all did. We all expected a third world war with the Soviet Union. I certainly did. The Soviets had set up Salzburg as a major base. They had eighteen KGB officers . . .
SON: In Salzburg?

FATHER: These Soviet operators, *rezidents*, as they called themselves, would take a train out of Salzburg, go to Paris, and run an agent. How were we going to follow a guy from Salzburg to Paris on a train without losing him? And they'd send a guy here, they'd send a guy there, all over Europe, Yugoslavia. Running agents out of Austria. So that's why they wanted somebody there in Austria.

SON: You were the sole . . .

FATHER: I was the only guy there.

SON: Rebecca Wellington was the consul?

FATHER: She was the consul.

SON: There were basically the two of you there.

FATHER: No, it was just me.

SON: I mean Americans.

FATHER: Oh no, Rebecca Wellington had a huge staff. There was a guy for refugees, a guy for consular affairs, all kinds of people. It was a big consulate. But only one guy to chase these KGB fellows around.

SON: How much did your business overlap with hers?

FATHER: Almost none.

SON: Did she employ your services?

FATHER: She did, but I only did what I wanted to do. She got upset because she would ask me to do things, and I would say yes—but then I didn't do them.

SON: You were just like the guys who wouldn't do what you told them to do.

FATHER: She found that unbelievable, but as I was the only guy in the whole consulate who spoke German, she was stuck.

Rebecca Wellington had two little dachshunds, and I played with them when I went to her house. One day she gave me an enormous tome—*Max und Moritz*, a treasury of cartoons by Wilhelm Busch. Max and Moritz were unbelievably sadistic, as were the ghoulish and self-righteous adults who dogged them and occasionally caught them, which gave rise to a whole new cycle of terrible vengeance. The drawings were grotesque, depicting dirty tricks and acts of physical torture between the two kids and all the grown-ups. I was impressed and mystified by Consul Wellington's act of generosity toward me, and went on fervently studying the horrible exploits of *Max und Moritz*.

SON: She didn't speak German?

FATHER: No, no. Her German was perfect. Your mother had known her in Berlin and we had very good friends in common. It was a big family reunion. I was the only one in Salzburg she knew from before. The others didn't treat her with due respect. The administrative officer didn't send a car to meet her in Munich when she arrived—what a fool! He was totally lacking upstairs. And so I was a breath of fresh air. The fact that I never did anything she told me to do was minor. She invited me to all her dinner parties 'cause she wanted somebody who could sit with the Austrians and chat with them and carry some of the social burden. We had a great time together. She came to visit us in Israel; she wasn't too mad at me. [*laughs*]

SON: You enjoyed Salzburg.

FATHER: It was great fun; the skiing was great, but of course if you're talking about a career it was a dead end. A total zero.

Salzburg is where my clear memories begin and where my worldview was formed. We lived in an old house on the side of a mountain with a balcony that faced the town. The mountains rolled down in front of us to the great Salzach River, which wound through the valley like a glittering snake. On the other side of the river the town grew more compact, and taller, with church spires, toward the rocky hill that was like the top of a giant's head popping up out of the earth. The old castle, the Schloss, sat like a crown of medieval stone walls and crenellated towers on top of the giant's head. Hohensalzburg. Near the tops of the tower walls, several open-air dungeons hung out over the town.

They were made of iron bars curved like the tines of a fork, which covered tiny openings in the wall, closed with prison doors. These cold, vertiginous cells held those who ran afoul of the feudal status quo. I pictured bad people like me hanging out there in the cold for all below to see, terrified, cramped, and humiliated, and hoped I would not end up there.

Our house belonged in a fairy tale. The balcony and the trim on its eaves were carved in old gingerbread style. Big rocks sat on the roof. I think the place had once been an inn. It was the house of my dreams. In fact I began to have wonderful house dreams, with new rooms I'd never seen before. It was a bright contrast to the other type of dream I'd always had, which brought me to the end of the world, usually by bombing. I had a little wooden bench with arms and a back. I stored my most important things—my metal trucks and puppets—inside the trunk of the bench, under its hinged seat. When I dragged it out to the balcony it became my pirate galleon. My father made me a Jolly Roger flag: a wonderful treasure made with black paint on white cloth, a huge skull and crossbones—nothing childlike about it.

My brother Alex had been born before we moved to Salzburg and was now a toddler, a funny and charming little person. He had a puff of blond hair on top and wide, puzzled eyes. When Barbara and I

went to kindergarten in the mornings, we would look up at his window as we were getting into the car and wave good-bye, tragically, as if for the last time. He looked out from his crib by the high window, waving slowly. Barbara and I would collapse in laughter and affection. It probably scarred him for life. But he was our little kid. The three of us were a separate squad in the family unit.

Outside was a world of wonders. Deadly snakes called *Kreuzotter* (crossed vipers) lurked in a stone retaining wall on one slope of the yard. They were known by a white cross in the middle of their foreheads. On the other side of the house, down the hill, the woods invited me into its shadows. At the entrance to an old path that must have been many hundreds of years old, a big old tree raised its great arms in salutation. A salt lick and a hayrick for deer marked the transition from the world of people to the equally structured but more mysterious world of animals and numinous entities. Beyond that lay freedom and the wide world. Ancient paths wound through the forest, passing occasional small monuments. Foxes and pheasants lived there, and maybe bears and wolves, though I never saw them. Berries and flowers of deep bright colors dotted the way. Every now and then some old stone house would nestle alongside the path, surrounded by gardens.

Tulips of all different colors surrounded our house, close to the wall, in the spring. I reached down to pick up a piece of old rope one day when a couple of glittering eyes appeared on one end of the rope. It slowly raised itself to look at me. There was a cross on its forehead.

SON: I loved that mountain house.
FATHER: It was a wonderful place. But some bastards from Vienna bought the property at the top of the hill and started building a house. They had all these trucks parked in my driveway there. And I called the police to have them hauled away. And the man lost his temper. He came up to me and said, "Do you realize that if I can't park here I have to walk up to the house?" He was a great big, fat banker. And being a diplomat, knowing that nothing could ever happen to me, I poked him in the tummy and said, "You know, walking up the hill would be good for this." [*laughs*] He

got so furious he couldn't speak. He turned on his heel and left. And of course he never spoke to me again.

The town was enchanted, too. Archetypal characters appeared in folk-tales, songs, puppet shows, and skits, and spirits filled the air. I saw old stone castles at night; rowed in lily-covered moats; heard the old primitive music on viols, bells, harmonica-accordions, and hammered dulcimers; and was overwhelmed by the beauty of the mountains and the dark blue skies in the wintertime against the soft white snow. I was drawn to the darkness of the world there—the shadows of the forest and the fear and sadness in the stories. The Salzburger Mario-nettes, who performed *The Magic Flute*, came from another dimension. I remember the scene in which Papageno and Tamino walk through a wild, blazing inferno, for a long time, much longer than was possible, relying on faith alone, singing their hearts out.

Der Krampus, an ancient folkloric figure, a Christmas demon, the shadow side of Saint Nick, or a scary version of my father, haunted me

all year long, though he only appeared at Christmas. His name struck terror into every Austrian child's heart; he had license to be cruel to you if you'd been bad that year. I expected horrible things to happen to me: coals put into my shoes instead of candies, a willow stick in my stocking for lashings, and worst of all, being exposed for who I really was. It was almost worse when these things didn't happen. I knew I'd been bad, and I knew Der Krampus had his eye on me.

We visited the salt mines, where people would dress in protective bodysuits—white if you were a woman and black for men and boys. Sexual differentiation was extreme and a little charged. Down we would plunge, in big groups, either in rickety little railed carts or straddling smooth wooden banisters, everyone holding on to the person in front like a great millipede, sliding down into the earth on the special leather seats sewn into our suits. There was something intensely Jungian about the whole exercise. In one strange underground cavern we met the heads of various devils with fangs and horns.

A sexual feeling permeated the air in Salzburg, from lewd laughter that emanated from the cocktail parties at night to the antics of the folktale players in the city squares. I remember an evening at an outdoor restaurant by the lakes in the Salzkammergut. An oompah band played on one side; in the middle of the space there was a table on a small platform set up for a contest between couples who volunteered to play. My parents mounted the platform and sat face-to-face in the spotlight, everyone watching eagerly while they were ritually blindfolded with large black cloth. A bowl of something like burnt marshmallows stood on the table between them. The idea was to see which couple could feed the other the most burnt somethings per minute, as the oompah rhythm accelerated. The crowd cheered and laughed as my parents' faces turned black with char, as they would miss the target and smear each other's faces. It seems harmless to me now, but at the time I thought my parents were going to hell, as though I were watching one of the plays at the *Marionettentheater*, surrounded by laughing strangers who didn't understand that my parents were real. I screamed bloody murder, as I was well equipped to do (I had a good strong soprano voice) and the whole thing ended in general confusion.

I think my mother stopped the game by taking off her blindfold before the time was called, to see what was happening to me. I remember the laughter and the oompahs dying out as I screamed, feeling a little surprised that I'd been able to stop it, and noticing that everyone was embarrassed, as though it really had been some kind of satanic ritual.

My father must have enjoyed taking me to theatrical events. I saw vaudeville-style fairy tales played out in grungy little places: for instance, the magnificent story, "Seven in One Blow." I remember laughing at a donkey played by two guys who couldn't agree on which way to walk underneath the donkey costume, an ancient comic bit. And I remember *Jedermann*, the Max Reinhardt production that still plays every year in Salzburg,[47] a medieval morality play that fits like a glove in the square by the Cathedral, under the shadow of the castle, torch-lit, figures in black robes intoning warnings about sin and death.[48] And there were street performers and all kinds of crazy stuff. And a tightrope walker who crossed the Salzach River, high, unbelievably high up in the air. It seems in that distant memory that all the town was watching, wondering if he would survive it.

I am struck by how utterly different my father's experience of those years was from mine. We lived in different universes. He went to the office, dealt with shady characters, working with some, nailing others, and felt that he was wasting his time. For me life was a phantasmagoria.

---

47 Max Reinhardt was a brilliant theater artist (known in this country for directing the Hollywood film of *A Midsummer Night's Dream* with Mickey Rooney) who co-founded the Salzburg Festival and bought the palace at Leopoldskron. He took twenty years to restore it and introduced the world to a new form of theater in which the audience saw a play while walking through the rooms of the building, the precursor to modern site-specific theater. Leopoldskron became an important gathering spot for artists of all kinds. Reinhardt fled the Nazis, who confiscated the estate in 1939. He died in the US before the end of the war, and his place now houses the "Salzburg Global Seminar," a forum for international seminars.

48 Looking it up I see that the event attracts famous actors and directors and that it has become a place to show the best of cutting-edge contemporary theater. The Salzburg Festival is also world-famous for its opera productions. I've seen a video of a 2007 *Traviata* (performed by Anna Netrebko) that is stunning in every way, a superb combination of all the arts.

SON: You say that you survived all the machinations and the backstabbing by not taking it very seriously, but I remember that you took the whole thing quite seriously. For instance, I remember you fanatically listening to the radio in Salzburg, when the results from the Kennedy election were coming in.

FATHER: But that was curiosity, not . . .

SON: It was more than curiosity. It seemed like a lot hinged on it. You needed to know exactly what was happening, up to the second.

FATHER: Well, I had to be aware, I had to talk to people. But that's very different from being a participant. I had to know what was going on.

SON: You talk about all this as though you were a casual observer, but I know there's more to it. There's your father, who lost so much of his spirit when he was wounded in the First World War, who ended up working for the atom bomb and died of anxiety and a broken heart—and there's your uncle, John Lloyd, who played with you when you were very small, while he was dying slowly of mustard gas, because he quit the seminary to go to the trenches as a foot soldier, to give whatever comfort he could—there's a lot of sacrifice for something you believe in. And you became a soldier too and ended up working in the dark, without any fanfare, and it was good hard work, and here you are at the end of your life in a rage, seeing the whole thing go sour. Was it worth it?

FATHER: Not just me—a whole lot of other people. Those ten thousand crosses in France.

SON: Are you not interested in what goes on inside?

FATHER: You mean inside of me?

SON: Yeah.

FATHER: No, I'm not.

SON: But what does it mean to you?

FATHER: I don't know. It's just a matter of luck. We come out of nowhere, we rent a room for the night, and then we're gone. One guy has a martini on a porch swing in Connecticut and another guy crawls around under the wreckage of a bomb. Good God, Mrs. Weissmuller, you don't expect it to make sense, do you?

CHAPTER 5

The Highest Bidder

"The dog that trots about finds a bone."

—Golda Meir

One day in church, in Washington, DC, my mother whispered to me that we were moving to Israel. I felt a rush of excitement. We'd been in the States for another two years and now we were heading back out. I was already addicted to going away, plunging into the unknown. My father must have felt the same way, though I never knew much about his inner life. But he must have been beside himself with joy and relief. Finally, an interesting post in a world that was new to him—and it was a move up the ladder; now he was chief of station.

When we stepped out of the plane at Lod Airport, the dry heat hit us like an oven. After the first shock, I decided I liked it. For the next four years I spent all the time I could outside, either at the Sharon Hotel poolside or at the beach, pickled in the Mediterranean, and fried by the sun. Israel was as safe and weightless as a womb for me. I loved the sandy earth, the saltwater, the waves, the kids I hung out with, and the dry, hot air that enveloped me every day.

My father enjoyed being there too. He was his own boss now, and Washington was far away. All kinds of people wanted to talk with him. The King David Hotel in Tel Aviv was a good place to meet for lunch, where he would buy them martinis and listen to them talk. It was a pleasant and colorful life. There was nothing he could do about the overall relationship of the two countries, which runs on the poisoned fuel of politics in Washington, but he adopted a philosophical approach. It's a natural partnership: Israel is run by Westerners, emigrants who share our social values and logic. She is a Western outpost in a strange and mostly hostile land, she has enough proxy financial backers to force powerful leverage on a single issue ("yes" on Israel), this strip of land on the Mediterranean has always been an important crossroads to the rest of the world, and last but not least, there is oil in the Arabian Peninsula.

On the other side, three hundred million Arabs of widely differing traditions and persuasions, traditionally cool toward each other, have united against the presence of the tiny Jewish nation (six million), which is in their minds an infidel intruder that has stolen the land of Palestine and poses an unacceptable threat to all her neighbors. Israel wields an unholy stash of weapons, conventional and unconventional; she is a relative behemoth on a small and fragile piece of land next to the sea. The Arabs generally agree that the state of Israel must be eliminated no matter what it takes. We pour money and arms into Arab countries to appease them and make them dependent on American dollars. (War is excellent business, but that's another story: the story of how military corporations ride cultural and political riptides to the bank, causing massive death and destruction to peoples and places far away from us.)

Israel's position is clear. She is beset by enemies and does what she must to survive. Her leaders have regularly referred to the "Samson Option," the nuclear deterrence that not only assures mutual destruction but serves as leverage to obtain massive conventional materiel from the West. Jews the world over have spoken the words "Next year in Jerusalem" for thousands of years, and Jews throughout history have been hated, persecuted, and murdered in countries in which they have prospered. The Israeli military historian and author/professor Martin Van Creveld has said,

> We possess several hundred atomic warheads and rockets and can launch them at targets in all directions, perhaps even at Rome. Most European capitals are targets for our air force. Let me quote General Moshe Dayan: "Israel must be like a mad dog, too dangerous to bother."[49] I consider it all hopeless at this point. We shall have to try to

---

49 Moshe Dayan, the heroic and picturesque Israeli general, was defense minister during the Six-Day War; later, as foreign minister, he was instrumental in making peace with Egypt.

prevent things from coming to that, if at all possible. Our armed forces, however, are not the thirtieth strongest in the world, but rather the second or third. We have the capability to take the world down with us. And I can assure you that that will happen before Israel goes under.

My father never presumed to fault either the Arab or the Israeli positions—he saw the problem as insoluble, driven by powerful traditions and mythologies that are not subject to rational thought. He was, however, intensely critical of American politicians on both sides of the aisle who take money to quell debate and deliver the Israel vote, principally via AIPAC,[50] acting essentially as foreign agents (a transaction he well understood) and delivering enormous military and political support to Israel. He considered the unconditional codependence bad for both countries: Israel would become overconfident and more and more isolated, especially as American imperial power waned, and American sovereignty as well as her reputation were absurdly compromised. He added other incendiary factors to the mix: the proportional rise of the Arab population in Israel, which will eventually challenge the democratic system of the Jewish state, and the rise of radical extremism in Israeli politics, driven by fundamentalists and West Bank settlers.

It's a nuclear tinderbox waiting for someone to light a match. Right up to his death, Pop expected the Middle East to go up in flames sooner or later, and take the rest of us along for the ride.

*   *   *   *

SON: How did you first hear about the Israel job?
FATHER: Well, I'd been working in Washington, for Bissell.
SON: The technical guy.
FATHER: The U-2 guy. And then he was fired out of hand, for the Bay of Pigs thing. And that put me into the executive office of the chief of

---

50 America-Israel Public Affairs Committee, one of the most influential lobby groups in Washington. There are other groups that spend as much or more money for votes, but AIPAC conducts business with matchless efficiency.

operations, with Helms and Critchfield.[51] It was a desk job, you know—
pphhwwwt—I didn't really want to do that. So I kept pestering Critchfield,
"Can't you find me someplace overseas?" I just kept pestering. Finally
Lamott[52], who was in charge of the Israel account, came along and said,
"Do you know anybody who can go to Israel?" "Well, Jesus Christ, take
Hadden out of here." So that's how I got there. It was pretty quick. They
told me in September that I had to be there in October. Lamott would
be my liaison with Washington, and he was under Angleton, an awkward
partnership. I had to go buy a book of pictures to see what Israel looked
like. And I studied the alphabet, and a lot of files in the office, such as they
were, and then Helms said, "Hadden, keep your nose clean," and that was
it. Good-bye. It was a bit chaotic. I remember I lost all the passports and
the tickets in the taxicab when we got ready to go.

SON: What was your main interest in Israel?

FATHER: Well, I interested myself in everything. [*laughing*] Nothing was
too unimportant for my interest. As I say, you make your own job.

SON: And what did that turn out to be?

FATHER: I talked to as many people as I could. Architects, archeologists,
farmers, professors, opera singers, athletes, as well as businessmen and so
on. Most of these people had nothing to do with what I was there for,
but this is how I forced the guys who were watching me to waste their
time keeping tabs on a bunch of tennis players and opera singers. Some
of my favorite people in the world. There was Teddy Kollek[53] . . .

SON: The mayor of Jerusalem, yes, I remember visiting him.

---

51 At the time, this office was charged with Castro's overthrow and monitored
the Cuban Missile Crisis. Richard Helms was Pop's patron and boss throughout
most of his career. He was the first director of Central Intelligence (DCI) to rise
from the ranks, and he held the position longer than anyone else, next to Allen
Dulles. James H. Critchfield was a decorated WWII veteran who had led the
recruitment of Nazi War criminals to spy on the Soviets.

52 Name changed.

53 Kollek was elected to six terms of office between 1965 and 1993. He was
sympathetic to Arabs in the city after Israel annexed East Jerusalem from Jordan
after the Six-Day War, and was considered pro-Arab, although he himself felt he
had not done enough for that constituency. He was replaced by the future prime
minister and Likud member Ehud Olmert.

FATHER: . . . and Haim Blanc[54] . . .

SON: Oh my God, the blind professor, he was amazing.

FATHER: . . . and Yadin,[55] the wonderful archaeologist, who let me spend those two weeks with him on the Masada dig. Boy, that was one of the high points. And then do you remember Yossi?

SON: Sure, the really small tennis player, sort of a beatnik. I liked him a lot, and he had a really nice wife. Greta, right?

FATHER: I let things happen. You start looking for something, you won't find it. It's like Brecht, you know, if you go running after it, it's probably right behind you. That's espionage. Be careful, 'cause it's right there. You just don't know it. There's that wonderful quote from Conan Doyle— "There's nothing more deceptive than an obvious fact." That was my mantra in Israel. Don't trust the obvious facts. And then I had—[he mentioned a list of impressive contacts]—I mean, these were fabulous people— and then I was dealing with all the intelligence guys and they were great.

When Pop became expansive, chances were good that he was evading a question. It gave him time to think: How can I get out of this? Quoting Conan Doyle, playing on my interest in writers. Smoking a pipe was a useful part of his CIA behavior. When someone asked him a question he didn't know how to answer, he would start to respond and then mumble as he played with his pipe tool, reaming the pipe and fiddling with tobacco, to mesmerize the questioner with pipe business, which gave him time to prepare his evasion. What he said was usually plausible, and interesting enough to distract a person from the target.

Some animals practice deceptive behavior, pretending to be dead or wounded, changing colors or using camouflage, mimicking a predator—monkeys, for instance, practice tactical deception, which is conscious and deliberate; but in monkeys, the cost of being discovered— outed—can be high. Rhesus monkeys will physically punish a monkey who "lies" about where food can be found. Conscious deception in animals is rare, but it does happen. It seems to be most common when

---

54 Professor of Arabic languages and literature at Hebrew University; died at fifty-eight in 1984.

55 Yigael Yadin was a colorfully independent warrior and scholar who had equally distinguished careers as a political figure and as an archaeologist.

the cost of ignoring the lie is worse than the lie itself. A tufted capuchin will make a false alarm call so when the other monkeys run off,
he can steal their food. It works in capuchin monkey society because a
wrong guess on the truth of the alarm signal can be fatal.

Deception was a central issue for me and my father when I was a
young boy. Lying was the sin of sins, far worse than other wrongs. He
caught me at it from time to time, a dreadful thing, but I never thought
to question the truth of what he said until much later.

SON: What did you actually do when you went to the office in the
morning?
FATHER: There were two Israelis assigned to the embassy, and their job was
to translate things for the Political Section, the Economic Section. Anybody who wanted an article translated from the Hebrew, they would take
care of it. One was a guy named David, a very nice guy who was interested in stone artifacts in Israel. He thought Roman coins from Caesarea
were much too modern; he wanted Stone Age stuff. He was a nice guy,
sort of a Peace Now type. We used to go hunting for artifacts with him.
The other guy had come from Edsel and he was violently right wing. So
there are these two guys in the embassy, sitting opposite each other. In the
morning I would go down there and watch these two guys argue.

There was a guy called Ze'ev who drew a weekly cartoon for
Haaretz.[56] A full-page political cartoon. And it had everything that had
gone on during the week in it, from a cartoonist's point of view. Ze'ev
knew a lot about what was going on; he had characters saying things
and doing things, and I hadn't the foggiest idea what they were talking
about . . . but I would get these two birds to tell me what each word and
line in this cartoon meant, who it was aimed at. And then I would go
back and write a letter to Lamott, in Washington, and tell him exactly
what was going on.

Nobody else paid much attention to them, but I paid a lot of attention
to them. I would talk to them and they would give me the key phrases
in Hebrew that were of the moment, so I could toss one of these phrases

---

56 *Haaretz* ("The Land") is Israel's oldest daily newspaper. Founded in 1918, it has
always represented left-leaning views. Israel's other major paper is the *Jerusalem Post*.

in at lunch with some minister, to persuade him that I knew a lot more than I did.

If someone thinks you know more than you do, he wants to prove that he knows as much as you do, so he's not betraying anything by telling you—because you already know. It's human nature, camaraderie. At its best, no one even knows they're working for you.

I was careful to always sit outside . . . I never went into anybody's office. I always had lunch in different places, made sure there was nothing in the flower bowl, you know [*reaching out to finger an invisible flowerpot*]. 'Cause Mossad was following me all the time. Like that lamp in the living room over there. When they presented me with that lamp, in this big ceremony, Jesus, I had the guys from headquarters give it the works, 'cause I was sure they'd put something in the middle of it. And of course they tapped the phone; they listened to every phone conversation, and they trailed me all over Israel. And Israel is only two hundred miles long and a few miles wide and in the four or five years I was there—what, '63 to '69, I had a Ford . . . what were those little . . . ?

SON: Falcon.

I recently found out from one of his contacts in Israel that Pop drove another car in Israel that we didn't know about, a Hino Contessa. He must have been thinking of it when he said, "those little . . ." I never saw it, or if I did, I didn't know it was his.

FATHER: A Ford Falcon. I put 40,000 miles on it, and they had to follow me everywhere.

SON: So nobody ever got caught.

FATHER: My old friend Amit,[57] the Mossad head at the time, guessed that I'd recruited some Israelis. He put them in jail and he interrogated the shit out of them—they told me later. He never caught me. He tried to. He was

---

57 Meir Amit was the brilliant head of Mossad from 1963–1968. He was born in 1921 in Palestine, was a major general in IDF, a protégé of Moshe Dayan, earned an MBA at Columbia, and after his time with Mossad (while simultaneously head of Military Intelligence) he went into politics (with Yadin's briefly successful reform party DASH) and became a cabinet minister under Begin.

a great guy. But there was nothing that he could do. 'Cause I never made any formal arrangements. I just talked to them.

SON: You never paid anybody?

FATHER: Goodness, no. It was politically too dangerous to get caught with an actual agent in Israel. We did have a walk-in from Dimona. To see if he was real, I made arrangements for somebody else to meet him—in Athens. But he never showed up. Amit was just trying me out, seeing if I'd take the bait. [*laughs gently*]

I had a friend, a young Israeli named Shlomo Argov, a foreign service officer who'd been educated in the United States. He took me and a couple other people from the embassy on a road trip along the Syrian border so we could see what was going on. And down along the Jordanian border. Well, what was going on? Christ, you could see them shooting at the armored Israeli tractors as they were plowing the fields. I mean there it was right in front of us, like an arcade game. It was an interesting trip.

Shlomo. I got to know him very well. His English was perfect, which is why he got a job in Washington later. We would play squash at the YMCA; we had a lot of fun. He had a very good career; he became ambassador to London—we visited him there once. And then a month later, he was walking down a London street, and the Palestinians shot him. In the back of the head. He wasn't killed outright but his brain was gone, he couldn't function anymore.[58] He was a very good fellow. He had a lot of dignity.

SON: Had things with Israel been quieter before you arrived?

FATHER: Well, Truman started the period of friendship with Israel, and that went on until Eisenhower got mad at them because of Suez.

SON: In '56?

FATHER: Yeah, that was a break, but the Israelis made nice and got back on track with their special relationship to the US. Then Kennedy came along and he got upset with them about the nuclear facility at Dimona—he kept wanting to inspect Dimona to see if they were making bombs, but the Israelis wouldn't let him do the inspections. They'd made a deal with Eisenhower that they wouldn't pursue a nuclear capability, and in exchange for this promise, we would give them all kinds of tanks and Phantom jets and stuff, as much conventional materiel as they wanted. They took the planes and everything, but they kept making the bomb anyway. This was going on just before we got there, and of course in November Kennedy was shot, shortly after we arrived. Johnson walked into office and he was looking down the road four years, at re-election—and if you want to be elected you don't want to upset the Israelis—so he just knocked off the whole inspection business. Let them have their bomb, along with everything else. So it was smooth sailing between Eshkol[59] and Johnson, the new heads of state.

I learned the history of the founding of Israel in sixth grade Hebrew class. According to the "New Historians," Israeli scholars and journalists who gained access to the archives after many years, much of what

---

58 Argov was in a coma for three months and stayed in a hospital for twenty-one years, until he died. The 1982 war against the PLO in Lebanon was Israel's response to the attack on Argov, even though it was an Iraqi hit. From his bed in the hospital, Argov dictated an open letter of regret about that war, and about war in general.

59 Levi Eshkol was Israel's third Prime Minister, from 1963–1969, when he died in office of a heart attack.

was taught was false. Nevertheless, it made a strong impression and I remember it well:

The Jewish state was only fifteen years old. Palestinians had led a sandy existence there for eons, alongside a scattering of Jews, Christians, and the Druze. For thousands of years, repeated persecution of the Jews had fueled the dream to establish a Jewish national homeland and protect it at all costs for the following thousands of years. Herzl and Allenby and other earlier Zionist heroes inspired a wave of migration from all points; the wave grew much larger as a result of the Holocaust.[60] Many of the survivors made their way, most by unbelievably tortuous routes, to the fringes of the Holy Land, laying the foundations of the Jewish state, to be stopped at the very doorstep, this time by the British, who had held the region under the British Mandate established in 1920.

The British, who had fought hard against the Nazis, now imprisoned Jews traveling illegally to Palestine. There were many Jews living there before 1948, in relative harmony with their Arab neighbors, in Haifa, in Jerusalem, along the Jordan River and in Jaffa, the beautiful old city that became the suburb of Tel Aviv,[61] but this old life came rapidly to an end. Jews filled old rotten cargo ships to bursting and came ashore at night, in small rafts, or sometimes swimming in from the horizon, past the British guards, in a movement of illegal immigration called the Aliyah Bet.[62]

The 1948 War of Independence between the Arabs and Jews began when it was clear that the Jews were there to build a nation. The future Israelis engaged in madcap heroics. No firearms were allowed by the British, and very few were available. But the Jewish fighters would run around an Arab village, shooting a single gun from different positions, to give the appearance that there were many

---

60 Theodore Herzl was the founder of modern Zionism; British Field Marshall Edmund Allenby liberated Jerusalem from the Ottoman Empire in 1917.

61 Jaffa has been inhabited for 9,500 years; Tel Aviv was a small settlement founded about a hundred years ago.

62 Bet is the second letter in the Hebrew alphabet; Aliyah Aleph ("a") was the limited immigration allowed by the British.

guns, and the villagers would surrender. Men and women would go out at night with building materials into the desert and erect an outpost, defensible by morning, and add to it the next night, and the next, joined by women and children, and the first kibbutzim were established—communal villages dotting the future borderline of a new state. Milk trucks armored with improvised steel shields made daily trips to Jerusalem, winding through hilly roads, and were continually ambushed while getting food through to Jews in Jerusalem. Old wrecks of the trucks that were destroyed line that road to this day, reminding travelers what it took to win a life of freedom and sovereignty.

It's a story so full of pathos and triumph that even at the age of twelve I was strongly moved by it. Later, when we visited the new Holocaust Museum in Jerusalem, a beautiful monument with a black wall offset at the entrance—my father joked: to keep out non-Jews, the *goyim*—the large photographs showing the hollow despair and starvation of kids my age gave me an unearthly feeling of evil and suffering I would never forget.[63] We also visited an internment camp the British built to hold the Jews caught during the immigration. It was uncannily similar to a concentration camp. There was, for instance, an execution room. It was a primitive indoor gallows; a trap door gave way under the prisoner's feet.

I was in a class of seven or eight students in sixth grade at the American International School in Kfar Shmaryahu when we learned much of this history in Hebrew class. A stern-faced woman, Mrs. Ivrit (I always thought this can't be her name, since it means "Hebrew" in Hebrew), gave us the basics of the language and the history of Israel. The textbooks were illustrated in a ubiquitous Israeli style, drawings in ink and quick watercolor strokes, depicting Israeli children with cocky smiles and "cova tembel" hats, working the soil and doing other socially responsible tasks.

Mikael and Gabby Levin were more or less the same ages as my sister and I. They lived in a beautiful house on the cliff overlooking the beach. Their parents were both best-selling novelists. Meyer Levin had

---

63 Yad Vashem, the name of the museum, is taken from the Bible, meaning "a place and a name."

written thick novels about the Holocaust and other topics, and Tereska Torres, who was French, wrote diaries and novels, mostly about her experiences in the Free French Forces under de Gaulle. Both husband and wife were beset with controversy, he because of a copyright battle he fought for many years over the diaries of Anne Frank,[64] and she over the supposedly pulp erotic nature of her work. They were very nice to us, and to everybody. I was given an honorary task at Mikael's bar mitzvah, which I performed with a sense of awe. Gabby, a beautiful gymnast, was one of the Boy Scout leaders. Because of Gabby I was a Boy Scout for a while. I learned to tie knots and memorized the mottos, got an official Boy Scout pack, and went on long bike trips.

The kids in my class changed from year to year, depending on the diplomatic families that came and went, but the personality of my class somehow remained the same. There were between six and ten of us, mostly Americans. We were lively, talkative kids, interested in Shakespeare and current events. Our teachers were young and dedicated. Mrs. Shapiro, teaching history, smacked the blackboard with her chalk, pulverizing one stick of it after another. Mr. Robinson refused to discipline us and said that we would decide ourselves what we would learn and who we would become. A lovely young French teacher, Miss April, flirted mildly, upping the sexual ante of the universe, and we learned French like there was no tomorrow. I don't remember taking math in those four years—and I never caught up.

Other Americans lived in houses specially built, bigger or smaller, according to rank, but since my father was not supposed to be identified according to rank, we lived in regular houses in Israeli neighborhoods, and were viewed as unconventional. There was one main highway from Tel Aviv to Haifa that we were not allowed to cross. One year we lived on the school side rather than the ocean side of the highway; this meant that I couldn't play at the beach or the hotel that year. There was a stable across the street from the house where I

---

64 Levin had been instrumental in discovering the diary and having it published, but Otto Frank rebuffed Levin's adaptation for the stage, bestowing the rights upon a more tepid version by Frances Goodrich and Albert Hackett. Feeling that the accepted version distorted the story, blurring the era's sense of Jewish identity itself, Levin fought the case for decades.

befriended Jomo, a slender black horse who had been mistreated. We became very close. I spent hours talking with him after school, preferring his company to that of people.

The last house we lived in was the prettiest thing I'd ever seen. It was a combination of rectangular blocks of different shapes and sizes in white stucco that looked like adobe architecture. There was an empty lot next door that was part of the unspoiled dunes. I loved the dunes. I loved the feel and crunch of the granular sand underfoot, the scrubby plants, the heat bouncing off the surface, the strange whiteness of it, and its gentle undulation. We played all kinds of games there. We were left on our own and sometimes got into trouble. In a mock battle, I got hit in the eye with a handful of sand and had to have my eye flushed out by a doctor with a garden hose. My brother Alex, six years old, digging one day, felt a squirmy movement in his hand. Instead of closing his fist around the unknown thing, he pulled his hand out flat. It was a yellow scorpion, a "death stalker," disoriented. He let it fall harmlessly to the ground. It was one of several narrow escapes Alex has somehow passed in his easygoing, strangely blessed life.

When it came time for war, in June 1967, we dug a right-angled trench in the dunes next door. If the planes came in one way, we would get into the trench perpendicular to its path; if they came the other way, we would scoot around to the other angle. All our headlights were painted out with black paint by volunteers at intersections, leaving only small slots of light, so that we wouldn't be seen from the sky at night. I wondered if there was a handbook of things to do when war comes. Everybody seemed to know exactly what to do. There was an incredible feeling of heroic tension and solidarity in the air. All the men, women, and many boys not much older than me had been mobilized into camps in the dunes for weeks and were practicing maneuvers. Old people and young girls were running the country. It couldn't go on like that indefinitely. If something didn't happen soon, the Israelis would have to attack or pack up, otherwise all the grocery stores would grind to a halt. Most of my American friends had been evacuated weeks before and were living it up in hotels in Rome.

Finally, Nasser's blockade of the Gulf of Aqaba, and the mobilization of Arab forces from Egypt, Jordan, Iraq, and Syria, gave the Israelis reasonable justification to strike. At dawn on June 5, 1967, a hundred Israeli fighter pilots flew into Egypt under radar detection, blew up the Soviet-supplied MIGs that were unprotected and parked too close together for easy takeoff, and flew home. Egypt had lost almost her entire air force in less than an hour. By noon, in three waves, with seven-minute turnarounds for refueling and rearming, the Israeli Air Force had disabled most Arab airfields and destroyed most Arab combat aircraft, gaining complete control of the skies while suffering only minor losses. It was amazing to us kids that the Israelis, who couldn't fix your windshield wipers without losing the bolts to your hood, or, as we joked, would return your car with the doors on backward, could take a French Mirage or a Phantom jet into the shop and improve its precision and speed, and fly it like nobody else in the world.

When it was time to go to school that day, I faked some awful sickness because a paper that I had not yet begun was due in Hebrew class. I was practically the only kid left in the class, and I was counting on the war to get me out of it. Barbara and Alex, however, were ushered on their way, carrying their books and lunch boxes, nine and twelve years old, to the bus stop. They trudged dutifully on abandoned streets toward the school after giving up on a bus that was not going to come. Some old people from the neighborhood pulled the two of them into an air-raid shelter where they spent hours wondering what was going on.

Though it was the opening day of the Six-Day War, nothing much was happening in our neighborhood. Every now and then the air-raid sirens went off. My mother and my youngest brother Jamie and I and our neighbors ran out into the trench, but that was about it.

Only two planes ever made it across the border, and they weren't able to do any damage. Egypt was finished; we heard stories of reluctant Jordanian forces fleeing their tank squadrons in the desert, leaving all their equipment and their boots behind. There was some intense skirmishing over the next few days in the Golan Heights, for Syrian high ground, but the West Bank fell quickly, as did the Gaza Strip.

My father came home to tell us we didn't have to go anywhere; Israel was the safest place in the world. He left it up to us. By now Alex and Barb had made their way home. I was desperate to be evacuated: not only was my nonexistent paper for Hebrew class due, but my seventh grade girlfriend was riding around on a Vespa with a precocious Roman boy. My mother looked at me and decided we should go.

We boarded a plane at the airport and sat in it for hours while, I remember—and my memory is surely wrong on this point—they replaced the wings. It was a prop plane that shuddered in the air for several hours before it finally landed in Cyprus. From there we went to Athens, visited the islands, were photographed and put in the newspaper as a family in flight, tennis racquets in hand, as though the war had interrupted our game, and ended up in Rome. But we only stayed in Rome for a day or two before we were flown to Washington. We passed a muggy summer in a Maryland suburb before I went off to school. Fun and games in other people's countries were over, it seemed.

SON: You said that you tried to delay the Six-Day War. How could you do that?

FATHER: It wasn't easy! In May before the war I got called in by Amit to discuss the situation and I said, "You've got to wait three weeks, you've got to give Johnson three weeks to try to broker peace with Rusk's Navy that you know and I know won't work, but we've got to let him try, so that he can stand before the world and say, 'I tried,' and save face. If you go to war now he'll be in the position of not having kept you under control and not having tried to keep the peace. Let him go three weeks and he'll give you the green light and you can do whatever you want." And Amit lost his temper with me. He said, "You're condemning six thousand, twelve thousand Israelis to death by making me wait three weeks.

They're all going to get killed." And I said, "I don't think so, I think you'll have fewer casualties than you had in the '48 war, and whether you do it now or later you're overwhelmingly powerful." And he says, "Not a bit of it, we're under the gun here and we may lose the whole thing." He lost his temper.

SON: And waited three weeks?

FATHER: And waited three weeks. They thought I'd been given specific directions by the president or some goddamned thing. All I was doing was reading the State Department traffic back and forth and I knew that Johnson needed the time.

MOTHER: But you also went to Washington.

FATHER: Yeah, I went with Amit. It was McNamara who gave him the green light, and Amit finally got what he wanted. The US would not interfere.

SON: Like the Iraqi invasion of Kuwait?[65]

FATHER: Yes, actually! On the Saturday before the war, when I flew from Rome to Lod Airport, the first class El Al compartment was full of cases of morphine ampoules. It was clear that the Israelis were prepared for major losses and that we had only a few hours to go . . . You want to keep going? You want to go to chapter two of disobeying orders?

SON: Yes.

FATHER: Well, it's the middle of the Six-Day War. I'm sitting there in Israel and the code clerk comes running into my office with this hot cable. It was a direct order from Fitzgerald, the chief of operations in Washington:[66] "Go at once to the chief of Israeli Intelligence" [Amit]—and it was one of the crucial days of the war—"and advise him that we think it's okay to go ahead and bomb Cairo." I took one look at this thing and just dropped it in the shredder; I paid no attention to it at all, absolutely none. I was going to wait and see what happened. It was over the weekend, so Lamott didn't see it before it went out, but when he did come in and saw this order, he

---

65 US Ambassador to Iraq, April Glaspie, in reference to Iraqi troops amassed at the Kuwaiti border, passed on to Saddam Hussein assurances from Secretary of State James Baker that the US was not concerned about Arab–Arab conflicts, giving a tacit green light for the invasion of Kuwait, which was followed by reprisals from the US—the Persian Gulf War of 1991.

66 Desmond Fitzgerald was deputy director of plans who had been in charge of the Cuban Task Force to overthrow and/or assassinate Castro.

took the thing and rushed to Helms, "My God, what do we do now?" And Helms said, "Tell Hadden if he hasn't handed it over, not to hand it over, and we'll see what Hadden does." So I got another cable saying, "Disregard cable XYZ! Have you taken action?"

SON: Was this from Helms?

FATHER: This was from Lamott, but of course it was signed by Helms by that time. Meanwhile Fitzgerald is sitting right there. Of course Helms caught him up at once and told him to knock it off. What the hell did he think he was doing?

SON: On whose authority was he doing it, on his own?

FATHER: Exactly. He was just that kind of guy, he was one of these gung-ho guys who didn't realize that the war was over, you know, bees in his bonnet, burrs under his saddle. The days of the proconsuls in the American Empire was burgeoning. Crazy, just crazy. So I sent a quiet cable back saying I had so far been unable to carry out the order. [*laughs*] Whereupon they wiped the sweat off their brows and carried on.

SON: And Fitzgerald stayed in place?

FATHER: Oh, nothing happened to him. And I never told them that I had paid no attention to this cable. They never asked me.

SON: When these cables would come in from Washington, what sort of obligation would you feel toward them in general?

FATHER: Not much, because they didn't know what was going on. The guy on the ground knows much better what questions should be asked, and people in Washington never had much idea what the real priority questions should be ...

MOTHER: Even Lamott?

FATHER: Lamott didn't bother me much. Anyway, we worked together mostly through letters that Angleton would never see. I would write a personal letter to Lamott, and he would write a personal letter back. We would just keep all that stuff out of our official communiqués that had numbers on it that Angleton could busily decode.

SON: You said once that the Six-Day War was not a war at all, that the war is ongoing.

FATHER: Yeah, it's been going on since the late eighteen hundreds. These are skirmishes.

SON: What's the solution?

FATHER: There is no solution to the Arab-Israeli problem. It might be solved when some greater problem swamps it. World War III, say, or nuclear war in the Middle East. Then we'll be nostalgic for the old problems, won't we? This war has a Greek quality to it. It has nothing to do with the facts; it's beyond logic. It's about the feeling of the people, the mythologies. Both sides have impregnable moral positions. People are wrong when they think they can solve it. For the most part, the whole so-called Peace Process tends to make matters worse.

SON: When did you first become aware of the Israeli atom bomb and the trail of how they got it?

FATHER: Before I went, in '63, in the office there, they were interested in where Israel was going with the bomb. I'd certainly never heard of it—I'd hardly ever heard of Israel.

SON: But Angleton had the Israel account under his wing. I thought you said he wasn't particularly interested . . .

FATHER: No, he was hopeless, unconditionally pro-Israel. But Lamott knew the files and the files were there. I was able to talk to him and that was my briefing.

SON: Was Helms similarly uninterested?

FATHER: No, no, no. Helms really understood that whether or not the Israelis had the bomb was a high priority intelligence target. Because for us to get caught with the Israelis one day, say, testing the bomb and us sitting there with egg all over our face in front of the president and the Congress saying we didn't know anything about it? Well, that's bad news for the Agency.

Angleton—his thinking was so odd; he was very strange—his whole focus was on counterintelligence, so he never thought about any positive intelligence regarding the Israelis. That was totally out of his head. He wasn't interested in it; he wasn't worried about it. His obsession was with the Soviet Union, his anti-Communism. He was a professional anti-Communist and it blinded him, you know, as it did all those people. So they couldn't think of anything else. There was Israel out there, an anti-Communist state in a sea of places where the Soviets were making headway and we weren't. Of course we weren't making headway—we were in bed with the Israelis. But he didn't understand that.

SON: Or chose not to. Would you say that once that American support for Israel became unconditional . . .

FATHER: Yeah, from that day on it simply got worse and worse and worse and worse. We lost any kind of middle position there in dealing with the Arabs and the Israelis. As mediators, from that day forth, we went steadily downhill. Till finally today: with Bush it's absolutely out of the question. Mediating? Clinton was pretty bad, too, playing peacemaker at Camp David when his top negotiator, Martin Indyk,[67] was an Israeli agent. And of course Arafat knew that.

The Arabs will never trust us. Ever. Ever again. And the Israelis only slightly. Because Eisenhower kicked them out of Suez in '57, promising that the Straits of Tiran would stay open. And the Americans reneged on that in '67. The Israelis don't trust the US government. They did once—they never will again. They will never take any promise we make as a bond they can rely on. And of course the Arabs just hate us. Just despise us.

SON: More every day. What do you think it is, that makes people interested in killing each other?

FATHER: Suffering, then persuasion and training. The pre-statehood period is instructive. The early activities in the Haganah[68] before the '48 war established the Israeli military doctrine that you don't wait for the enemy to come and attack you. You go out and kill him first.

SON: You're talking about the night squads, that Dayan and even Rabin[69] fought in.[70] Would they have been different people if they had spent that time in a music camp instead, say, singing or studying the cello?

---

67 Martin Indyk has led a distinguished and sometimes controversial career as a scholar and practitioner of Middle East politics. Twice US Ambassador to Israel, senior research director for AIPAC, top negotiator/advisor on Middle East peace talks under Clinton and Obama, he was recently critical of Israeli intransigence, naming West Bank settlers as a key cause of obstruction.

68 Haganah was the largest Jewish paramilitary group in Palestine before 1948, formed to protect settlements, which provided the core for the Israeli Defense Force (IDF) after independence. For a brief period, Haganah worked in collaboration with the British against the more radical Jewish groups Irgun and Lehi.

69 Yitzhak Rabin, the fifth prime minister of Israel, was a commando in the Yishuv and its top commander during the 1948 war, but was not a member of the Night Squads. Rabin won the Nobel Prize for his support of peace during his tenure.

70 The Special Night Squads were organized in Palestine in 1938 by British Captain Orde Wingate, who recruited Jewish Haganah fighters and British sol-

FATHER: Oh, of course. They wouldn't have learned this military doctrine. Like all the people who studied Clausewitz[71] who have an attitude toward making war that people who don't study Clausewitz don't have. There's an interesting counterpoint. Take the Civil War: the South studied the French theorists of war—oh Christ, the names are gone. And the North studied Clausewitz and the Prussian theory of war. Sherman took it one step further. It was one of the reasons for the North winning. One of the many reasons . . .

SON: And yet Rabin was urbane, conciliatory. How did that come about?

FATHER: Dayan, too. He was nothing like these single-minded right-wing radicals they have now. It's a paradox. You can see it right here in this country today. If you've seen combat, if your soul is partly shattered by it, you understand the cost of war. Very few of these neocons have been there, that's part of their problem.

When we lived in Israel, after the first excitement wore off, time went along with its usual ups and downs. I went to school and played with friends. It was only in retrospect, lying in my dormitory cubicle in New England, that I saw the time in Israel as a period of blessed ease and luxury. During my second year at Groton, my father returned to Israel, and we went to join him for the summer. It was 1969. The air was humming with change. I carried three (vinyl, LP) records with me: *Cheap Thrills*, by Janis Joplin, the best of Dylan, and the soundtrack to *Hair*. The music and the words made their way into my bones. I started to consider almost everything in a new light. The summer in Israel came like a reprieve, an opening. I was ready to go back to the sun.

As in earlier years, membership in the embassy community entitled me to instant friendships that were just as instantly dissolved when the time came for someone's departure. There were always lonely teenagers in American families overseas. I hadn't had as much as a conversa-

---

diers to attack Arab insurgents, especially preventing them from sabotaging oil pipelines. Vicious cruelty and ruthlessness were their hallmarks of success.

71 Carl von Clausewitz was a Prussian general during the Napoleonic Wars who wrote a philosophy of war, *On War*, which because of its psychological insight is still studied today.

tion with a young female person for two years, since I'd been at school, occasionally going home to the Maryland suburb where I knew no one and had no way of meeting people. I turned sixteen a few days after our arrival in Israel and my days suddenly brightened with new friendships and the intense pleasure and amazement of sexual discovery.

Once I went with a young woman who'd taken me in hand to Caesarea—she was two or three years older than me and had a car. We found a little cove in the ruins and floated out into the Mediterranean. The waves circling in from Egypt and deflecting off Cyprus were slowed and softened in the cove by old submerged walls. Below our feet, as we were gently lifted up and down by the warm saltwater, lay undiscovered vials and caches of coins, vases, and the lost utensils of ancient Arabians, elite Romans on vacation, Byzantines, Crusaders, Bosnians, and Ottomans, all resting together on the peaceful bottom. It seemed to us that the place was alive with the spirits of other lovers, and that they were smiling at us, enjoying the idyll of two young people bobbing gently in the waves of the buoyant water, surrounded by the fallen magnificence of the past. Toppled black columns pointed this way and that; they were no longer obliged to delineate the edge of a courtyard or a temple. The water grew warmer between us until our bellies touched.

One night she took me by the hand and pulled me into my parents' room while they were sleeping. I rarely went into their room, never while they were in bed, but my friend seemed to know her way around the adult world. Laughing, she tugged them out of bed, exhorting them to come swimming. It was an odd hour, just before dawn. It was the only time in my life I did anything with my parents purely for fun. She was a magician. I could see her in the half-light when we entered the surf. She led the way toward the horizon, her hair skimming the water as she dissolved into the waves. I saw her through my father's eyes and wondered if there was something she wasn't telling me.

The weeks passed. The novelty of incessant loving wore off for me and I began to wonder if there were other adventures in the little time I had before I would have to return to school. My father said, "Say, if you're interested, I can see if they would take you on as a volunteer at a kibbutz up north." "Sure, that sounds interesting."

I didn't expect my lovely new friend's reaction. Why was I going? There was no good answer. I didn't know how to be adored and I didn't understand yet what it was to lose someone.

The kibbutz, Kfar Blum, was in the Golan Heights above the Sea of Galilee. I lived in a small shelter made of concrete, a room with a cot, a door, a window, and a sink that doubled as a pissoir. It was the first home of my own. Every morning at four I would get up and get on the back of a truck with a load of other volunteers and trundle out to the apple orchards. We were issued canvas baskets that were harnessed around the shoulders and hung down by our stomachs. We climbed ladders into the trees and picked apples until eight, stopping for an occasional cigarette or a snack of toast and tea. We were warned not to eat too many apples. Though delicious, they would give you *shilshul*, endless bouts of diarrhea.

Breakfast was at eight at the communal dining hall, a big, open, camp-like place where everybody gathered to talk and eat three times a day. It was noisy and it smelled good. We sat on long benches. Everything had a utilitarian simplicity. We feasted on tomatoes, olives, onions, and cucumbers, toast, more tea and cigarettes, and then it was back to the orchards for another three or four hours of apple-picking until it was too hot to work, and then the workday was done.

After lunch, a substantial meal with chicken or fish, I made my way up the hill to a large swimming pool with a high dive. The pool was supposedly an integral part of the kibbutz's irrigation system. It was gloriously situated with long views over distant hillsides and old Arab settlements. Once or twice I saw little puffs of smoke in the distance—afternoon bombings. I loved poolsides, and this was the best. The water was fresh and cool, fed by the Jordan River, also nearby. I liked to swim underwater. My goal was to be able to stay under indefinitely, so I practiced ways to extend the time and distance. I started at one end, bobbing in and out of the water, taking deep breaths and exhaling slow bubbles to fill my body with oxygen, and to relax, and then, using as little effort as possible, I slipped down and shoved off toward the other end. I carried only as much air in my lungs as was comfortable and wouldn't float me to the surface. I made just enough movement with my limbs to keep me in motion. I slowed

my metabolism and stayed under a long time. I wanted to live in that suspension.

I took to smoking the cheap Israeli cigarettes that were handed out with other supplies, wrapped in blue paper, with the design of the jet stream of a Mirage Fighter on it. The sensation of the Israeli smoke in my lungs and the air and the sun and the outpost sense of mission, made me feel comfortable in a way I'd never felt before, like having less gravity to contend with. I had more energy than ever before. I was surprised that the smoking didn't slow me down.

The kibbutzniks told me they were pleased with my work. It was the first time in my adolescence that I'd been complimented for my work, and because of this, I put everything into it. Soon I was moved from the orchards to the chicken coops, to shovel chicken manure. As I was the only volunteer pulled from the orchards, though I was the youngest, and the only non-Jew, I took it as an honor, and undertook to shovel the shit with diligence. It was a Sisyphean task. The chickens were confined in split-level wire cages suspended above huge troughs that filled with their viscous leavings and overflowed, crusting slightly, onto the concrete aisles where human workers walked between the rows of cages. My job was to stem the tide. I scooped it with a wide shovel into a wheelbarrow and emptied it over a downward slope outside. It was repetitive work that felt good in my muscles, a new feeling, and gave my mind the freedom to wander. I'd found my niche. When I appeared all jaunty, humming a little tune, at the poolside after work that day, my friends (it was a summer blessed in new friends) made me go jump into the river to wash away the stench that I'd become used to.

I was promoted again, this time to the fishponds. I was issued a large pair of flaring blue cotton shorts, kibbutz fashion, that could have fit a grown kibbutznik in each leg. By now I had adopted the habit of going without underwear. It felt more comfortable and simplified the laundry. But on this occasion it proved inconvenient. I was given a short-handled net and told to enter a concrete lock into which all the fish from the pond had been drained. There were three steps down into the room-size pit filled with writhing fish. I stepped down until the fish were up above my knees. The fourth step was a long one that dropped off to the floor of the fish chamber. I sank down slowly through the mass of fish until my feet touched the bottom. Now the fish were up to my armpits. I was expected to scoop the fish into my net and hand them up to another worker, who dumped them onto a conveyer belt that took them up to a tank truck. I did this while the fish squirmed all around my body, not only my torso, which had always been unreasonably ticklish, but in and out of the legs of my shorts, squishing up against my testicles and taking little nips from time to time.

There were two kinds of fish: carp, which were large and gray, slippery, the size of a fat billy club, up to two feet long, and sunfish, which were smaller and prettier, but whose dorsal fins cut like broken shells. The sunfish made little red, crosshatched scrapes all over me, and the carp nipped. Now and then one of them made a heroic leap from the boiling surface, squeezed from between his fellows like a huge watermelon seed. One of these leaping carp thumped me right in the solar plexus. At the end of the day I asked if I could return to the chicken coops, and my request was granted.

This time, my job was to take sickly chickens—I could recognize these by the state of their feathers—to the kitchens, where they would be slaughtered for lunch. At first I would open their cage doors and pet them and soothe them before picking them up the way I would a cat, gently, but no matter how I treated them they would raise an unholy fuss and peck at me. For about half a day I tried different techniques to make them feel safe and loved—I was good with animals—but nothing worked. After breakfast I got more efficient. I reached in for the ones I wanted, grabbed them by one leg, and shook them if they tried to peck. By the second day I was holding five or six chickens in each hand and stuffing them into the rolling box that took them to their final destination.

One day I assisted a man whose job it was to chop off the ends of their beaks. This was to prevent them from killing each other, which they often tried to do, living in such cramped and unpleasant quarters. The man had a rolling table with a crude, red-hot guillotine. The blood from the cut beaks became sticky and waved from the blades of the guillotine like ribbons. I thought of the French Revolution. It was gruesome work. But I had discovered an appetite for experiencing as much as I could of real life—anything outside the school in Massachusetts—and wanted it to go on forever.

Volunteers were assigned to kibbutz families for the length of their stay. Pop had arranged for me to be taken in by an old acquaintance of his, Lennie Friedman.[72] Lennie treated me like a son. In the afternoons some of the volunteers would join their adopted families. Adults in the kibbutz had their own little two-room houses, tiny and simple: a hot plate, a veranda, and a bedroom, enough for basic private needs. All meals were served at the central dining hall. Entertainment from string quartets or theater groups was available at the outdoor amphitheater or the recital hall. Kids were housed in their own dorms. They grew up identifying with the kibbutz as much, or more, as with their families: everything except solitude, lovemaking, and family conversation could be taken care of in the bosom of the community. There were relaxed hours in the private cottages designated to talk, play chess, listen to music, read the paper, and have snacks, before the next part of the communal cycle would begin.

I went to see Lennie and his family in the afternoons. I enjoyed talking with him in a way that felt different from the way I had talked with adults before. I wasn't continually aware of the inferiority of

---

72 Not his real name.

youth or of the need to defend my emerging little self. We all had a place in this particular corner of the universe, old or young, American or Israeli. I began to see that these distinctions were more permeable than I'd thought. It was time to reconsider all the assumptions.

Volunteers were supposed to be at least eighteen and Jewish. This made me something of a curiosity among the women volunteers, self-sufficient women who had trickled down through Turkey or who knows where, to take a break in the comfortable routine of kibbutz life. In addition to plenty of worldly experience they always had excellent hashish. On odd afternoons they shared it with me, and passed me around like a toy. I fell into a longing for the youngest of these women, a sullen and solitary person, but she showed no real interest in me. Another one said she was in trouble with her visa and I gave her my father's phone number.

As the summer waned I indulged myself with hash, sex, and cynicism, to store up for the inevitable business of a cold fifth form year in Massachusetts.

FATHER: What were we talking about? Something about the bomb.

SON: Well, you were talking about the Bergmann brothers, how the first brother, David, was the nuclear physicist and the obsessive pursuer of the bomb.[73]

FATHER: Yeah, the nationalist. And his brother, Shmuel, who, by contrast, was a philosopher, sort of a Martin Buber guy.[74]

SON: Did you know him?

FATHER: No, no. I didn't know either of them. I read about the bomb endlessly and Bergmann of course was leading the charge. And his brother was a scholar, a peacenik, and a real humanitarian. I was interested in how

---

73 Ernst David Bergmann was a German-Jewish chemist who came to Israel after the war to found Israel's nuclear programs.

74 My father had his Bergmanns slightly confused. Shmuel Bergmann was an important philosopher and humanitarian, sympathetic to Palestinians, a best friend of Max Brod and Franz Kafka, but he was from Austria-Hungary, from a different background and time. One of David's younger brothers, Arthur, was a lawyer who defended Palestinians and started a program for blind Palestinian children.

two people from the same family could turn out so differently. Cain and Abel.

SON: We were talking about the ruthlessness of Israeli groups—the Stern Gang,[75] for instance—how they blew up that ship in Haifa with their own people onboard to get the sympathy they needed, wagging the dog. We were comparing terrorists.

FATHER: That's right. That was the kind of fact that suddenly stuck, that had some point, some meaning that other facts didn't have.

When I came home from school as a hybrid flower child after the fall semester, in 1969, my father and I eyed each other across a chasm of mistrust. I'd come to realize that I could veer away sharply from the path set by adults around me. I could decide to wear whatever clothes pleased me, I could pay attention and commit to things that actually interested me, I could feel what I felt without shame, I could stand against violence and war in any form, and I could choose my own heroes. I felt exhilarated, like a new person. I would never go to Harvard (a fortuitous decision, since I would never have gained admittance anyway) and I would never work in an office. I wrenched myself away from my parents and by doing so felt closer to the rest of mankind. I defined myself as human rather than as a WASP, though there was no getting away from the WASP blood that coursed through my own veins—but I hated that part of myself instead of the wayward part I'd previously been ashamed of. There were a thousand colors on my side and a sea of gray on theirs. I've grayed up a lot since then, and dropped a few petals.

The generation gap is a disturbing cliché; it is a sign of humanity's discomfort with itself. In Israel, the gap was more in body than mind. The children of the death camp survivors were tanned and athletic, clear-eyed and confident, playful and free next to their pale, stooped, Nazi-tattooed, taciturn parents. But which one shows the true face, the parent or the child? Doesn't one live underneath the surface of the other in either case? It was the Israeli parents who had made fantastic leaps to freedom in the long and tortuous journeys from the camps to

---

75 Lehi, or the Stern Gang, was a self-described terrorist group committed to fight against the British in the years before independence.

the Promised Land, battling the elements as well as British Mandate police to accomplish the illegal immigration, the Aliyah Bet. And it was the strong Sabras[76] I knew who lived under a siege mentality: the renewed legacy of two thousand years. And these heroic, highly conscious people have replicated the harsh ghetto conditions they themselves suffered, in Gaza and the West Bank. Israel, the Promised Land, was supposed to do for the survivors what Peace and Love were supposed to do for us.

---

76 Sabra, the word for a native-born Israeli, is Hebrew for cactus: tough on the outside and tender within.

Chapter 6

Dog Days

"In America we got food to eat, we don't have to run through the jungle and scuff up our feet."

—Randy Newman

By the time I was fourteen, I'd spent only a few vague years in America. My impressions were erratic. After Berlin and Hamburg, when I was three, we moved to Falls Church, Virginia. I remember very little about Falls Church. Something about my father and a big model train layout he wanted to build. I got metal yellow trucks one Christmas, which came in terrific new boxes that excited me almost as much as the trucks. I remember a backyard that seemed exotic in its exact resemblance to other backyards. The Twins, who lived next door, were an evil influence, but I don't remember why. Best of all, again, was the low-slung fleetness of the fancycars.

I wanted to be a cowboy. Once, on our way to visit cousins in California, we stopped over at a Texas airport. I expected to see all the men dressed in ten-gallon hats, chaps, and gun belts, as I was, but I was the only one. When we came back to Virginia, I found a stick horse in a convenience store. I rode it all around the store, and I wanted to have it more than anything, but my mother made me put it back. It was an early lesson that I mustn't make a show of wanting something. Or that I mustn't want things at all. At the beginning of the next home leave period, after Salzburg, when I turned seven, we stayed in a small apartment in a large brick building that smelled of old cantaloupe rinds. It was a tenement for transient diplomatic families. My father was absent; my mother and the three kids were stashed there until further notice. There was a TV! We watched *I Love Lucy*. Lucy was great, as splashy and weird and exciting as the rest of this American life.

Then my father appeared and we drove north to spend part of the summer with my grandmother in Connecticut. Here was the America I'd always heard about. We drove in our Volkswagen bug, sent from Austria, on the Merritt Parkway, which in late spring was beautiful, perfect for cars.

Barbara and I were enchanted with Lucy, and the Merritt Parkway, and fancycars. But as we rode in the back-back of the VW, we swore we would speak to each other only in our Salzburg dialect. We arrived at a little house in Darien, on an inlet of the Long Island Sound called Holly Pond.

There was a beach and another TV. My father made me write a paragraph every day, each on a different topic, to practice writing in English so I wouldn't be too far behind in school. Otherwise, we spent our time swimming and sailing. One of the great-uncles had given Granny Hadden his old Sailfish, a big board with a sail, a centerboard, and a rudder. Pop set up a course out on the pond and put us through our paces, which included capsizing and rolling back upright. When he was satisfied that we knew enough to be safe, he let us sail on our own to our heart's content. At night I listened to the laughter of the adults through the door as they watched *Perry Mason* and westerns. We were not allowed to watch TV, so of course I was fascinated; it seemed like magic.

We went back to Washington and moved into a little white brick house on 49th Street. The house had two tiny dormers upstairs facing the street, like eyes. It was compact and symmetrical. The yard was the epitome of a yard and the house was the epitome of a house, something like what I'd thought American houses were, without the picket fence. Now I felt an enchantment, as though my real life was about to begin—this feeling happened every time we moved, and it became addictive.

The houses were tightly placed in square blocks, away from the larger city streets. MacArthur Boulevard was a big river of traffic nearby, with fantastic stores where I later made my first purchase: a catcher's mitt. Jug and Dick lived nearby, one around one corner and the other around the other corner. Jug was a little unsavory, which made him amusing and attractive to me. His older sister was crazy

about Elvis, and they watched *Howdy Doody*. To go into their house
was like visiting another planet. The colors were loud and everything
was covered with thick, clear plastic. Dick's life was more conservative.
They had a lot of darkly stained pine. I don't remember as much about
Dick, but he was a solid little boy who wore plaid. His mother was the
den mother of the Cub Scouts.

I prevailed on my parents to let me join the Cub Scouts. The
pack leader doubled as the choirmaster. I joined the choir because it
was either that or Sunday school. My mother had been raised Irish
Catholic so we had to do something about church. I went to Sunday
school once. The teacher drew a ladder reaching to heaven on the
blackboard. She explained that if we were good, we could climb the
ladder, but if we were bad we would fall off into hell, which was full
of fire and damnation. It was not the first time I'd heard about hell
but I'd never seen it depicted graphically, with hardware store para-
phernalia. In Salzburg evil had a much more colorful aspect. I didn't
want to know much more about it, maybe because I thought I was
the type that would fall off the ladder, prone as I was to break the
TV rule and so on, and climbing up didn't seem all that appealing
either. I was allowed to quit Sunday school to join the choir and the
Cub Scouts.

I went on a camping trip with the Cub Scouts. We bounced along
the rolling road into Virginia so fast that it felt like our insides were
leaping up to our throats. We all begged the choirmaster to go faster
still. He did; he even let us take the wheel, sitting in his lap I suppose,
and we were nearly airborne over those little hills, laughing like never
before.

One night I was over at Dick's house after a den meeting in his
remodeled basement, watching *King Kong* on TV. It was thrilling. My
parents called to see why I hadn't returned home after the meeting and
I told them about King Kong. They ordered me home immediately,
and made me quit the Cub Scouts. Dick's mother was quite upset over
the affair, but what could she do? Years later I heard that the Cub Scout
choirmaster, who I am sure was a completely good fellow, had been
implicated in some hanky-panky with young boys. He'd disappeared
like a drop of water on a hot skillet.

Barb and I gained admittance to Potomac School, in McLean, Virginia. The school was fun. In my third grade class we studied Vikings all year—I still remember all the Norse god stories—and played with neat little sets of blocks in some variation of New Math. We learned morris dancing and Renaissance songs. I played a very rudimentary violin part in the lower school's year-end performance of *Noye's Fludde*. But even in such a nice school, I began to notice how mean little kids could be, especially boys.

Barry and Christian both went to Potomac and they lived in our neighborhood, so we got be friends. They were of a higher social class than Dick and Jug—I think I already knew something about that. My new friends and I formed the Swamp Fox Club, Barry's idea. Christian had access to cherry bombs. I remember we set one off in a bottle in the woods near his house and the fire trucks had to be called to put out a small forest fire. Christian and Barry liked to throw rocks inside snowballs at cars on the highway from an overpass. We were supposed to grab at each other's testicles to make them hurt. I sank in the hierarchy of three when I didn't find these pastimes hilariously entertaining. Christian was beautiful and rich, the son of the German ambassador, and Barry was butch American. I tried to be interesting and tough too, but I couldn't match them. One night I confessed to Barry, who was sleeping over, that I was in love with a Russian girl from the school. I really was. The next day it got out and everyone had a good laugh. Barry had sworn on his Swamp Fox pledge never to breathe a word to anyone.

I could never apply my father's dictum—never to trust anybody— no matter how often he told me. Unwisely, or perhaps to defy him, I trusted everybody. I revealed myself. It put me at a disadvantage again and again. These days I'm a little more cautious, for survival's sake, but I still don't see the great wisdom in concealing things. If we all knew that we were amusingly screwed up in one way or another, life would be more entertaining, we would know a lot more about the mechanics of screwing up, we would be less likely to hammer one another for failing to live up to unrealistic standards, and we would want to do the right thing because it ultimately feels better. We would know more about what the hell the right thing was.

How to do right: Why don't we spend more attention on that aspect of our education? How to be considerate of other people, how to understand the terms of integrity, and yet be tolerant toward our own and other people's failings—it's complex territory, worth looking into even if only for intellectual exercise.

As I was growing up I often wished I'd been born in a precolonial American Indian culture. Theirs always seemed a good life to me, and still does. It's a white man's fantasy, but still: they lived in the wild, in rough harmony with nature. They took the mysteries seriously, their answers were less definitive than ours, and their elders guided the young. Whatever happened to our elders? In modern America we have tribes, replete with tribal rivalries and primal imperatives, but our mechanisms are determined by money and status rather than value and merit, and the closest thing a man has to the traditional guidance of the elders is the relationship he has with his boss or his gang leader and those circles of power. By a series of tests and humiliations he becomes an elder himself, or a flunky—or an outsider.

Powerful men address us on the TV, but for the most part, unless we're hooked, it's impossible to believe what they say. Walter Cronkite once said it would be useful if every authority who spoke on TV had a subtitle stating who pays him and how much money he gets for saying what he says. If motives were transparent, we would know better how to vote and our policies would improve. If we improved ourselves we might cause less harm, and other countries, less violated by us, would be less inclined to mount tidal waves of fury against the American devil.

*   *   *   *

SON: Why did you always want to be out in the field? What was so bad about being in Washington?

FATHER: I'll give you an example. I've mentioned Bissell, haven't I? Bissell had invented the U-2 spy plane and conducted overhead surveillance of the Soviet Union, and had made a big name for himself. So Dulles picked Bissell to be chief of operations. He was a big hero, but he had no intelligence experience at all. He'd never heard of a spy. Well, Helms was the ADDP, the number two in operations, and they literally never spoke. There was no connection between what Bissell was doing and anything else. And he didn't want to have anything to do with spies, so Helms ran the spies without telling Bissell, and Bissell ran these technical operations without ever telling Helms. Bissell was also into covert action, especially in South America, you know, overturning governments and that kind of thing—that was Bissell. He was up to here in the Bay of Pigs; he thought that was a wonderful idea. The guy had never been in uniform, he had no idea what a landing was like for troops, or fighting, or air cover . . . he didn't have the foggiest idea, so of course the thing was doomed from the very start. Anyway, that was the situation.

Somebody told Bissell that he didn't have anybody on his staff that had ever run a spy, so they did a computer search and my name fell out. This guy calls me up and says, "How would you like to be on Bissell's staff?" I said, "I don't know, let me find out and I'll call you tomorrow." I called [a friend who knew about such things] and I said, "Is this a good thing, for me to go into Bissell's office?" And [my friend], thinking that it might be a good thing to have someone keep tabs on Bissell, suggested I accept. And there I sat in Bissell's office.

One day Bissell looks at me—he had one of these eyes that was totally wild, so he could only look at you with one eye, the other one ranging around the room, and it was quite off-putting—says to me, "Well, what are some of the problems you operations people have?" And I said, "There's one very simple one. Ever since 1948 the State Department has refused to give us diplomatic passports, so any Soviet bureaucrat can just look at this list and he knows right away who all the CIA people are in the embassy, like that, bingo. They don't have to have a spy in there at all. That's pretty dumb, don't you think?" And he said, "Yes, take it up with Mr. Helms."

Helms had been trying ever since 1948 to get diplomatic passports for us, with a total lack of success. So I go to Helms and say, "Bissell thinks it would be a good idea if we had diplomatic passports." Helms threw me out of the office [*laughing*], he lost his temper, he went absolutely berserk. So I went back and told Bissell I'd done my best but didn't think I could be much use to him.

MOTHER: But you did stay.

FATHER: Oh yeah, I stayed.

SON: For how long?

FATHER: Oh until Bissell was fired. Helms took over as chief, and then I worked for Helms. Bill Hood[77] asked me, when he was writing Helms's [auto]biography, if I could shed any light on Bissell and Helms. When I told him this anecdote, he collapsed with laughter. He said he never expected anything could be funny about the two of them.

SON: The theater of the absurd.

FATHER: Then there was the Cuban Missile Crisis. That happened on Helms's watch while he was chief of operations there. By then I was in his office. I quickly became totally convinced, having watched the Soviets since 1948, that they weren't going to do anything. If they hadn't done anything up to 1962, they weren't going to do anything now. It was all bluff. Nothing was ever going to go off. That wasn't in the cards anymore. Even I could see that. It was just part of the Russian character, to bluff, like the way they used to pull out their guns in Berlin. It didn't mean anything. The Americans kept shooting them when they did that back then and it caused all kinds of misunderstanding. And so I didn't send you guys out of Washington either. I could have sent you down to Richmond to stay with the cousins. I could have done any number of things if I'd felt the least bit uncertain. But I knew nothing was going to happen.

Helms put me in charge of the war room. For the Agency, for the Missile Crisis. I had to track the coordinates and set up maps all over the walls. You know, every Soviet ship, every American ship. There was a file for state cables and a file for all the incoming and outgoing agents—Moscow, Cuba, Florida, internal agencies. It was time-consuming because you had to keep everything up to the minute in case someone came waltzing in and wanted to know what was going on that very minute. That was me.

SON: Did any of this end up in a study or a paper?

FATHER: Not really. When the whole thing was over everything was all packed up and went to the historical section. Where they disappear in a distant haze.

SON: But while you were in the thick of it, people were jumping like . . .

---

77 Bill Hood worked for OSS and CIA and then retired to write spy novels.

FATHER: Grasshoppers. Reading all this stuff, going in and out, talking about it . . .

SON: . . . talking about invasions and the bomb, assassinations and all kinds of things.

FATHER: Yep.

SON: They never asked what it looked like from your point of view?

FATHER: Yes, and I told 'em . . . As I recall, everybody agreed with me. I don't recall anybody being . . . nervous or anything.

SON: So they were just excited about getting a good reason to strike?

FATHER: Who, the Soviets?

SON: No, the Americans. Dulles and the Kennedys.

FATHER: Oh, everybody was excited. Curtis LeMay thought we ought to nuclear bomb them, no hesitation. That was the military point of view. Kennedy was dead set against that, thought that was idiotic.

SON: The recommendation was to bomb Moscow?

FATHER: No, no, Cuba. Not Cuba, but the missile sites in Cuba—take them out. That was the word—take out. We take them out. Meaning to kill anybody within a twenty-mile radius [*laughing*]. So that was silly. Kennedy didn't really want to do anything. So then they looked for an appropriate response. The quarantine came along—you intercept—we knew that the warheads weren't there yet. We knew that. So the idea was to intercept everything that might bring a warhead in. And the Soviets didn't have any air carrier capability, of bringing them in that way, so there was no interdiction. There was no point in worrying about aircraft.

SON: 'Cause the planes weren't big enough?

FATHER: They just wouldn't make it—too far. So they had to bring the missiles in by sea. It was very logical—let's just intercept the boats. Turn them around. We didn't have to sink them. But we had to threaten to sink them, so they would turn around and go away. It made all kinds of sense. Essentially.

In the end both Kennedy and Khrushchev were able to make themselves look pretty good, staring at each other "eyeball to eyeball," supposedly, before they both backed down and established improved relations—Kennedy had to withdraw some missile sites in Turkey—and everybody went back to work winning elections.

SON: What was your feeling when Kennedy was shot?

FATHER: I didn't know what to think. We were in Israel. I was out at a dinner party when the news came through that the embassy had called. One of my communications guys called me and said, "Kennedy's been shot. What do you want to do?" 'Cause you could never go anywhere without letting people know where you were. I went to the office but realized there was nothing for me to do. Nobody knew who was behind it, or whether it was a conspiracy, or who did it or anything. What are you going to do? So I turned around and went home. It was a very sad . . . a very sad . . .

SON: You thought Kennedy was okay, as a president.

FATHER: He and his brother had behaved so badly in Cuba that I didn't think much of him. Still, it was a shock. By the end of November Kennedy was dead.

SON: You always said you never voted.

FATHER: No. How could you serve your commander-in-chief if you'd voted against him?

SON: But you liked Kennedy at that point.

FATHER: He was a charismatic figure, and a young man, and he hadn't had a chance to prove himself, so who could be too critical of him? Look, he'd just been elected and by '63 he was gone. He hadn't even finished his first term.

SON: What did that mean to you, when he was killed?

FATHER: It was very sad, for the country, and for everybody. And one wondered how stable things would be. Johnson was an unknown, as far as I was concerned, a total unknown . . . But he took over on the plane to Washington, and everybody swore allegiance to him, McGeorge Bundy[78] and the rest. I thought Johnson was a better president, better for the job than Kennedy. But then he had his problems, didn't he? Kennedy had gotten us into Vietnam—that was great. That was a big plus, wasn't it?

SON: Weren't Kennedy and McNamara talking about getting out?

---

78 McGeorge Bundy, who went to Groton and Yale, was National Security Advisor to Kennedy and Johnson, later president of the Ford Foundation. Hawkish on Vietnam at first, he quietly regretted the war and became a spokesperson against the use of nuclear weapons and was influential in the SALT II treaty. He was on Nixon's "enemies" list.

FATHER: They didn't do much about it, did they? That was great thing to say, but nobody knows what Kennedy would have done. Presidents don't like to be pushed out of places. That was Johnson's trouble, too, he felt that he was being pushed out. People told him it wasn't in our national interest but he paid no attention to them. It wasn't Kissinger, you see, it was Johnson. He wouldn't listen to anybody else, he couldn't see how to get out.

SON: Did you know Kissinger?

FATHER: There was a thing called the 20 Committee. Every political action operation had to be presented to and passed by this committee.

SON: Was that the same thing as the 40 Committee?

FATHER: They kept changing the name, to keep it quiet. And it consisted of Kissinger, Helms, Packard from the Pentagon, and Loy Henderson from the State Department, the administrative chief. They would meet and Helms would bring his staff guys with him depending on what the problem was and so I would go to a meeting with Helms, and if he wanted me to put in a word or tell him something, I would be there. There would be these chiefs in ties and shirts, button-down collars, and there would be Kissinger, feet up on the table, sleeves rolled up, tie loosened, no coat, looking at these guys. He had them all lined up. Nobody had the president's ear except him.

SON: I saw a film recently that makes a pretty strong case that Kissinger is a war criminal. It shows how Kissinger, in '68, just before the elections—who knew he had a big job coming to him no matter who got in, Johnson or Nixon—sent a secret message to the South Vietnamese to boycott the Paris peace talks that were going on then, just because that would sink Johnson. Of course, Johnson withdrew from the race.

FATHER: Like Reagan and the hostages in Iran . . .

SON: To screw Carter, yeah. So the peace talks failed, Nixon got in, and Kissinger got what he wanted. Then when the peace finally was signed . . .

FATHER: Nixon got the credit.

SON: Nixon got the credit and Kissinger got the Nobel Peace Prize. The terms were no better than they'd been in the first talks, but umpteen thousands of people had been killed, there was the illegal war in Cambodia, an entire ecosystem ravaged and poisoned— So here's a guy who for relatively miniscule personal gain . . .

FATHER: Political gain . . .

SON: . . . allows the whole thing to go up in smoke . . .

FATHER: . . . more deaths . . .

SON: . . . and more rending of the American soul.

FATHER: Yeah.

SON: A lot more.

FATHER: Yup, true.

*　　*　　*　　*

The universe sometimes sends a cascade of signs, as if to cry to the slightly awakened creature: See? See? Do you see?

I was staying at an apartment in Cambridge, Massachusetts, preparing to accompany a dear friend, my old roommate, to his father's memorial service at the church in Harvard Yard. My friend's father had been prominent in the life of Harvard and had been a member of the Kennedy and Johnson administrations. He was one of the architects of the Vietnam War, and had privately expressed regret about his part in it to his son. He was one of the only other parents I knew at the school and he treated me with kindness. I missed him; my friend was bereft.

I went to look around Harvard Yard the day before the service so that I could get my bearings and be there on time. I'd always liked the buskers, the street people, and the old Orson Welles cinema. Cambridge was a countercultural hot spot; Baez and Dylan had been there. I lived in Boston for several years and I was drawn to Cambridge, but I avoided the Square and I'd never gone into the Yard. Maybe I was afraid to run into someone from Groton or I was intimidated by the ghosts of a dozen ancestors who had been there. The famous landmarks—Memorial Church, Weidner Library, Lowell House—seemed familiar to me though I had never seen them before. The breeding grounds of power are lovely, wonderful places.

Back at the apartment, a pile of CDs on the floor beckoned to me. I picked one up. It was a recording of a Simon and Garfunkel concert in Central Park. I put it on.

"When I think back on all the crap I learned in high school/It's a wonder I can think at all . . ." Long forgotten sensations washed over me. Through the years, my friend and I had shared long talks about our fathers. The conversation is ongoing, and we are grateful for each other's interest and understanding—and grief, on many levels. I thought of all the talks we'd had at school, and how the music had been such a comfort to us both.

I looked around at the books lining the room in the shelves, and saw *An Unfinished Song*, by Joan Jara, a book about her husband and the Chilean coup in 1973. The book had affected me deeply, and had led me to write my first play. I reached for the book, another friend, tears running down my face. I felt blessed in friends.

SON: Do you think Kissinger is a war criminal?
FATHER: No, no, no, he was doing what the president wanted him to do.
MOTHER: But you just finished saying that Nixon was doing what . . .
FATHER: The future president. Well, that's what he was there for, at least in his mind. A war criminal is someone who intentionally kills people. A man who thinks that the country is better off if he can personally establish himself? It's hard to say.

After the Chicago riots and the escalations in Vietnam and the Civil Rights confrontations, all accompanied with senseless violence, things really started to change. There was a pivotal point Pop might not have noticed. As he said himself, it's sometimes hard to see what's right under your nose. But events and feelings began to flow in a new direction, like the changing of a tide.

Young voices rose in volume and power and found a new common ground all over the world, rejecting consumerism and war. Kissinger himself in his memoirs claims that he understood "the young people's" perception that there was a lack of meaning in the post-industrial age. Even at Groton School the administration saw the traditional influence collapsing—and chose to get tough. They fired a lenient headmaster in '69 and kids were expelled left and right. One senior had been reading aloud, magnificently, in a ringing, low, slow voice from the Tibetan Book of the Dead every morning in Chapel for a week—intellectual curiosity was not yet discouraged—but he snapped one night at supper. He pushed his chair out and waited for his moment.

The muffled din in the Dining Hall died down and came to a halt. He intoned in his best Chapel voice, "FUCK!" and was promptly removed to the infirmary, the usual way station before the final boot.

Ewell Gibbons, the author of *Stalking the Wild Asparagus*, once came to speak. The speech itself was unremarkable, but the very fact that a man who represented a counterculture point of view had been invited to the school was stunning. He had been driven to the school in an old Chevrolet by a younger man who was an ACLU volunteer. I took the chauffeur on a tour of the school, showing him the dorms, wondering if I could get the ACLU interested. I couldn't—we were all there voluntarily. But the man talked about life on the outside, what was happening in the Movement. He knew the Berrigans, who were regularly going to jail for wonderfully imaginative acts of civil disobedience with their Plowshares Movement, damaging nuclear warheads or defacing draft records with their own blood.

On the other side, Curtis LeMay was itching to pull the final trigger, soldiers in the National Guard were being trained to kill students in Ohio if necessary, and the damned Gooks wouldn't go down, no matter how much poison and napalm you dumped into their jungle villages. People just wouldn't see that we were right, that we were the only ones left that stood for freedom and the rights of man. But a lot of people, and not only young people, were allowing a different possibility to enter their heads, the possibility that we didn't have to bash everyone into grateful submission.

I worked in the kitchen to earn a little money, to get to know the townies who worked there, and to escape the stifling routine of meals in the Dining Hall. I loved being in the kitchen, working with the steam dishwashers, finishing work after everyone in coats and ties had left the building. After work a fellow dishwasher and I drifted downstairs to have coffee in the sumptuous faculty lounge. The coffee was kept hot in a fabulous silver urn. We drank the masters' coffee in exquisite demitasses embossed with the Groton seal, smoked an old roach, and reveled in the small break from the routine.

SON: You were back in Washington. You were still working with Israel.
FATHER: I had what they called the Israel account.

SON: Lamott had been your liaison when you were in Israel, and now you took his place.

FATHER: Yeah.

SON: Who went out to take your place?

FATHER: One of Angleton's guys.

SON: You didn't choose your replacement.

FATHER: No, Angleton did.

SON: The Israeli bomb was a big question and Johnson didn't want to touch it. What did you do then?

FATHER: Nothing, because that was the science attaché's job, a guy named Webber, who was really first-class. Dimona was his baby, not mine. He did the inspections.

SON: So they did do inspections.

FATHER: The Israelis swept everything under the rug when he was around. They would never allow him to bring any gear into the place, so they were never able to track anything. It was a hopeless waste of time. But he would go talk to the scientists and whatnot, and he knew what was going on. But nobody believed him, so it didn't do any good.

SON: But you talked to him.

FATHER: I talked to him. That didn't do any good either. What could I do?

SON: At least you knew what was going on.

FATHER: Yes. Webber was dealing with Bergmann, the head of the Israeli bomb project. So that was all useful background for me. But you know, even when I could prove they had the bomb, the political leadership refused to believe it—and refused to deal with it. Helms went over and told Johnson, and Johnson said, "Well, don't tell anybody." The day came when I was told to go over and brief the Secretary of State on the fact that they had the bomb, and why, and how they smuggled the uranium out from under our noses, with a little help from our friends, and that we could prove it. I went over there, and I forget who it was, Rusk— Dean Rusk, and he had a guy named Sisco,[79] whom I called the Sisco Kid, because he was rambunctious and wanted to be Secretary of State himself—well, *pphhhwww* . . . He had never served abroad, never been

79 Dean Rusk was Secretary of State under Kennedy and Johnson, until 1969. Joseph J. Sisco was undersecretary in charge of Near and Far East affairs, under Rusk and his successor under Nixon, William Rogers.

overseas. He was like one of Shakespeare's staff officers, who was it, the one who takes snuff?

SON: Shakespeare never mentions the guy by name. It's the scene in which Henry Percy goes into a rage in front of the king about how they're trying to get things done in the field, and this effete staff officer complains to him about the stench from the dead bodies Percy's men carry by. This fop, says Percy, takes snuff to mask the smell and pretends that but for the guns which he disdains, he would have been a soldier himself! Of course, Percy is digging his own grave.

FATHER: That's it. Just like that. The Sisco Kid thought he knew it all and he didn't know anything. There I am briefing Rusk and Sisco, that Israel had the bomb, and it was so clear that there was nothing they could say.

SON: This is after the Six-Day War?

FATHER: Yes, it must have been, just afterward. I'd been back in Washington for a short while. So Sisco turns to me and says, "If anyone finds out, can we claim an intelligence failure?" I just looked at him.

SON: He says that to you?

FATHER: I just stared at him. I mean there I am, finally, with the papers proving that they have the bomb . . . Brilliant. Brilliant. You learn a lot, listening to people. I just shook my head and didn't say a word.

I have been consciously looking at how my father and I negotiated the question of masculine dominance that ran through all our conversations. Now I see him facing older bulls himself. How did he deal with it? It's a little difficult for me to imagine—and I think this must be true for a lot of kids, looking at their fathers. Our fathers are like gods. Who's God's god? How does God do what he's told? I think this is especially difficult for those of us who were brought up in monotheistic societies. The Greeks, Norsemen, Hindus, and Romans had gods that constantly knocked each other aside, and I think because of it they understand our cosmic nuances and contradictions better than we do.

Pop did not automatically respect Washington bureaucrats; he didn't like being told what to do if he thought the order was wrong and counterproductive. In this case he had done some of his best work, carefully and discreetly compiling the report. In the end he was bumped out surely because it became clear to the bosses that Hadden was getting too big for his breeches. He had built a good record of keeping his mouth shut—if anything, he was too quiet—but they knew he was a bit of a loose cannon.

He was very careful, however, about the NUMEC affair. Whenever possible, he referred to information that was already out there, in headlines, history, and common sense, an accumulation of which would point to the same conclusion as the hard evidence provided. He spoke openly to one or two friends that I am only now learning of, but only after he was absolutely sure of their discretion.

He had reason to be careful. Mordechai Vanunu, for instance, an Israeli nuclear technician who worked at the Dimona plant in the seventies and eighties, revealed nuclear secrets to the Sunday *Times* (UK) in 1986, and was jailed for eighteen years, all but six of them in strict solitary confinement, for disclosing what he knew. He was kidnapped from Rome after his release, returned to house arrest, remains under a gag order, and is still jailed regularly for technical violations, though he no longer has any inside knowledge that could damage Israel. There's a personal side to how Israelis punish their adversaries, or friends who have gone astray.

"Nuclear ambiguity" is the official stance Israel takes on their possession of the bomb. They want everyone to know they have it but they don't want anyone to talk about it. Israel has consistently said that it would not be "the first to introduce nuclear weapons" to the Middle East. Israel has up to 400 nuclear devices, including neutron (thermonuclear) bombs. One advantage of maintaining silence on nuclear weapons is that Israel receives $2 billion a year in US aid that would not be legally available if she had overt nuclear weapons. The story goes that the first bomb to be made in Dimona had the words *Never Again* welded on its casing.

The stakes are high, because of history, mythology, the Holocaust, and the determination of Israel's enemies to destroy her. Israelis are forged in a hot fire, on a hard anvil. And yet there are a spate of books out about the Israeli bomb: *The Samson Option*, by Seymour Hersh; *The Worst-Kept Secret*, by Avner Cohen; *The Bomb in the Basement*, by Michael Karpin; and *The Apollo/NUMEC Affair*, by Roger Mattson. Mattson's research comes from his own long experience tracking the case, as a nuclear safety engineer and former AEC/NRC official and from recently declassified documents from the Department of Energy, where my father was finally called in to share what he knew, six years after his retirement.[80] Following some of these leads, Mattson came in October 2014 to look through the boxes of files from my father's attic with me and his wife, Donna, a savvy veteran of the nuclear business.

Avner Cohen, who teaches at the Monterey Institute of International Studies in California and is an ardent voice for nonproliferation, tells the following story in "The Avner Cohen Collection," published by the Woodrow Wilson Center for International Scholars:

> I will end this introduction with an amusing anecdote that [Avraham] Hermoni [technical director for Israel's nuclear weapons program, 1959–1969] told me that took place sometime during the period when Hermoni was the science attaché at the Israeli embassy in Washington D.C. (approximately 1969–72). One evening, during an intermission of a cultural event at the Kennedy Center, Hermoni noticed John Hadden, the former CIA station chief in Tel Aviv (1964–68), in the audience. Hermoni knew well that one of Hadden's most important tasks while in Israel was to monitor the nuclear project. As they recognized each other in distance, Hadden shouted, "Avraham, does it work?" to which Hermoni promptly responded, "One hundred percent it does." Both laughed.
>
> What does this little anecdote tell us, beyond a little laughter? Maybe it suggests that even in those early days, the big secret was not that big, and it was already "the worst-kept secret."

SON: Intelligence failure. It has a certain ring.

FATHER: All you can do with people like that is stare at them in disbelief. And that was sort of the end of the meeting [*thin laugh*]. Intelligence failure can mean a lot of things. There was another occasion, after Israel, when I was working in Washington, the people in the DDI, the analysts, were telling Helms what should happen in Israel, in detail, briefing him. And they were absolutely crazy, they didn't have the foggiest idea what

---

80 See appendix.

was going on in Israel. But Helms's whole approach to life was never to argue with anybody. If there was a disagreement he would get both sides to sit there in front of him and he would watch them battle it out and see who would win, like a tennis match.

He's talking to these DDI guys and he gets me on the phone and tells me to come up to his office. No explanation, no preparation, no paper, nothing, just, "Come up here and I want you to talk to these guys." I go up there and I listen to their presentation and Helms says, "What do you think of this?" I say, "Well, they're all wrong." He eggs me on: ". . . and?" I said, "Look, I've got notes on all this—let me go down and prepare a position paper, because I'm not ready for this," and he said, "No no, I want you guys to settle this right here." So then I lost my temper. I don't quite know how I got there, but I just lost it. I said, "You bastards have never been there, you don't realize that there's a war going on! These people are at war—they have been at war, to the knife, since long before 1948; they're still at war, and if you people think that anything is going to happen because of your ideas and your procedures, you can just pack your bags!" I was furious.

Helms sat there with a big smile on his face and said, "Well, gentlemen, I guess that settles that." [laughs] He said to me later, "You know Hadden, that's a side to you I've never seen before!"

I loved hearing him tell this story and I felt proud of him, but I didn't want to feed his ego. It's a little mean—but he never wanted to feed mine. Tit for tat. So I changed the subject. The stuff about Helms was too easy and I didn't trust it. My father grew up without the guidance of loving men, and when he grew older, a Shakespearean pattern revolved principally around two powerful men: Richard Helms and James Jesus Angleton. Patron and nemesis. Angleton and Helms. These names orbit the story of my father's career like large planets. They both go way back, always a little ahead of my father, the big kids playing around Europe and the Middle East, inheritors of the system as handed down by Dulles and the founding fathers of the big new game.

SON: I'm confused about Angleton. How did Israel fall into his bailiwick? Counterintelligence is about working against the Soviets and so-called enemies, isn't it?

FATHER: Oh no, counterintelligence [*laughing*] is against everybody, even US Congressmen sometimes.

SON: But am I getting this right? Angleton was backing the Israelis to the hilt because he saw them as a barrier to the Soviet Union.

FATHER: He felt that anything that the Israelis could get outside the Agency they ought to have. Anything that would strengthen their hand against the USSR. Israeli operations against the US never bothered him. In other words—let's take the bomb. Angleton thought they ought to have it. I mean what the hell? He didn't care where they got it. The fact that they stole it from us didn't worry him in the least. I suspect that in his inmost heart he would have given it to them if they'd asked for it.

SON: So one of his main peeves with you was that you wanted to account for all this.

FATHER: Oh, of course. He was totally against anything I was doing. He knew for example that I questioned all foreign reporting. I wanted to see how they were using this so-called reporting to steer the American government. Feeding us certain kinds of information.

SON: To what extent do you think that succeeds?

FATHER: Oh, to a great extent. These people are very bright. Surgical. They only do what is absolutely necessary to get what they want. . . .

SON: It sounds like steering a satellite. I mean it doesn't take much—a small nudge sends us on a vector to an infinitely diverged point.

FATHER: A thousandth of a degree makes all the difference. And that's been happening—

SON: Since when?

FATHER: Since Angleton first started in Washington.

SON: What were the mechanics of how the Israelis did this?

FATHER: They'd give a report to Angleton that'd been all dummied up. . . .

SON: Like what?

FATHER: Oh, an original Arab document saying XYZ . . . and then Angleton would take it and swallow it whole—on purpose—and make sure I never got hold of it.

SON: So it must have been very different to go back to Washington and deal with Angleton after your relative autonomy in Israel.

FATHER: Yes. In a word, yes.

SON: But you must have felt that it was important to make clear what was going on. Wasn't that your job in Washington, as you defined it?

FATHER: Goodness, no, it was my job to understand what was going on, but not to tell people how it was being done, no. For instance it was up to me to tell people how the Israelis got the bomb, but in such a limited way that it could never be published. Once you put out a report and put a number on it and a title, and source it and whatnot, Christ, the news media have it and it's out. Americans can't keep secrets. I never made a report. I never wrote a report. Never. I only wrote for Helms. And it would be a blank. Just like the things I write today. I don't put my name on it. It doesn't come from my office; it has no number on it; it has no title. I source it by talking to him and that's the way I did it. Sometimes he told me that he'd showed it to the president and whatnot. But he always took it back, he never left it.

SON: Yes, I saw your essay on the Israeli bomb—"The Nth Power." With the timelines and newspaper headlines and all . . . you're very careful to point to the tangential evidence all around and sort of lead the way in, without actually saying anything yourself . . . it seems like you could have written a simple paragraph and footnoted the reported data, but you didn't.

FATHER: No, no, no, that would have been counterproductive, because if it ever fell into the hands of a pro-Israeli politician in Washington, my God! There was a senator . . . How do I turn this off? [This senator] came to visit Israel on one of his junkets—you know how Congressmen are.[81] So the ambassador gave a dinner for him and invited some of us to come too. And also invited the Israeli chief of staff. It was a pleasant enough dinner. As we got to the cigars and the cognac, the senator turned to the ambassador and said, "Mr. Barbour, the general and I have some private things to discuss. I request that you and your staff go into the other room. . . ."

SON: Wow.

FATHER: It was that blatant.

---

81 Congressmen regularly accept lavish all-expenses-paid vacations to Israel from AIPAC. In one month in 2011, 81 House members took the trip. Lately, with all the lobbying against Obama's no-nuclear-bomb deal with Iran, led by Bibi Netanyahu and AIPAC, these junkets have gone through the roof.

SON: Incredible. How did this serve him? What was his interest?

FATHER: Where do you think these guys get their campaign money?

SON: At one point you mentioned a figure like $800 million a year.

FATHER: Oh Christ, that's just the UJA alone. I don't know what the figures are now, that was way back in the seventies.

SON: It's funny that everybody is knocked over by that $200 million in Bush's campaign chest. That's nothing.

FATHER: Peanuts! Peanuts!

SON: So you're talking about campaign costs not only for the presidency but for . . .

FATHER: A number of politicians.

SON: So when McCain tries to push campaign finance reform . . .

FATHER: He's pushing uphill. But be careful. You have to be very careful with that. Because they never use that incredible power that they have for anything but their own narrow special interest, so that they don't split their own constituency. Not that their own constituency isn't split, but . . .

SON: But on that one item, they expect action . . .

FATHER: They get the one vote they care about. And the politician knows it. As long as the politician gives him whatever he wants on that item he gets elected and then he can do anything he wants in any other direction. That's the way the US government works. Or doesn't work. And of course the other lobbyists buy up the votes on the other issues—oil, timber, taxes, subsidies, arms sales and whatnot. . . .

SON: Guns . . .

FATHER: Guns . . .

SON: So there's not much left over for the people.

FATHER: The people? Who are they? No, their problems don't figure much in the business of the government.

SON: What was Helms's position on all of this?

FATHER: His only interest was in getting information and making it available.

SON: So he had no personal interest in what was done with it or whether anyone would listen to him . . .

FATHER: Oh, I think he was as upset as I was, that foreign agents were running the US government, but that wasn't my business, nor was it his. So we were the same on that. It never bothered me that he didn't try to blow up the government with this kind of reporting, that would have been dumb, you know . . .

SON: How effective was your work, do you think, in general?

FATHER: Johnson told Helms that this was all very interesting and not to discuss it with either the Secretary of Defense or the Secretary of State [*laughs*].

SON: Why was Helms so cozy with Angleton?

FATHER: You'll have to read his book. He goes into that in detail. He mentions that some people thought that Angleton was off his nut. And he was. I mean, I'm not a doctor, I don't know what the hell was wrong with him . . .

MOTHER: But you also said that Angleton was kind of a genius.

FATHER: He was a genius. He would have been invaluable as some kind of advisor or think-tank kind of guy. But here he was the head of a staff in the chain of command, and he was absolutely worthless as an administrator. He had no leadership qualities whatsoever, none. He made up for it by being so brilliant in combinations. He could make any combination. His problem was that he made too many. What he needed was a chief to keep him under control, then he would have been invaluable, because he would have gotten people to think of things they never would have thought of otherwise. And he was a brilliant writer too. He was a published poet, you know. He wrote the eulogy for Allen Dulles, that Helms delivered at the funeral.

MOTHER: He was a big buddy of Allen Dulles. He carried the casket.

FATHER: Yeah, yeah. So.

SON: There was the trip to New Orleans . . .

FATHER: That was with the Mossad guys and General Amit. I set that up and Angleton came along. I said to Angleton, "Let's take them on a pack train into the mountains for a week, with a chuck wagon and cowboys— it'd be something they would never forget, an experience they would never get anywhere else in the world. Otherwise, what are they going to see, one more city?" "No," he said, "they want to see the hot spots and the night spots and they want to eat it up." What an idiot.

SON: What was the incident about the diamonds?

FATHER: It was on that trip. I was with Angleton and I just disappeared one day around the corner. I could tell that he was nervous. He was always nervous. So I came back around the corner and joined the party, and he said, "Where have you been?" I said, "You won't believe this, but a guy just came up to me and he had two diamonds wrapped up in a newspaper, and it was an offer I couldn't refuse." So Angleton looked at me in his superior way—he was known to be an expert on all kinds of arcane subjects—and said, "Let me see 'em." I took out my wallet. Your mother had given me two diamonds from her mother's wedding rings. He took one look at them and said, "Glass!" Oh, I said, "Oh, isn't that terrible—well, you win some and you lose some," and I wrapped them back up in the newspaper and he looked at me with that patrician smile, and we went on with the party. When we got to Los Angeles, I said, "You know, there's not much going on tonight, they're going to have supper downstairs and go to their rooms. Do you mind if I go see my sister-in-law? She lives nearby and my wife has asked that I go see her, because she has a little favor for me to do for her." And his curiosity got the better of him—for one thing, he knew both the sisters in Rome—so he said, "What was that?" I said, "Well, she gave me two diamonds to have set." And he got red in the face, he was so mad he couldn't speak. [*he laughs uproariously*]

SON: Why were you playing with him?

FATHER: 'Cause I knew he would say they were glass.

SON: I know, but what were you up to?

FATHER: I wanted to prove to him that he didn't know what he was talking about. He just made it up. All the time. He just wanted to be one up on people.

SON: He was after you for some reason.

FATHER: Always. Always. But he was always after everybody—everybody beneath him. Never anybody above him. He'd play with facts and he'd deal them out like cards. He'd say, here's something that you never knew, and that's why you don't know what's going on. Terrible. He was always playing games. And it was all crap, it was to no purpose, just for his own ego, just to be one up.

SON: What was his whole obsession with the fifth man?

FATHER: Angleton had worked very closely with the British in OSS. He'd gone to school with them in England.

SON: With that whole upper crust public-school group—Philby, Maclean, Burgess, and the others?

FATHER: That's right, Angleton saw himself as an aristocrat. He belonged.
He'd gone to Yale. Skull and Bones. *Pphhhwww* . . .

SON: So when Philby defected . . .

FATHER: Philby was head of MI6—or the Soviet division of MI6. And he
had trained Angleton, for God's sake, when he was first sent over in OSS.

SON: Was Philby running the investigation against himself, getting closer
and closer . . . ?

FATHER: He wasn't running it, but he was privy to it. They eventually
fired him out of hand. And then they sent him to Lebanon on a job for
the London *Times*, as a journalist. But he was on his own. They wouldn't
put him up. And more and more piled up against him. MI5 wouldn't let
go. And finally they sent one of his best friends, Nicholas Elliot, to say,
"C'mon Philby, we know you work for the Soviets, come on, tell us what
you did."[82] And he stonewalled. Two days later he was on a freighter out
of Lebanon bound for the Soviet Union.

SON: And was that the first domino that led to Burgess and Maclean?

FATHER: No, they'd already gone earlier. In fact, that's what started to
unravel for Philby. He was the last one to see them, and that's what nar-
rowed it down. MI5 deduced that Philby had tipped off Maclean and Burgess, so they knew without a doubt. It was supposed to be just Maclean
defecting, but Burgess decided at the last moment to scamper, and that's
what really blew it wide open. Sort of a harsh moment for him, don't you
think?

SON: Harsh moment for Angleton, too, since he'd put so much stock in
that association, told Philby everything through the years. Is that why he
was so crazy about tracking down the other two? To counter the stigma of
his friendship with Philby? To make up for what he'd given away?

FATHER: I don't know how it worked itself out, hard to say, because he
was paranoid anyway.

SON: Did he ever think you were a mole?

FATHER: Oh, yeah.

SON: How did you know?

---

82 Nicholas Elliot, who was close with Philby, felt the betrayal very personally.
Elliot had a long and interesting intelligence career during the war and afterward,
mostly as a field officer.

FATHER: He accused me directly. He brought me into his office. He'd give these three-hour lectures, so I would sort of nod, yeah, yup, that's really interesting, ho-hum. But on this occasion he'd set it up like a stage play. All the curtains were drawn, the place was black, and there was this one desk lamp, lighting his face from below, and I was sitting there nodding, half asleep by now, a totally worthless waste of time, getting me nowhere, and he was . . . I think it was one of those periods when he was convinced that the whole Sino-Soviet conflict on the border was disinformation, and had been wholly made up by the KGB to put us off our guard. Absolute madness. I mean you didn't have to be a student of Russian affairs or Chinese affairs to know that there was a Chinese-Soviet war going on right there on the Ussuri River. They had photographs!

I was nodding away, and then he chose his moment. He leaned across the table and said, "Hadden . . . WHEN DID THEY PITCH YOU?!" And I burst out laughing, I thought it was the funniest thing I'd ever heard. It woke me up, I will admit that. Here was this serious man, telling me that I'd been recruited by the Soviets. I just couldn't help it. And it made him furious. He couldn't take anybody laughing at him. He had very little sense of humor. He was a great wit, but that's different. That's one thing I learned from Angleton, the difference between wit and humor. And he said, "What are you laughing at?" He was practically throwing things.

And I said, "Jim, if the Soviets have been pitching me, they've been so subtle that I don't even know it." And he said, "Get out of here!" [*laughing affectionately*] But he finally got rid of me. We were oil and water. It was hopeless. There was no way we could ever see eye to eye on anything.

Ever since I'd seen Philby's name on the file in my father's office in Tel Aviv when I was eleven, I'd been fascinated by him. Philby had grown up overseas, watching the British Empire crumble, and had been appalled by the British treatment of foreign people on their own soil. It was something I recognized. His father was an emissary to India who later became a mentor to Lawrence of Arabia and to Prince Ibn Saud, wore a kaftan and kaffiyeh, married an Arab woman, and accumulated a lot of power in the Middle East via oil and cultural politics.

Like his son, he was born overseas, in Ceylon, and like his son, his loyalties were not necessarily with the West. Kim Philby became a Communist while he was still quite young, rose quickly in British Intelligence, and did his best to undermine the whole capitalist machine.

I started to fantasize that my father really was the Fifth Man. It
didn't seem so absurd. Angleton had a lot of power over a long period
and he was by all accounts a brilliant analyst, head of counterintelligence—and *he* thought it was a possibility. Helms installed my father
in Angleton's office. Why? Was he supposed to watch Angleton? Was
Angleton supposed to watch him? Very unclear. In any case, Angleton
thought my father was a mole, and accused him of it. He thought he'd
caught him finally, and my father had burst out laughing.

So: did my father expect this? Did he set it up? Was he playing with Angleton? Did he prepare that surprised outburst of laughter? Was he delighted that Angleton had fallen into a trap? He talks about other little games he played with Angleton. It doesn't disprove the possibility. He didn't deny it, did he?

But in time my fantasy fell apart. Blunt, the fourth, was found while he was serving as the curator for the queen's pictures at Buckingham Palace, and the Fifth Man, who was thought to be John Cairncross, was confirmed ten years later by a Soviet defector named Gordievsky—and by that time I'd sort of lost track of the whole thing. In any case, Pop wasn't one of the five.

SON: Then Blunt came out . . .

FATHER: They got Blunt, and then Cairncross.

SON: The fifth guy?

FATHER: Some years later. But that was after I was gone. Philby blew when I was in Israel, that's how close it was to the end for me. And Blunt was picked up afterward.

SON: Yes, I remember that. The queen's paintings. But that was only four. Was Angleton still there when they got the fifth?

FATHER: No, Angleton left in '74. He was fired by Colby out of hand, about a year after I left. That's right, because when I came back in '75, it was Colby I dealt with. He was DCI then. My, he was bitter against Angleton, holy Jesus. You mentioned Angleton's name and he could hardly speak. Everybody hated him. It was crazy. Angleton never had anything to do with much of anybody except the DCIs.

SON: DCIs?

FATHER: Directors of Central Intelligence. Angleton's great feat in life was the care and feeding of DCIs. He had them all in the palm of his hand. That's why his peers hated him so. Of course, when one of his peers got to be chief, he was fired out of hand. That was Colby. And that was the end of Angleton.

SON: I'm so confused about Angleton and Helms and you. I don't understand why Helms was as loyal as he was to Angleton; I don't understand why you didn't talk to Helms about your experience.

FATHER: Because of Helms's loyalty to Angleton. I knew that . . .

SON: But you had nothing to lose. You were quitting anyway at that point.

FATHER: Ah, what good would it have done to upset Helms?

SON: It would have given him a clearer view of . . .

FATHER: That's not my business. To open Helms's eyes? I would leave that to someone else. I would only have told Helms if he had specifically asked about it.

SON: But he was asking you—

FATHER: He wasn't asking me about Angleton.

SON: He was asking why were you leaving, wasn't he?

FATHER: There were two parts to it. Angleton had gone so far as to swipe one of my own case officers. And he told my subordinate not to tell me things, and of course the guy told me about it. Well, if I went to Helms with that, my subordinate would have been in all kinds of trouble. To no purpose, 'cause I was already on my way out.

SON: Why didn't Helms pick up from this legion of officers who were screwed by Angleton what was going on? Wasn't he an extremely perceptive man?

FATHER: Good question. I have no answer to that. You can read Helms's book. The two really grew up together, you know, in OSS. They'd been very young in the war. And they'd worked closely together for thirty-two years, seeing each other every day. I knew I didn't have a chance. If it was me or Angleton it was going to be me, you know, so why bother? There was no point in it. So I left. It was very simple. I had checked, of course, to find out what the conditions of retirement would be, and it wasn't so bad. Sixty percent of my highest salary, and it would go up with the index every year, and I would have medical for life, along with my wife—well, what the hell, what was I doing? If I had stayed on I'm sure that I would have died long ago. I never would have reached eighty.

SON: Why?

FATHER: It was not a healthy life.

SON: Stress, and . . . ?

FATHER: Whatever. Alcohol, and whatever. Besides, I hated Washington anyway. And by that time, I couldn't get a job anywhere else in the Agency, because everybody so hated Angleton, that anybody that worked for him was *finito*. I had a good friend who was kicked out of the Agency, just for having worked for Angleton. It was dumb. So there was no point in my sticking around.

MOTHER: Can I make a comment?

FATHER: Mm-hmm.

MOTHER: We were at a dinner in honor of Richard Helms one night and he turned to me and said, "You know, I don't mind a lot of people leaving, but I do mind John Hadden leaving." And I didn't say anything. But I should have said, "Well then, why are you letting him go?"

FATHER: That's just what people say when they don't know what else to say. Around that time, Helms called me up to lunch in his dining room, just the two of us. We ate together alone, and he . . . he never said, "I'll give you another job," he never said that. He kept asking me, "Why are you leaving," and I said, "Well, it's time." So I never told him, but he never suggested that I do something else, so . . . So I never said anything. We just sat there looking at each other.

SON: Kissinger says that Helms's smile did not include his eyes.

FATHER: Does he? Well, Helms played him as well as anyone could.

SON: But you must have thought that he would have figured out the situation with Angleton.

FATHER: I have absolutely no idea. [*At this point, he shouts irrationally, something about the dog outside.*] We've been through that.

SON: Did you know that Helms was on his way out by then?

FATHER: Goodness no, because he wasn't. In '72 he was doing fine.

SON: And what precipitated . . . ?

FATHER: Oh, the . . . the whole business of the . . . [*sighs*] of Allende came up, and there was the intelligence committee in the House, and the intelligence committee in the Senate,[83] and they were the ones who were authorized to get information about operations. And he told both of them, both committees, all that he—that the Agency had done in the Allende business was just paying newspapers to attack Allende. And when Nixon, oh . . . Well, you see, it went back further.

The real reason he got kicked out of the Agency was because of CREEP, you know the Committee to Reelect the President. Nixon had sent over a direct order to Helms to get the Agency to say that Congress

---

83 The Church Committee, chaired by Senator Frank Church in 1975, investigated abuses by intelligence services: the so-called "Family Jewels."

couldn't investigate where money to pay their cover-up lawyers came from, because that would interfere with CIA operations in Mexico. Helms established that it wouldn't interfere with any operations and told Nixon that no, he couldn't say that any investigation of this laundered money would interfere with operations, 'cause it wouldn't. So Nixon fired him. And then, to get him out of the country, he appointed him ambassador to Tehran. Well, to become ambassador to Tehran, he had to come up before the Committee on Foreign Relations. And those guys, wanting to make a political name for themselves, which is all that senators have in mind, started asking about the Allende case, and Helms just said, "Well we had nothing to do with that." Because they weren't authorized to get information from Helms about operations. And the other committee refused to stand up for him and say that he had briefed them, although he had.

He wanted to drag all this through court and show them all up, kick 'em in the face. Edward Bennett Williams, one of the most famous men in Washington, was Helms's lawyer. And he said, "That's a waste of time, you'll never get anywhere with that, not with the judges the way they are. They're all in the pockets of these senators—let me make a deal instead." And Helms said, "I don't want to do that, but it's silly of me to have the most expensive lawyer in Washington and not take his advice." So he came up before the judge and the judge fined him two thousand dollars and gave him a lecture, and that was that.

Helms went off to lunch at the Tuesday club, and they passed the wastebaskets around and [*laughing*] they collected all the money for his defense. More than enough. It was so much more, that he turned the rest over to the defense of some FBI officers that were being prosecuted in New York. But it brought a tear to his eye. Anyway, in the courtroom, he said, "Well, Williams, how much do I owe you?" And Williams turned back to him and said, "Mr. Helms, for a man like you I don't charge anything."

So that's why he left, and that's why he went to Tehran. But I was long gone by then.

I understand the sense of community one gets by being a member of a group. It's a primal feeling of belonging, of protection, of being in the right—but I am disturbed that my father, who was ordinarily a solo artist, fairly immune to the sway of good old boys, was vulnerable to this "gentleman's club for psychopaths, sociopaths, lunatics, misfits," as *Pravda* characterized the CIA after the Senate torture report came out in December 2014. I think he needed to love somebody and he loved Helms.

Helms was DCI during the Chile coup in 1973. One day my brother Alex had to do a report on the coup—which occurred on another September 11—for school. He had heard a Chilean eyewitness speak at his school and he could see that the CIA had been up to its ears in it. It was one of those occasions when the strife out there in the wide world came to the dinner table, only this time I was able to see it more objectively since my brother Alex was taking the heat. My father refused to admit CIA involvement. His loyalty to Helms, who carried out the dirty work (Operation Condor) at Nixon's bidding, was unfailing. And possibly blinding.

I think there were many things that collided in his head this way, when soldierly loyalty—or love and admiration, as for Helms—came up against plain evidence of what he found disturbing. In public or with friends and acquaintances he maintained a cool intellectual sang-froid, but his loved ones felt the heat of what was going on inside. He became violently agitated by these inner divisions; his muscles tensed, his face twisted into furrows, and his voice distorted with sounds of anger and complaint. In later life these episodes occurred less frequently. I was less combative, for one thing, and eight years of watching things unravel under the Bush administration clinched Pop's disillusionment with the political process.

He often referred to *The God that Failed,* a collection of essays by six ex-Communists, one or two of whom I'd read and admired, like Ignazio Silone, whose *Bread and Wine* had given me pleasure and inspiration when I was a teenager. He probably read these essays as he was gearing up to go to work against the Soviets; he probably didn't guess that later the idea of a God that fails could apply to America's surrender to money and power.

SON: They recalled you later, didn't they, for a special assignment?

FATHER: In '75. Kissinger was trying to get Prime Minister Rabin, who'd just finished being the Israeli Ambassador in Washington for years—it's a wonder Kissinger didn't know him better by then—to take a softer position against the Arabs and the Russians but he wasn't getting anywhere. So he thought he would get tough and go over his head and appeal directly to the Israeli people, and put the screws on him that way. But he didn't realize Rabin was being as soft as he could get away with. But Kissinger couldn't see it. That man, of course, was inept—and it was crazy. The pressures on Rabin from the right were far greater than anyone over here could imagine. That's why they murdered him in the end.

SON: Orthodox extremists, wasn't it?

FATHER: That was a sad day. For me that was even more discouraging than when Kennedy was killed. I knew him pretty well. Anyway, back in '75 I was sent over to see what was brewing. I had my little list. It took me three weeks to see everybody. It was fun; I was right back in the swing of things. Rabin knew I was there and they came to me and said, "Rabin wants to see you." "Okay," I said, "that's great."

When I was in Israel ten years earlier, Rabin was army chief of staff. And then we knew him in Washington and then we knew him as prime minister. It was a long-running association. We knew him well. Right from the beginning it was obvious that he was a shy man. At the ambassador's parties, he would get his back against a wall and just stand there and not talk to anyone, like a suit of armor in a forgotten English castle. But we had a common interest in military history and that helped.

He asked to see me, but what were we going to do, talk about the Civil War? We chatted for a minute or two, and then I said, "You know what? This visit can be quite useful to both of us if you'll do one thing for me." He said, "What's that?" "If you'll read this paper I've written"— and I handed him a two-page typewritten report on what I'd gathered was going on in Israel—"and tell me where I've gone wrong." He sat there and read it and said, "I wouldn't change a thing." I said, "Thank you very much," I went back and cabled headquarters and said, "This is what Rabin thinks." And sent the paper.

MOTHER: And was it well received?

FATHER: No. Not by Kissinger. He was quoted as saying, "Who wrote this thing? And who the hell is this goddamned John Hadden anyway?"

Although he did know who I was—I'd been with Helms in the 20 Committee with him. Then I got called in by Scowcroft,[84] and he understood what I was saying, so Kissinger was overruled. His approach would have been crazy, it would have brought the whole Jewish community down on his neck, and it would have ruined Rabin. Kissinger's a funny man.

SON: You were a subcontractor then?

FATHER: Yes. And then wouldn't you know it? The bureaucrats said they couldn't pay me, citing some technicality. But I showed them the regulation on page 3,003, column b. See that? And they paid me. Bureaucrats.

SON: Was there any chance that you would get more involved after that?

FATHER: No. [laughs] That was that. I came back to Maine.

SON: Well, I know there's more to it than just having a good hearty laugh at it all. Or is laughing a good way to deal with your disappointment?

FATHER: Oh, I have no personal cause for disappointment.

SON: You never felt underappreciated or let down in any way?

FATHER: No, goodness no.

*　*　*　*

In my play *Hard Rain,* about the folk singer Victor Jara, a young American boy named James Middleton, whose father is a high-ranking CIA officer, has been accidentally rounded up with several thousand people, during the Chilean coup in '73, into the capital's soccer stadium. The next day most of the people around him will be gunned down and dragged into the hallways, to be thrown into piles of dead bodies.

MIDDLETON (*to the audience*)

My father liked to be away from America as much as he could, and whenever we went home, he couldn't believe how much more crass and awful America had become. He was happiest working for an America that belonged to Lincoln and Truman, where you could stand on solid principle. It was best if someone else opened the Corn Flakes box before he did, so that he wouldn't have to face the fact that

---

84 Brent Scowcroft, a West Pointer and Air Force general, was national security advisor under Ford and the first Bush. He was a long-time associate of Kissinger, but was often critical of the policies of Nixon and the second Bush.

we were being cheated by the Corn Flakes people, who insist that the box is half empty because Corn Flakes settle to the bottom of the box.

Most people take cheating for granted. If you buy a two by four at the lumber yard, what you get is a one and a half by three and a half. And everyone calls it a two by four. Or take gas prices. Did Lincoln give his life for this? I mean, what are we doing here? Making the world safe for democracy? To the Eskimos, ice is important, so they have ten different words for ice. We have ten different words for brown soda pop.

I mean, I'm running around stuffing my head with information about the latest disaster, the latest inhumanity, the latest death toll, the latest eco problem, the latest killer virus, like I'm still trying to make some point at the dinner table. But I'm just running around. Like some lemming, trying to get there first. Only I know it's just the edge of a cliff coming, I know that. But now I can't run around anymore, someone's sat me down here in this stadium like I'm supposed to watch something, but nothing's happening, just everybody's going crazy. Like that guy, smashing his head against the wall. I guess he didn't want to know anymore so he took all that stuff in his head . . . and just . . . broke it against the wall. Too much pressure, so he just broke it open, like an egg.

[Pause]

I want to go home.

CHAPTER 7

Escher's Puddle

"A visor for a visor."
—Mercutio, *Romeo and Juliet*

A Guatemalan king-mask hangs on the wall, looking at me with steady, reliable eyes, comforting me with its stern demeanor. Reptiles hide in its beard and the top of its head has crenellated points like a crown, or like the fortification of a tower. I used to take it with me whenever I moved to a new place, even if only for a month; now it's stayed in one place for ten years.

Our faces act as social masks, shape-shifting to suit one situation after another. When we are in company, the mask rarely drops. Darwin writes about the origins of facial and physical behavior patterns as survival mechanisms. A complex range of displays, from camouflage to aggression, is deeply imbedded in our animal consciousness, and our facial muscles are always hard at work when in company, especially in uncertain situations. A fixed mask made of wood or plaster, on the other hand, can be oddly revealing. At the theater of Epidaurus, masks channeled the souls and voices of the gods. Today, actors use masks in training to explore their own archetypal selves—the cheat, the virgin, the fool, the vagabond, the lover, the king, the sorceress, and so on. From graduate theater programs to villages in Bali, a sense of ritual accompanies mask work, to show respect for the numinous power a mask can bring into a room.

An actor in training learns how to distill human experience to its most recognizable forms, training herself to be aware of her senses and functions, and to calm her automatic impulses. She trains to still her physical tics, let go of the habitual tensions in her face and elsewhere, and build a performance as minimally as possible onto a neutral base. It can be said that an actor's job is to drop her own social role, ordinarily full of evasions and accommodations, in order to reveal people as nakedly as possible. People generally think that actors pretend—and we do that too, when all else fails—but when I was a young actor, I found that I was able to say things on stage that would be impossible to say in real life. In order to drop a confining social role, we actors occupy a low rung on the social ladder and, in exchange, are allowed to be real for two hours a night in a "play." It is one of the bittersweet paradoxes of the trade. We are licensed to speak the unspeakable, like the fools in Shakespeare's plays.

Shakespeare, who was an actor himself, knew this and tailored his creations for the actors who were in that company—this is one of the reasons actors love to play Shakespeare—and I like to imagine who the actors were by tracing them through the roles they played. The actor who first played Mercutio was surely a wry and troubled soul. Soon to be stabbed, donning a mask to crash the Capulets' ball, he says that the masquerade will only mask his face, another mask. The layers of the truth/lie will go on and on. He speaks as honestly as he can, as a kind of personified Möbius strip, and we love him for it. He knows that we remain hidden, even from ourselves.

Before I knew what my father did, it was easy to say, "He is in the Foreign Service." After I found out, I tried, "He worked for the CIA," "He was an agent, he developed agents," or even "He was a spy," but they all felt wrong in my mouth. Either I was violating a taboo, or I suspected I was saying something crazy in order to make a splash. "He was a spy" was false in any case. Technically a spy is recruited, or "developed," by a case officer to pass information from a group of which he or she is already an accepted, native member, or is plausible in some way, has gained her bona fides, as my father used to say. Besides, the word "spy" made me think

of the rats in hats and trench coats, blowing each other up, furtive and maniacal, one black, one white, from *MAD Magazine*. Huge dark glasses made it impossible to know who was in there, to know what they were thinking. The cartoonist, Antonio Prohías, had seen enough in his own life, having fled from Castro's Cuba to the US, to make each side equally culpable, naive, impish, violent, and underhanded.

My father had these qualities, too, but during his career he wore his visibility as a cloak. No dark glasses. He played his character as an outgoing social being, garrulous, alternately pleasant and temperamental, and blended in with the noisy hum of human activity. In my world, people pay large sums of money after work to sit crowded together in a dark and usually drab space, to watch actors loudly pretend to be someone else in a castle or a kitchen made of quarter-inch plywood. Onstage, the way to go unnoticed is to match the usual, bustling dynamic. Stillness, however, is magnetic; it draws attention. I imagine that my father occupied himself with endless activity in order to hide the fact that he was doing next to nothing. He disciplined himself to watch and wait, to resist making a move. His stillness was masked by activity.

In his later years my father gave in to the role of old eccentric, on the edge of madness perhaps. It was a caricature performance. He played over the top quite a lot, sometimes on purpose, often by habit. More like one of Shakespeare's Fools than Pantalone, the classic dotard from Italian Commedia tradition. His surface bluster masked a quiet clarity that remained very much intact, maybe more than ever.

Early on in our conversations, facing his son and a tape recorder made him a little uneasy. Sometimes, when we came to loggerheads, our argument reached a level of sublime absurdity.

SON: This is the microphone here, okay?
FATHER: It's not going, is it?
SON: Yeah, it is.
FATHER: Shouldn't we turn it off till you . . . ?
SON: No, that's okay. I'll just get rid of this part.
FATHER: Oh, okay . . . [*eyeing the recorder with distrust*]
SON: That Lewis Carroll poem keeps coming to my mind, you know, "You are old, Father William, the young man said . . ." I feel like that guy.

FATHER: Which one are you? I know which one I feel like.

SON: Me? I'm the young man. How do you stand upside down on a ball, balanced on your nose for eight hours a day? And why? All these questions. Father William finally says, "Be off or I'll kick you downstairs!" I'll just keep going till you kick me downstairs.

FATHER: Have at it.

SON: I wonder what you think about this whole project, these interviews . . .

FATHER: Oh, my mind is a total blank. You're writing with chalk on a totally blank blackboard. I haven't had any thoughts, no.

SON: You said something at lunch about how I should dip from the puddle?

FATHER: Yes! Yes, that's what I am; I'm just a mud puddle.

SON: I see. What kind of mud puddle comes to mind?

FATHER: Do you remember that wonderful Escher drawing of a mud puddle? And the leaves are reflected in . . . and it comes in and out of the mud puddle . . .

SON: Those are tire ruts, aren't they?

FATHER: Yes! A car had driven into the . . . had made the mud puddle. Yeah. Well, anyway, I'm just a puddle reflecting whatever it is you're saying.

SON: What do you make of that picture?

FATHER: Well, of course he's a great artist. A great graphic artist. And I suppose a wonderful architect, because his things were mostly structural [laughs]—you know, steps going both ways up and down, in the same plane . . . yeah.

SON: But back to the puddle . . .

FATHER: Oh, dear . . .

SON: You've chosen this Escher puddle to compare yourself to . . .

FATHER: Yeah, you're supposed to dip into the puddle and whatever you want . . . you can splash it around . . .

SON: I know, I'm dipping now: I'm saying you've got this picture of yourself as this Escher puddle . . .

FATHER: Well, the dip has to be a question!

SON: Okay: why does the Escher puddle in particular come to mind?

FATHER: [looking at me as if I've lost my mind, speaking slowly, his irritation growing] You asked me what I was thinking of, and I said I don't have any thoughts about this thing at all. It's all yours! And that I'm just a puddle for you to splash . . .

SON: But not just any puddle—Escher's puddle.

FATHER: Well, then I went from puddle to Escher . . .

SON: Exactly. And here I am. We're pursuing this.

FATHER: . . . and I guess that's the end of the line.

SON: Well, to me the Escher puddle is much more . . .

FATHER: Oh, Jesus . . .

SON: . . . is much more specific than just any mud puddle. For one thing, it reflects perfectly . . .

FATHER: . . . whatever it's reflecting. Well, there it is. You see, I can't reflect anything except what you bring in on top of the puddle for me to have a reflection about. As it is, there's no reflection at all.

SON: Well, just so you know, this is very interesting to me. For instance, the fact that the ruts are made by a tire . . .

FATHER: Yes, but that's . . .

SON: It's a mechanical violation of the landscape that creates a new kind of beauty.

FATHER: But I . . . I hadn't remembered how the puddle was made! So that's your input.

SON: Okay, I concede. Back to the other thing. Your mind has been a blank.

FATHER: Yes! There you go. Now we're talking . . .

SON: I don't believe you.

[*Stalemate. We stare at each other, eye to unbudging eye. The room is tense.*]

SON: Are there things you won't say?

FATHER: Oh, of course.

[*Another pause. I give up; we move on.*]

SON: You talked about Angleton's extreme fear of the Soviets. Where did that come from?

FATHER: [*sighs*] The war, probably, being in OSS during the war, and you fight—you know, it's war. In the fifties, we all thought the Soviets were going to attack. And people were committing suicide as a result because they couldn't see that anyone was doing anything about it. Forrestal[85]

---

85 James Forrestal was secretary of the navy under Roosevelt and the first secretary of defense under Truman. He was a controversial figure who personally visited the battlefield and was present at Iwo Jima. He advocated strongly for a conciliatory negotiation with Japan and against the formation of Israel. He was

committed suicide; Wisner[86] committed suicide. A lot of that is in this paper I sent you.

SON: So the Cold War was a high-stakes game that you played in which it was reasonable to risk one's life. And ask other people to risk theirs.

FATHER: Yes, that's right.

SON: I'm fascinated by something you haven't wanted to talk about at all, which is your relationship with the guys you recruited. I know that you don't want to say who they were in any way, but I would love to know from a more personal point of view what those relationships were like. I imagine that you really loved these guys. You were the contact, the recruiter, but in some sense you were more than that, almost a father figure. And I even thought it might be fun—or harrowing—to role-play a situation. Say I'm a newspaper reporter . . .

FATHER: Look, you have a much too glorified idea of what the hell I did. I wasn't a great case officer and I didn't recruit a lot of people—that just isn't what I did. What I did was to talk to as many people as I could and put together what I thought were things of interest, not based on recruited agents. For example, I was in charge of the Polish section in Berlin and we were recruiting Poles to send back to Poland, come back and report what was going on. And I was recruiting support agents for that activity, Germans, East Germans, who could support that kind of thing across East Germany and into Poland and back.

SON: So that they would have places to stay along the way and so on?

FATHER: People who could guide them, who could act as letter drops, all the support junk that . . .

SON: It sounds like pretty complicated logistical . . .

---

forced to resign due to increasing mental instability and eventually succumbed to apparent suicide.

86 Frank Wisner was part of OSS and CIA; appointed by Dulles to form OPC; covert action including domestic infiltration of the press (Operation Mockingbird, one of the "Family Jewels"); and worked closely with Bissell and Helms. Hoover at the FBI hated "Wisner's gang of weirdos." He and Senator McCarthy tried to implicate his group as Communists, but Wisner countered with a smear operation of his own against McCarthy, and prevailed. Spy vs. Spy tactics held even when the adversaries were from the same team. Wisner suffered from mental breakdown and died by suicide.

FATHER: It was very low-level stuff, support work. Because my German was pretty good and I'd worked with Germans all those years, they suddenly put me in the Polish section, ostensibly to straighten it out. Well, the guy who was heading it up had been the head of Polish operations in Berlin for years. Was I going to tell him what to do? No. So I told him to deal with the Poles and I'll deal with the Germans. That's the way we did it. But then another guy came in and built the Polish section up until there were about five case officers. And then he left and they made me the head of the Polish section. And I went through the thing, case by case . . .

SON: He'd recruited the case officers?

FATHER: No, they were sent by headquarters, they were Americans.

SON: They knew Polish.

FATHER: They were Polish-speaking Americans.

SON: Who knew the business.

FATHER: I wouldn't say that; they were a pretty poor lot. I went through it all and came to the conclusion that the whole thing was totally worthless. I saw it as my job to terminate every single operation that was going on in Berlin against Poland.

SON: So they were not only worthless, but they were compromising every . . .

FATHER: Yes. They were being run by the Poles, not by us, they were all doubles. Well, the other case officers caught on to what I was up to, and that's what started that mutiny that I mentioned. But they were all thrown out. I could see that it was idiotic to try to run operations across East Germany into Poland. These people were going to get caught and we would just have more doubles. There was one guy left, who'd stood by me, and we spent our time recruiting Germans. That's when we got this chauffeur for a Stasi colonel.

SON: You talked about him.

FATHER: Yeah. Very sturdy fellow. And there was another Stasi colonel—this was the most entertaining thing we did: we had learned that this colonel was recruitable—I forget how we learned that but we did. So we sent the man a goose for Christmas with a recruitment pitch in a letter in an aluminum tube shoved up the ass of this Christmas goose. [*laughs*] And the pitch was that if he was interested at all he was to turn up in a subway station between one and two o'clock in the morning. Headquarters would only allow us to go so far as to see if he would turn up. If he didn't turn up, they wouldn't let us talk to him. So they dressed me up as an infantry captain in full uniform. In my trench coat and the bars on the trench coat and on my cap and my combat boots, I got all dressed up again—it was fun.

SON: Like the old days.

FATHER: Like the old days. And so at two o'clock in the morning there I was, walking up and down, and train after train came by. There was just nobody there. Finally another train came, a guy stepped out. And I walked up this way and he walked up that way and then we passed, and I nodded to him and he nodded to me—we didn't exchange a word. Time passed. And after about forty-five minutes he came up to me and said, "Are you expecting meet somebody here?" In German. And I said "No, I'm waiting for a girlfriend and I don't know what's happened, she hasn't shown up and I guess she won't show up. Anyway, it means a great deal to me to see her so I'm just going to stay here and see if she turns up." So we walked up and down some more. And he was furious, shaking his head. Finally he got in a train and disappeared. And I went back and reported that the guy showed up, because there was no question—he had some password that I got. And then they went on from there.

   And then I can't remember why—but the chief of police was one of our agents in West Berlin, and we would go to a safe house and have dinner with him. It was sort of a joint thing.

SON: You went with your chief?

FATHER: He was chief of police, West Berlin.

SON: He was from your office?

FATHER: No, no, no, he was the agent.

SON: The Stasi guy?

FATHER: No, no, no, no! This was another guy.

SON: Another guy.

FATHER: A West Berliner.

SON: But the man you went with, he was the . . .

FATHER: He was our number two in the station.

SON: He was the number two guy. Oh, Hecksher.

FATHER: He was an interesting fellow, because he ran that coup in Guatemala. Later. He ran it very well. He did what they wanted him to, which of course was something they shouldn't have wanted him to . . .

SON: But you said you never recruited agents.

FATHER: Not in Poland.

SON: Just as we stopped before—you were saying that intelligence was a puerile occupation—

FATHER: A game.

SON: A juvenile game—and you were just beginning to say why you couldn't possibly do it now, now that you have more perspective.

FATHER: Well, there was the Soviet Union with its half million KGB people—and here we were with just a few thousand in our outfit, and they were far better at it than we were, they had a long successful tradition of espionage. Their people were naturals, but look what happened. It didn't make any difference at all. They lost in a walk—they just collapsed.

SON: You're saying that not only is it a puerile game but it doesn't do any good.

FATHER: For the most part, no. The Israelis, of course, are a special case, because they're so small. Besides, they're at war all the time—and there's a big difference between peacetime intelligence and wartime intelligence. You can do things in wartime that you can't do in peacetime. Of course, the Israelis are at war all the time, so they can go out and murder people, and do anything they want. They can torture people and get information and do all kinds of things that we can't do. They get a lot done.

SON: So it's a capacity for ruthlessness that . . . ?

FATHER: Espionage requires a byzantine mentality, living in a world of secrets, and Americans aren't suited for it. They talk too much. The idea of keeping a secret never occurred to an American—out of the question. [*he stops and rolls his eyes*] Bongo, bongo, bongo . . .

SON: But is intelligence useful at all?

FATHER: The smaller you are the more useful it is. It's almost useless for us. Of course, Israeli intelligence is our main source of intelligence. Unexamined—and that's another problem . . .

SON: What made the Soviets so good at it?

FATHER: In Soviet Russia espionage was a way of life. It started way back in Tsarist times with a man named Azef.[87] Azef was a Tsarist agent who penetrated the dissidents of the time, the Narodny,[88] and made him into a revolutionary. Christ, they even went so far as to have him murder Plehve, who was the minister of the interior, to establish his bona fides with this group. They would do that. It was one way to get rid of troublesome bureaucrats, as well as establishing the credentials of your so-called revolutionary. When Azef had the whole group, they rolled the whole thing up and shot them all.

SON: Just like chess. Sacrifice a pawn, and *pfft* . . .

FATHER: Except in chess, white stays white. In the twenties, after the Revolution, the Allies were of course very keen to overthrow this Bolshevik regime. The Bolsheviks had made peace with the Germans[89] and done all these things that the Allies didn't like and there was no dearth of hostility between them, so the Soviets built up this whole operation known as the Trust. Same thing: they got hold of a White general and they turned him. They showed him that the Allied intelligence services were just murdering his own people because they were so inept, and they proved it, and they said, "If you work for us you'll save Russian lives." So he did. They called it the Trust, thinking that would appeal to the capitalist mind, you see—wonderful people!—and then this whole huge phony organization grew up within the Soviet Union that was aimed at overthrowing their own regime. They had couriers going back and forth to London and Paris, black [with phony papers] across the borders, carrying secret documents, and they had this huge organization and they got thousands of patriotic Russians to join it, thinking it was real, and that's how they swept them up, you see?

---

87 Yevno Azef lived in exile during his twenties, as a "revolutionary," making strong connections with dissident groups all over Europe, during the late nineteenth century. When he returned to Russia, he worked undercover for the Okhrana, the Imperial secret police, carrying out acts of terror and assassinations to provoke and justify violent repression by the police.

88 Narodniks began to agitate for social reform in the 1860s, after the emancipation of the serfs. Mostly an *intelligenzia* group, they considered the peasants to be the future reformers of the tsarist regimes.

89 Treaty of Brest-Litovsk, eight months before the end of World War I, in November 1918.

Son: Did the Allies think it was real?

Father: They financed it! It was Dzerzhinski[90] who did that; they financed Soviet espionage for years with this operation, by pouring millions of dollars in gold over the border. Espionage outfits have their expenses, you know, and the Allies paid for the whole thing—and it was all phony. When they'd finally taken out a whole crop of the top émigré counterrevolutionaries and were playing it a little too close, they rolled the whole thing up and shot everybody and that was the end of the Trust. The Trust! After that they just kidnapped the rest of the White generals right off the streets of Paris, whipped them off to the Soviet Union, and killed them and whatnot. It kind of discouraged the others.

Son: So there was an elegance that appeals to you.

Father: They were thoroughgoing bastards, but yes, there was an elegance. Oh yes. Especially getting the other side to pay for your operations, you can't beat that. After the Second World War, the Soviets did exactly the same thing in Poland. This time they played against the Americans. People never learn. I was in Berlin and they fed us this story about how one of these Armia Krajowa colonels,[91] traveling black, had been arrested by the East Germans. But the East Germans didn't know who he was, see, and couldn't we get the Gehlen Organization[92] to spring him and save his life, you see, and get him to the West? So they sent this greasy Pole . . .

Son: What was the Gehlen Organization?

Father: That was the Nazi espionage outfit operating against the Soviet Union in World War II. The Nazi files became the spine of our Cold War intelligence, of course. But it was penetrated up to here by the East; the East Germans were in it like worker ants, like worms.

---

90 Felix Dzerzhinski, or Iron Felix, was a Polish-born Communist who founded the Soviet secret police, known as the Cheka. He espoused and implemented the Red Terror, purging Russian society of so-called counterrevolutionary elements by massive executions without trial. He also built orphanages, fought typhus, and established a Soviet film society.

91 Armia Krajowa, or AK, was the Polish resistance movement or "Home Army" during WWII, allied with the Polish government in exile.

92 Reinhard Gehlen, an ex-Wehrmacht major general in military intelligence, was recruited by OSS after the war to put a group together to penetrate the Soviets. He worked in that capacity, eventually assembling a group of 4,000 undercover agents, for both CIA and Germany (BND), until 1968.

The idea was to get Gehlen to spring this phony colonel. They sent this guy up from Munich to arrange it. He had these two whores who were supposed agents of the Armia Krajowa people, and they were going to brief the Gehlen guys as to where to go, to spring this guy. Goodness, 'cause they were from Frankfurt Oder, it says here, these two German women. I took one look at that, and it was a lot of crap. But I was told to make this thing work. The Gehlen people sent me this wonderful officer, a real guy for a change, one of these aristocrats, a young fellow, from a good family and whatnot. They called him Mr. Taylor—Mr. Taylor Von Steuben maybe, but [*laughs*] anyway, it wasn't Mr. Taylor. Anyway I was Mr. Haynes, and he was Mr. Taylor, and so they put us in touch and we had meetings about this business. Right at the beginning I said, "Don't touch this thing with a ten-foot pole. Anybody you get involved in doing this is going to get killed. It's a lot of crap. There's nothing there. Now, I have to make my presentation and ask you to do this. If you want to get out of it that's up to you. How you do that is your problem. I can't help you with that. I'm betraying my own side in this, and if you want, you can end my career tomorrow by telling my people what I've just told you. But I hate to see people get killed for no purpose." So I jumped.

We got along very well, and this is what he did: he got an ex-Prussian police interrogator on board, and we had a meeting with the greasy Pole and these two German ... these German whores. The Germans ran this; I was just looking on. It was magnificent. They separated them and kept them in separate rooms. They called the Pole in and quietly asked him questions, and he began to sweat, and they sent him back to his room. Then they got one of the girls in and quietly asked her questions. It took about an hour before the whole thing fell apart. They just didn't have a straight story in any possible direction. And old "Taylor" looks at me and I look back at him and then that was it. *Pft.* We sent the Pole back and said, "This guy is lying to us," and we proved it, because we had the transcript of what he had said.

You might think that would have tipped the thing, but no. The Americans thought the Pole had been hoodwinked by the two women, and they put him right back in. He was working for the Polish UB[93] for Christ's sake, and they couldn't see it down there. When he first came up,

---

93 Polish Security Department, MPB or UB, analogous to the East German Stasi.

he talked to Hoffman, who was the previous head of the Polish section, and Hoffman said to the unit case officer, who was a West Point colonel—and he was in the thing because he could speak Polish, or because he was an expatriate—Hoffman said to him, "Now, Colonel, you've got this bird here, what do you think? In a case like this we usually tap his phone and read his mail, and keep a check and see who he goes around with here in Berlin. We don't know who this guy is, and I don't know if you do or not, but why don't we just check?" And this West Pointer drew himself up to his full five feet height and said, "Certainly not, you must be crazy. This man is from one of the best *szlachtas*, one of the best Polish families, you must be crazy, we couldn't do a thing like that, mistrust one of our officers?" But the next day he comes in to Hoffman and he says, "You know, your suggestion about checking this guy up, his mail and phone, and where he goes and who he sees and how he spends his time here in Berlin? Well, I asked him and he said it would be all right!" Now, you were asking me what little grains of sand began to bother me about where we were going? It was things like that.

MOTHER: You were saying that you'd disobeyed your orders in this . . .

FATHER: Yeah, I betrayed the whole operation to this Gehlen officer, telling him not to do what I'd been told to do, and in doing so, I'd deliberately disobeyed an order. But nobody ever found out. He never split on me, and of course I never said a word. [*laughs*]

SON: Just as we were finishing up yesterday you started talking about people dying for no good reason.

FATHER: People do, of course. But then they also die for a reason. It's a mixed bag, isn't it? For example, Nathan Hale was such a clown. He sat there with a Britisher at a tavern table and told him the whole story. And of course they picked him up and hung him. I mean jeepers, what kind of a show was that?

SON: Maybe the show was more important to him than his life.

FATHER: Well, he was a naïf; he didn't know what he was doing. That's a terrible waste. Then there are those who are very clear, but the game becomes too important for them. For example, Penkovsky.[94] We knew

---

94 Oleg Vladimirovich Penkovsky was a GRU (Soviet Military Intelligence) officer, a key informant who told CIA about weaknesses in the Soviet nuclear arsenal and Cuban missile capabilities.

that Penkovsky was in deep trouble and was about to be compromised. We gave him an order to get out, and he wouldn't, and of course they killed him. That happens. He was just so enraged at the Soviet Union, he couldn't stop working against them. They'd killed his father, you see . . .

Did you ever see that film, *The Sorrow and the Pity*?[95] About the German occupation of France. You can't understand World War II until you've seen that film. There was a guy who was being run by the British against the Germans. He was a homosexual, and he took up with a German colonel and picked up everything about the Western fortification zone on the coast there. He passed as a Belgian businessman, selling concrete. That's where the colonel got his concrete. In London they could see that the Germans were getting closer and closer, so they ordered him out. But he refused to leave. He didn't get caught, he escaped with his life. When he saw that he was about two feet from getting caught, they landed a plane and picked him up at night, but it was a close call. . . .

* * * *

Pop used to take me to the James Bond movies. They tickled him to no end. He also took me to see *Yellow Submarine*—because it was anti-Communist! And to the strange Czech film, *Closely Watched Trains*.[96] He took me to fantastic spectacles all through my childhood. I saw the marionettes and the street shows in Salzburg, and later in Washington, *MacGowran in the Works of Beckett* and several Shakespeare plays at the Arena Stage. I saw my first *Twelfth Night* there. And a wonderful production of Brecht's *The Resistible Rise of Arturo Ui*. On the other hand, we never had television or comic books, which seemed a cultural deprivation to me.

These experiences provided the bedrock of my imagination and gave me a longing for that peculiar magic that could be found, among other places, in the theater, which was to become my nationality, my

95 Two-part 1969 documentary film by Max Ophuls, using interviews and footage to show how anti-Semitism, greed, and sycophancy figured in the Vichy government's collaboration with the Nazis during the war.

96 Jiří Menzel's superb 1966 film, a satire on sex, officialdom, and resistance to the Nazis.

home. I have no idea what these outings meant to him. Did they appeal to his interest in oddities? Or did he see that there was something real going on under the artifice? Or, almost inconceivably, did we go for fun?

One day, not long before he died, Pop quoted Shaw: "Every man is a revolutionist concerning the thing he understands. Every man who has mastered a profession is a skeptic concerning it and, consequently, is a revolutionist."[97] My father talked about his own departures from the official line, but I wonder how much of him got buried under all the stuff he couldn't buck. Maybe he got away with more than I imagine. Maybe he played dumb sometimes, or acquiescent, and just went his own way as quietly as he could.

As I piece together my father's story, there's a Zen aspect to it that intrigues me. He was careful not to draw attention to himself, except in social roles. If he was doing well, nobody knew it. There would be no reward for a job neatly done if there was no evidence of anything done at all. Accolades were a sure sign that a field officer's work was sloppy, leaving as much of a trail as an out-and-out botch. And yet, the splashier officers rose to the top. Of course, he rose to the top, too, in the end, and that confuses me. Maybe Helms was his protector after all, and protecting my father was evidence of Helms's good angel at work—or my father didn't tell me everything.

In this and other things, we made a strange pair. As an actor, my work is to reveal what goes on inside, to find moments to let the character's mask slip. When an actor is said to have presence, it is because the actor is simply there; he is present. All the technique in the world goes to waste without this basic alignment. The trick is to blend the fictional moment with the actual reality in the theater.

On stage, the moment-to-moment voyage is both heightened and ridiculous. As I wait in the wings for my entrance, I am afraid. As the entrance approaches I walk, leap, or stumble through the "tormentors," the drop curtains that shield the wings. We are paid to make the transition from being safely hidden to being fully exposed, found out. Every actor I know lives in fear of being discovered a fraud and yet

---

97 From *Man and Superman*, *Preface to the Revolutionist's Handbook* (1903).

there is something powerful about the barefaced admission of fraud-
ulence. Fear is important. An actor who is not afraid cannot summon
the weird energy required to engage an audience. There's something
reminiscent of ancient rites in the air, like blood sacrifice, that an audience has paid good money to witness.

Maybe my fear of exposure was similar to my father's. In both
cases it was the fear itself that had to be managed, if not tamed, to
pull off the role with seeming ease. We both obsessed over codes that
had to be deciphered—words of a script or an intercepted message, or
what people said or intended, layered with meaning and deception.

But our differences were obvious. To begin with, the stakes were
different. When he failed, someone died. When my career fell apart, I
signed on as a carpenter somewhere. I've rarely had a regular income
and, except onstage, I've hardly ever worn a suit. When my father
retired, he had a nice pension. His hair was greased back neatly; mine
was unkempt, though later our hairstyles reversed. He was a member
of the inner circle; I live on the outer margins.

My father played a conscious role for thirty years and was continually on the move. For a long time after my childhood with him I
continued to ricochet from place to place. His moves were those of
a pawn, placed here and there on the board, doing what he could to
manipulate the assignment but following the master plan determined
by the bosses in Washington; mine are the random moves of a traveling
player. But the metronomic beat of change he gave our family lent my
life a restless momentum that couldn't be stopped. For some years I
remained in one place no longer than a month or two, sometimes less.

As he did, I've also felt that obscurity was key to my success: a
strange choice for an actor. But an anonymous actor can watch the
world to see how things work, and has the leeway to become different
characters, more easily than one who is known.

But things change. In his last years he wore ratty old clothes and
rarely combed his hair. He became a woodcarver, an artist—and I surprise myself occasionally to find myself in a position of responsibility. I
became a father thirty years ago, thirty years after he did when he was
thirty. Contrasts and similarities chase each other back and forth like
nervous schools of fish.

My American friend in Israel, Ryan Golding, when he was twelve, stood about six foot three. He collected scorpions from the dunes and pickled them in formaldehyde. We were best friends. One day a couple of Israeli TV producers visited our Current Events class at the American International School in Kfar Shmaryahu. We looked more American than the others, and we were the talkers. There were only a few boys in the class and the competition was not stiff. In any case we were chosen to play Moshe and Yoram in an English-teaching program. It was a four-part series called *The Spy*. As one of the only TV productions in Israel at the time, it was aired repeatedly and got a lot of exposure.

I remember the first paid line of my acting career: "Look, Moshe, look at the MAN. He is reading a neewzz-paperr." Cut to a picture of the *Jerusalem Post* captioned "Newspaper." We were called Moshe and Yoram so that schoolchildren could relate to us, but we wore long Bermuda shorts to match our overdone American accents.

The story was that all along we had been following the wrong man. The man we thought was the spy was actually the detective who was after the spy. Unwittingly we helped him make the snag. The Man congratulated us at the end of the story. When the credits were shown under "The Spy," there was my entire name: John Lloyd Hadden, Jr. The real spies in the country had a good laugh. "Look, Moshe! THE SPY!" My father could say nothing, but afterward I got the impression that the surreal coincidence amused him. In retrospect I am amazed that he was so cool about it, given his reaction to the Marco Polo affair on the night Kennedy was killed, but I guess by that time he was no longer a new boy.

After it was all in the can, Ryan and I were each given a check for a hundred dollars. It was good money for a twelve-year-old in the sixties.

SON: Spy technique in Israel was a slightly different ball game than in Europe, yes? You say you just talked to people.
FATHER: No, it was pretty much the same. People would tell me things. By talking to everybody, see, soldiers, businessmen, judges, archeologists and farmers and opera singers and everybody, they couldn't tell who was talking to me and who wasn't.

SON: So having a formal arrangement is a vulnerable . . .

FATHER: It's not important and very often stupid and counterproductive.

SON: Then how do you get them to talk?

FATHER: People always want to talk. A person will be most likely to talk if he's somebody who hasn't been properly appreciated—the best people are often left behind because they make people uncomfortable, they're too smart for their own good. Then he really needs somebody to talk to, somebody who'll understand how good he is.

SON: So you used friendship to get what you wanted.

FATHER: I was very friendly, yeah. I would agree with anything anybody said. And when you deal with two people you learn something from one that you can tell the other, that he didn't know, so then the other thinks you know more than you really do, and then he tells you things, and then—well, it's like a Ping-Pong game.

SON: But there comes a point where you're close to a mother lode of information and they have access to it . . . Then what do you do?

FATHER: Well, then you have to wait. I did finally recruit somebody . . . and, ah, yeah. It worked, it was . . . Yeah. It was the best thing I ever did. I got . . . Helms liked it so much he took it to the president and . . . That was one thing, that was my one real . . . good one, yeah.

SON: And was your personal relationship different with this guy?

FATHER: I winkled him out and then I had somebody else dealing with him, under my control.

SON: So you stayed in the background.

FATHER: Oh yeah, Christ, I couldn't have the Israelis knowing that I was doing things like that.

SON: So he went to other people and they passed it on to you.

FATHER: I only dealt with third parties.

SON: Were these third parties in danger?

FATHER: Not that they knew it, no. In Hamburg, all I did was . . .

SON: But you knew it.

FATHER: Well, that was what I was there for. In Hamburg all I did was talk to people.

SON: Did you know any of them well? Did you get into their lives, and . . .

FATHER: I would see them all the time.

SON: You must have gotten to know about their families, their sex lives . . .

FATHER: I suppose. Your mind sifts that stuff out very quickly.

SON: For them to have somebody to talk to . . .

FATHER: Especially if they think you're friendly and if they think you agree with them anyway . . . so that you don't have to be convinced of anything. Once you get into an argument with somebody, then you don't learn anything. Then it's gone.

SON: In order to be convincing, you have to become really interested in them . . .

FATHER: Yeah, you keep nodding your head . . .

SON: And then you bring them a book that you think they might like . . .

FATHER: Oh, gifts are the sine qua non.

SON: You have to give the right gift.

FATHER: You have to figure it out. I used to spend a couple of days at the Savile Book Shop in Washington, before Christmas, picking out a book for each one of these birds. There was an endless list.

SON: And you have to know the culture, the language.

FATHER: That helps. There was a guy in Israel named Karmon, who told his people never to speak Hebrew in front of me. I couldn't speak enough Hebrew to get out of a paper bag, but he thought I was faking it. We went to a dinner party one night and I was sitting across from him, and there were two Israeli ladies sitting at our little card table, because that was the kind of dinner party it was. Halfway through this meal one of the ladies said to Karmon in Hebrew, "Pour this guy a lot of wine, maybe he'll tell you some secrets." Of course they all knew who I was. And I picked up the only word I distinguished in all of that, *yayin*, the word for wine. For some reason I had learned a phrase from my two guys, my cartoon interpreters, which was *"Nichnas yayin, yatzeh sod."* Which meant, in goes the wine, out pops the secret. And Karmon turned white, because of course he thought I'd understood everything they'd said, and of course I hadn't understood a thing. [*laughs*]

MOTHER: He was a good friend. He stopped to see us here.

FATHER: He was, he was a wonderful man. It would be people like that I would talk to. He was in a position where he didn't have to worry what he said to me. They left it up to him as to what he would tell me. It was up to me to listen.

SON: And would you feed stuff back to him, to make it worthwhile for him?

FATHER: I would try. Intelligence is a kind of currency and you have to spend it. There's no point in keeping it locked up in a safe. You lead a little bit and you take a little bit, you win some and you lose some. My young friend Shlomo Argov had gotten a pretty good post in Washington, when I was head of section. He had become a senior officer when Rabin was ambassador there. So we made a deal. I said, "I'll get my guys and you get your guys, and that'll give me the cachet to set the whole thing up, and we'll go to Gettysburg and we'll both see it like we've never seen it before, and maybe we'll have fun. I think Rabin will enjoy it too, because he has a big interest in the Civil War." So out at Gettysburg, we were met by three limousines with drivers, and each one had a guide that would take us all around the valley and the battlefield. Then we had a super lunch, and then they took us to the museum—it went on and on. It was an all-day tour of Gettysburg. I was with Rabin most of the time and I knew enough about the subject so I could tell Rabin what was right and wrong about what the guy said. We had a great time. That's how you get things done, indirectly. Having fun loosens people up.

SON: Outside, as you said, away from offices and people listening . . .

FATHER: That's right. Then we gave a party for Rabin. I'd invited the DCI and of course Angleton was there, and all the Mossad guys were there, and Mr. and Mrs. Rabin and all the wives. I hired a steamboat that went up and down the Potomac doing parties, and we spent all afternoon into the evening, of a summer's day. And that was another nice way to get to know people.

SON: When you say friendliness, you're not talking about real friendship, are you?

FATHER: Intelligence agents have no friends. It's like international affairs. Nations have no friends. They have relationships. Sometimes they're close, and then? Then things change. But that's the thing about espionage, and especially liaison, you have to be on their side, you have to speak their language, you have to see their whole way of looking at things, and address yourself to that, and take it on as your own. At the same time there has to be a little corner of your head that remains loyal to the United States— and it's not entirely easy. People who don't know where the line is go overboard. We had an ambassador in Israel, when we came there, who was an Israeli as far as that was concerned—worked for them. There were people who couldn't do liaison work; there was always the tension they felt because they were working against these people, and they couldn't get into bed with them. It required a certain . . . a certain touch.

SON: You seemed to like people more overseas than at home. Why is that?

FATHER: I never got along with Americans at all. Ever. I expected too much from Americans, and coming from West Point, when I was in charge I thought people ought to do what I told them to do. But Americans don't like to be told what to do. Foreigners, on the other hand, don't know any better and I was much more tolerant, so I could put up with anything as far as foreigners were concerned. I was never in charge, either; I was never in a position of total control. So.

SON: You'd also made yourself see things from their point of view.

FATHER: You have to get into bed with them, and be one of them. Yeah.

SON: Meanwhile you would get these orders from Washington.

FATHER: Yes. What the hell. For instance, Bobby Kennedy was always after us to kill Castro. So we thought up these dumb ideas to kill Castro. You do what you're told. Or you get out.

SON: You said before that Americans don't like to do what they're told; would you include yourself in that?

FATHER: No, because I was a soldier, I always did what I was told. When it was obvious that I knew more than the person telling me what to do, and it was going to be a disaster if I did what I was told to do, then I deliberately disobeyed orders, but you can do that only just so often. But any bureaucrat with a drop of conscience has to disobey orders from time to time. In any case I did, and I was damn lucky not to get caught. But the point is that this is how "political action" began. It was with these cowboys who thought bombing and assassinations were the way to get things done. For one thing, presidents demand it. Diplomacy takes too long, and they can't always go to war, so they need something in between, something they can deny if it comes up. These puerile shenanigans, which have taken over the CIA, have caused us nothing but grief and harm, and they have nothing to do with espionage. They damage our intelligence. In more ways than one.

SON: You said before that you didn't consider yourself a successful intelligence officer. How would you define a success?

FATHER: Secrecy was tops. Cool judgment. He had to be an intellectual to think of all the possible combinations and yet, active enough to take huge risks. I was never willing to take risks of any sort, really. So I didn't. But you can go overboard. My God, there was one officer we had who was so scared that he might say something that he kept himself locked in a safe in his office and was never able to function. I looked upon information as cards in your hand, and the trick was to play the information cards to get the maximum exchange in return, and of course, like any poker game, sometimes you don't win and you get less back than you gave, and sometimes you get more back, in which case you congratulate yourself—but information is like money in a bank. It's for a purpose. Stuffing your money in a mattress is a dumb way to handle money. A dumb way to handle information is never to use it. You can't use it all at once because then you don't have anything. You just have to use a little bit, a little at a time.

Information by itself is meaningless. A pile of facts is just raw material. It's not a piece of work until you carve it into something. Otherwise it's just a piece of wood that you might toss into the fire. Until you've done something with it, until you've worked it, it hasn't done anything. And words are like that. What good are words until you've put them together in some understandable fashion so that you can communicate an idea? The words themselves are nothing. It's only when you string them together in an interesting way that something happens.

SON: And facts are never isolated; they are attached to people. What about them?

FATHER: People? Which people?

SON: The people you work with, who take such huge risks with their lives, and with the lives of their families . . .

FATHER: All on your behalf.

SON: . . . on your behalf.

FATHER: Of course you pay them, and try to help them in every possible way, but it's like a company commander in combat, or a platoon leader—follow me!

SON: Did you have to keep your own feelings in the background, or remind yourself that they were not your friends?

FATHER: I never thought in those terms, you just . . .

SON: . . . got involved?

FATHER: . . . do the best you can. I never analyzed these things at the time. I don't think that'd be a good idea.

SON: You have to gauge the risk to the person but you have to detach yourself, don't you, because it has to be a game, right?

FATHER: Oh yeah, that's one big trouble, because when they kill one of your agents you have to be able to take it, you know. For example, you were talking about killing people yesterday. And I thought about that. And then I really thought about Bill Coffin,[98] with whom I'd gone to Buckley. You know, he was in the Agency. He'd started in OSS during the war as a very, very young recruit. And after the war he was recruiting Russians— he was bilingual in Russian. And he was a great guitar player. He was a great artist, musician.

SON: He was a great antiwar speaker during Vietnam. I used to listen to his sermons on the radio. He was a neighbor of yours, wasn't he?

FATHER: He was in New York—we played cops and robbers as little kids. And then I met him again in Germany. And he did that wonderful Cossack dance where you squat and you kick out—very athletic. And while doing this kicking dance he would play the guitar and sing Ukrainian songs. Well, he was down there recruiting these guys to drop into the Soviet Union to promote underground activity and they all were killed, every last one, murdered. First turned, and then killed. Every last one. Because of Philby, you see. They were waiting for them each time. I think everything that happened to Coffin after that was in reaction to that experience.

SON: He felt responsible.

FATHER: He was responsible. I never had anything like that.

SON: Never?

FATHER: No, I never had faith in those operations.

SON: What were you going to say about killing people?

FATHER: I had an agent in Berlin, and the East Germans caught him and put him on a railroad . . . uh track, and they found his head, you know . . .

SON: And you had developed him?

---

98 William Sloan Coffin, from one of the most prominent New York families, was on his way to becoming a concert pianist when he enlisted in the Army during the war. He had a brief career in the CIA before becoming a minister and well-loved peace, civil rights, and nuclear disarmament activist.

FATHER: I hadn't developed him, but I was running him, yeah. So you always wonder, was . . . was that my fault? What happened? And you never know. It gets to be quite a problem. Especially for young Americans. The old hands, the Czechs, the old Poles, the Soviet stars that worked with us are much more attuned to this kind of a life, especially the ones that grew up in occupied Europe. You know, people die . . . but Americans get bothered, they get off the track. They get neurotic about it.

SON: How many others were there?

FATHER: I don't know. It's hard to say. You're asking things that are covered in time and I don't . . . You have to have . . . you have to have a certain . . . a certain ability to take the good with the bad, and not get too upset. You console yourself with the idea that someone else might have done it worse, might have killed more people, who knows.

SON: So when you're running an agent, you feel quite responsible.

FATHER: Oh, God, yes, it's terrible, yes, it's a strain. It's stressful in two ways. One, it's stressful professionally because you screwed it up, and the other stress is human. You've gotten quite close to these people, and you . . .

SON: How so?

FATHER: Oh, Christ, you talk to them hour after hour after hour, to make sure they don't make a mistake, walk them through each step of the way, and make sure that they feel useful, and valuable, and valued, and that what they're doing is worthwhile, even though you don't think so yourself . . . It's hard . . .

SON: So it's impossible to avoid a personal bond of some kind . . .

FATHER: That's a huge part of it. Absolutely necessary.

SON: So how did you get by?

FATHER: I don't know, I tried, but I'm an American.

SON: You talk about how the children in the Middle East are trained to be killers from the moment they were born.

FATHER: Yeah.

SON: Was I a future soldier in your eyes, when I was born?

FATHER: I never thought about that and hoped that it would never happen. Happy is the man who has a male child who gets to the age of eighteen and there's no war going on.

SON: You always thought that?

FATHER: To see a child go off in uniform? I couldn't bear it. Remember your mother talking about [a good friend] seeing his child go off to Vietnam and realizing that the child was trying to impress him? Oh, God. How do you live with that? Allen Dulles was totally in favor of the Korean War and his son was this brilliant, brilliant, brilliant young man who wanted to make his father proud—he went off to Korea and had the back of his head blown off, came back a vegetable for the rest of time— boy, how do you live with that?

*   *   *   *

Even when I was very young, there were little misunderstandings between my father and me, although, or maybe because, I worshipped him. I was so blindly unquestioning that sometimes I put myself into ridiculous quandaries. Once, when I was five, I waited for an hour at the bathroom door as I'd been taught, for him to be done in there, without knocking, only to find there was no one inside. I was sure he'd gone out onto the balcony through the window, just to play a trick on me, and I still think that's what it was. Around the same time, after I'd been helping him make something in his wood shop, he patted me affectionately on the fanny. I burst into tears, thinking I'd done something wrong. I was reacting in the prescribed fashion. Later, when I was eight, when we were on home leave, at a posh little garden party, I asked for a cookie. He told me to run around the house. I did, looking forward to the double reward of cookie and accomplishment. I asked again, he sent me 'round again—and after the fifth or sixth go-round, my mother stopped it. I was supposed to wait until the cookies were *offered*. I had entirely missed the point.

But in general we understood each other quite well. I knew he was a strict disciplinarian and he knew I was out to make trouble. One day I broke into helpless giggles in the middle of a serious spanking, and that was the end of spankings.

These punishments were invariably administered after I'd been found out in a lie. I lied about everything: I said I'd done my home-work, I said I had to go to the bathroom (to spit out the gristle in the meat at dinner), I said I had not drawn all over the walls with crayons while they were away. The punishments did not stop me from lying. Instead they confirmed my self-image as a liar and a cheat, made sense of my terrible guilt, and made me a more skillful liar.

His dictum, never to trust anybody, played out between the two of us. I trusted him; he never trusted me; I never trusted myself—and I don't think he thought very highly of himself. I think he wanted me to be safe and trustworthy, and find an honorable line of work, in the law, for instance, but he just didn't know how to make that happen.

I was with him in his car one time in Israel—I was about eleven years old—and he told me, "Don't ever let anyone else tell you what to think." That felt really good, like he was giving me my life. I took it seriously—and I never again let him tell me what to think.

Several years ago I took him out for a sail in a small catboat he built for my sister. When we were well downwind of the dock, and it would take a couple of hours to tack back against the wind, I took out a ten-page letter I'd written him. It was a letter I had not found the courage to send—instead I wanted to be able talk about it in his presence, and ask him questions. What was *his* relationship like with his father? And so on. He guessed what it was as it emerged from my jacket pocket—our letters sometimes exuded a certain ten-page vibe—and he said, drily and with great eloquence, "Oh, shit."

We had a great conversation. He claimed that he'd been a lousy father, that he had no idea how to be one, and that his father almost never talked to him. He could count the words, and remembered them all distinctly. He had also worshipped his father, that was clear, but had never received the simple message from him that he was a lovely young person, a good boy. My grandfather was too shell-shocked to notice. And yet, by looking at Christmas cards his father sent out during the Depression, one can tell that my grandfather adored his youngest son. Adoring someone and sharing oneself, however, are two different things.

My father and I talked at great length later in his life. Not always with great understanding, but there are things he has said to me over the years that have given me that magic permission to be myself, that he perhaps missed from his own father.

Did I learn never to trust anybody? Yes and no—perversely, I went around foolishly trusting everybody; the more suspicious, the more I trusted them. I think I liked suspicious people. Did I stop lying? I tried to. I became painfully conscious of my habit of falsifying or exaggerating reality. *Am I lying to you now?* I used to ask myself.

I went home, a rare event in those days, for my twenty-first birthday. We were finally out of Vietnam and Nixon had retreated in disgrace, but many of us still felt that our fathers had poisoned our world and that the main battles were yet to be fought in our own country, even in our own homes. We finished up the birthday ritual after dinner, and my father picked up a book and began to read, out loud, "The Man Without a Country,"[99] the story of Philip Nolan, an officer who had been convicted of treason. When the judge asked if he had anything to say before his sentencing, he said he hoped he would never see or hear of his country again. The judge then sentenced him to spend the rest of his life aboard a naval vessel. The sailors were instructed not to mention anything about the US, and the flag was never to be flown. Nolan never again heard a word about his country, just as he had asked, and passed his days in wretched loneliness and remorse.

As my father closed the book, there were tears in his eyes. I had been growing more and more irritated as the hour passed, and finally said that Philip Nolan probably didn't miss his nation or its flag, he

---

99 A short story written in support of the Union during the Civil War, by Edward Everett Hale, in 1863.

missed his country, his people, the woods and hills of his home. He missed that part of the earth that conceived him and nurtured, among other things, his particular antagonism to the government and its policies. There was something sadistic about his sentence.

There was a dreadful silence. My father laid the book on the table and turned toward me. His face turned pale and his fists knotted. I stood facing him, ready for the first time to fight it out. But he turned at last and slowly left the room.

Later that day, he turned on me with Angletonian ferocity, to blurt out his conviction that I'd been recruited by the Communists! It was amazing to see how far off he could be. It was an almost exact replay of his scene with Angleton. I almost laughed at him. Didn't he know, for one thing, that I had no money?

The next summer he came to see me in a production of *Antigone*. I played Haemon, the son of Creon, the king. We were in a small outdoor space, in the afternoon. As Creon and I went through the epic confrontation between father and son, the chorus bending or pounding long bamboo poles behind us to emphasize a point won or lost, I caught sight of my father in his seat, following the story with great interest and sympathy.

SON: When you were telling me about Angleton saying, when did they pitch you? It reminded me of the time you asked me if I'd been working for the KGB.

FATHER: Oh yes. I wondered if you'd been approached by Lennie Friedman.

SON: No kidding. Lennie Friedman? When you sent me to the kibbutz? But you sent me to him . . . he was really good to me. He was KGB? Huh. 'Cause I had no idea what you were talking about. I mean, what use would I have been to anybody? I was barely sixteen, I didn't know anything.

FATHER: Well, you never know.

SON: I knew you must have had some grounds for asking me, so I kept going back over things, wondering if I'd ever had anything to do with the KGB—so, I had.

FATHER: Lennie Friedman was a Soviet agent from the Bronx. Did he ever admit to you that he'd been a Soviet agent?

SON: No, he was wonderful. He was very . . .

FATHER: A mensch. But he'd probably been told by the Mossad to see what he could get out of you. And he was there on sufferance. Everything was working together.

This one spun me around. I slowly realized afterward that it was about watching him, reporting on him . . . wasn't it? I'm doing that now, aren't I? . . . No, he set me up as bait, as an unwitting conduit, seeing if anything he leaked through me would come back around to him through his KGB channels. Or Mossad. And maybe it did. It must have. I just didn't know whom I was talking to.

SON: So the Soviet Union dissolved and the US became the only super-power, for the time being. Would you say that the US is the biggest threat to the globe today?

FATHER: It's pretty bad, I think so, very dangerous. But I think we're more danger to ourselves than we are to anybody else. Dangerous as we are to everybody else. That's why the Athenian example is so marvelous. The Athenians did it to themselves. Unnecessarily destroyed themselves. Your mother's terrified what's going to happen to you guys.

SON: About how we're going to support ourselves?

FATHER: No, I think she's worried about what the world is going to do to you guys.

SON: In this country particularly?

FATHER: Yeah, this country particularly.

SON: So what would you advise? Emigrate?

FATHER: That's up to you. I hope if I gave advice you wouldn't take it.

SON: But if it were you? If you were me?

FATHER: Not being you, I'm incapable of thinking about it. What you can ask is suppose if I were twenty—what do I think I would do? Of course I have no idea. There's no place else to go. There's Canada—and New Zealand is sort of a nice place. But if you get under the covers, who knows what tarantula you might find lurking there?

Indeed. Working on this material has made the old question of pos-sible catastrophe more real and immediate. Pop said you have to go down with your ship. He imitated a Monty Python captain who stays frozen in a good British salute as he goes under and his hat floats away. That's good, I think, but I'm no captain, I have no influence here. I'm a rat. A rat does no particular good if he stays aboard when the ship goes down. But I don't think the collapse of America would be an isolated thing—I imagine there would be chaos everywhere. Meanwhile, we pay our taxes to support plenty of chaos elsewhere. And the munitions industry is booming. How many yachts are paid for in blood?

SON: People hitting each other with clubs in the Paleolithic Age, or in Union Square, is one thing, but bombing innocent people . . .

FATHER: But that's the human condition, isn't it?

SON: At least conflict used to be hand-to-hand. You could see the person you were hitting on the head.

FATHER: People are more restrained when they have to do that than when they simply push a button and get rid of a thousand, or a hundred thousand people. That's true.

SON: We're getting more nonchalant about killing people, the more disembodied we become. While we pretend to be gentle and life-loving people. The most dangerous communities nowadays are the nicest ones. A lot of the people around Bush are very nice. There was a scene in the Michael Moore movie, Bowling for Columbine . . .

FATHER: I didn't see it. It's a sad day when Michael Moore is our shining light.

SON: It's a documentary.

FATHER: About the school shooting.

SON: Yeah. And he goes around and he asks Charlton Heston—you know, Moses, the head of the NRA—why does he make speeches in support of assault weapons right after these tragedies in the schools? In those same neighborhoods? Charlton Heston says he does it for freedom. The freedom to kill. Then we meet a guy who runs a missile factory right there in Columbine. There's a missile fifty feet long right behind him, as he talks very reasonably to Michael Moore. This guy sees no connection between building missiles to kill hundreds of thousands of people and what happened in his high school. He doesn't get the connection between violence and violence. Standing there in his nice suit, decrying violence in the school, he's dedicated his life to massive destruction. His kids grow up learning it's a good thing to kill people. It's your civic duty.

FATHER: That's the American solution—kill 'em. You have to destroy the village to save it. Yup, we're a violent people, we Americans.

CHAPTER 8

The God That Failed

"Things go better with Coke."
"We bring good things to life."
"I will work for your trust."
—Coca Cola Corporation; General Electric; George W. Bush

We still live in the shadow of the attack on the World Trade Center towers that happened fourteen years ago. For weeks after that September 11, sympathy for Americans poured in from all over the world. It seemed for an instant that we could all begin working toward each other's well-being. Instead we bombed Afghanistan, pointlessly enough, and then we invaded Iraq for reasons that proved entirely specious, and effectively destroyed that country. George W. Bush, a classic prep-school bully from Andover and Yale, a Skull and Bonesman, like so many in this story, played the manic, testosterone-fueled marionette to Cheney & Co.'s puppeteers. That group sent Secretary of State Colin Powell as hapless errand boy to the UN with a sheaf of lies, they authorized torture when it was clear that torture is not only illegal and inhumane but inhibits intelligence-gathering, and they killed thirty times as many innocent people in Iraq as died in the Trade Center. The ceaseless noise of bombers and helicopters in Iraq drove even the chickens crazy. In one hilarious scene, Bush paraded in a fighter pilot jumpsuit onboard an aircraft carrier in front of a banner that said "Mission Accomplished," the moment before the catastrophic repercussions began to tumble down upon us all. The list of offenses and willful stupidities our cowboy president and his gang committed went on and on. Not only were the actions in Iraq and Afghanistan like trying to kill a flea with a sledgehammer, but the decision-makers made terrible blunders—lying about Iraq's WMD capabilities (although according to confounding documents emerging from the recent James Risen affair concerning "Operation Merlin," they had given Saddam Hussein bomb plans and parts), conflating Al Qaeda with the Taliban, dismantling the Sunni military structure and so on—that made everything more chaotic than ever. Yet Bush won a second term, appealing to the basest instincts of the people and implying that he was God's Chosen. The US military reprisals for 9/11 struck at nations and civilian populations that had nothing to do with the Trade Center attacks, destabilized the Middle East, and unleashed a storm of revolutionary extremism in the name of Islam that is ever increasing in force and numbers. The chain of events has turned the US into an Orwellian total-surveillance state, corporations have taken the reins of power and left the people far behind, the top tenth of 1 percent of the people have more money than the bottom 90 percent, and divisions between right and left among the people are precipitous and likely to grow more pronounced and more violent. The media, owned by a small handful of oligarchs and corporations, feed on these divisions, many of them baseless, just as military industries, who (the Court has ruled them people after all), working with the current puppeteers, lobby hard for policies that spread chaos, and send electronic argosies of cash to their overseas bank accounts.

Soldiers, mercenaries, terrorists, and freedom fighters all know that killing and being killed is the whole point—that's what they sign up for; it's in the contract. But someone's little sister walking to school, hit suddenly by flying glass and bloody brain tissue and the sound of the world falling down around her, didn't sign up for this. What about her?

This makes us all crazy. We either get very angry, standing on one side of the fence or the other, or we contrive not to know, or we treat things philosophically—we're either crazy with anger or crazy in blank dissociation.

For as long as I can remember being aware of current events, as we called the shifting drama of nations when we were in fifth grade, my father and I saw things differently, though I learned how to think about these things mostly from him. By the late sixties, during the Vietnam War and the accompanying sea change we all went through, my father and I were barely on speaking terms. Looking back, I remember being very confused by his position on America. He seemed wise and logical about things in general. But when we got down to specific policies of the American government, I thought his broad perspective

started to narrow, and contradict itself. Maybe he felt bound by a loyalty that he himself was questioning. Maybe he clung to the last shreds of an American ideal while he watched its erosion day by day. Come to think of it, I don't remember him actually defending the American presence in Vietnam. I do remember him criticizing the movements for peace and justice, saying it would all end in a backlash from the right—and it looks like he was right about that.

The cost, to him, of having spent his career holding patriotic duty as a higher purpose in life—my country, right or wrong—must have cut deep. That principle was finally pushed beyond its limit, like a teacup knocked off a table to shatter on a stone floor. I am impressed that he was at all approachable in his later years, that his drinking didn't go haywire, that he kept something of himself reserved for simple tasks and relationships. I think whatever grace he could muster was extraordinary in the face of the failure of his god.

And he went further. I think he discovered kindness as a governing principle, and possibly found some inner peace. Family occasions became much happier than they were in the early years; his detonations were milder and less frequent than they once had been. It must have been as odd for him as for me that we were at last able to talk about these things with so little discord. It was a bittersweet peace, grounded as it was in such a tragic state of affairs.

*   *   *   *

SON: Where do the Bush people think they're taking us?
FATHER: Oh, these people can't think. Their only concern is their own personal ambition, their own personal future and their own obsessive ideas, which have no relation to the ideal.
SON: You mentioned Reinhold Niebuhr,[100] whose sense of humility and careful weighing of moral stakes is so lacking in our policies—you quote him in one of your papers.

---

100 Reinhold Niebuhr, 1892–1971, theologian popularly known as author of the Serenity Prayer, greatly influential as a balanced thinker on issues of war and politics, and founder of Christian Realism, which allows that one must use power to combat power.

FATHER: Niebuhr was an intensely interesting man, probably the most extraordinary religious thinker of our time at least. His recognition, for instance, that sometimes you really do have to go out and kill people. Amazing fellow, amazing fellow.

SON: I like his embrace of doubt, his mistrust of certainty. And about power—he says not only does power corrode . . .

FATHER: And corrupt . . .

SON: . . . and corrupt, but the corrupt seize power.

FATHER: Yes. Power corrupts and the corrupt seize power, yeah. It works both ways. It's a spiral.

SON: What prevented you from aspiring to power?

FATHER: Well, as I said, I never took my career that seriously. I really didn't. I should have—but it's one of the reasons I survived. I look around at people who did take it seriously, and see that they spun in; some of them killed themselves. If you looked at espionage as the last barrier to being overrun by the Soviets? If I thought that I'd have shot myself. Because it wasn't going to save us from Communism or anything else. It just wasn't in the cards.

SON: But still there's the hope that if you have power you can do some good.

FATHER: Oh, but that never interested me. I'm not an organization man. I really don't like people.

SON: And you don't care what they do?

FATHER: Not really, as long as they don't do it to me. I deplore that they do it to other people, but that's none of my business. I mean who am I to go out and tell the people of Maine how to run their government? For example, I had a colleague retired from the Agency who settled in Bath[101] and became the town manager. It killed him. He was dead in a decade. He had a heart attack and he was dead. You can't come from the outside and tell other people how to run their uproars. I never get mixed up in it.

SON: Do you mistrust anybody who's in a position of power?

FATHER: Oh, of course. Oh, they've got to be watched like hawks.

SON: Can you name someone in power that you trust?

---

101 Bath, Maine. For some obscure reason, or by pure coincidence, many CIA officers retire to Maine.

FATHER: Oh. Give me a couple of weeks and I might think of one. [*laughs*] I'm attracted to people like Jeffords[102] who jump the fence, who can change their minds. And strike back. I appreciate people like that. Fiorello La Guardia was a wonderful man—very powerful—but boy, you can count them on the fingers of one finger. Power is a terrible thing. That was the great genius of the guys who started this experiment, was that they made power impossible to wield. By splitting it three ways, each watching the other.

SON: It's interesting how the system still works sometimes. I think people don't like to be taken for granted. There's something beautifully perverse in human nature that says, wait a minute: You think you've got me pegged?

FATHER: That's very true.

SON: Like in the Supreme Court, people change.

FATHER: That's been the case in the past. Not so much lately. It's not true of Thomas[103]—he hasn't learned a thing. And that's the kind of person who is going to be appointed to the court from now on. Scalia hasn't learned a thing. Mrs. O'Connor has learned a lot. And of course the other lady, Ginsburg, knew an awful lot when she arrived. So she didn't have to learn so much. But that Western cowgirl [O'Connor]—she's learned an awful lot, about herself, about this country, and about power . . . But for the most part, power gets in the way. Johnson, for example, for that last four years of the war in Vietnam. Johnson really thought that the war was the thing to do. It wasn't Kissinger; it was Johnson. He wouldn't listen to anybody else. Neither can this man. Not that this man can see anything anyway. Hopeless. At least Johnson had some sense of helping people. He really believed in the Great Society. He did some very good things. There was that side of him. This man is just totally mean. A mean-minded, vicious animal. He has no side to him like that, none. None. Shrub, I call him.

SON: But I think it's a mistake to think of Bush as a cipher. There's some footage of him on the 2000 campaign trail, the press corps following him

---

102 James Jeffords, 1934–2014, Republican senator from Vermont, switched his party affiliation in 2001 to Independent and caucused with the Democrats, tipping the balance in favor of the Democrats.

103 Clarence Thomas, Supreme Court Justice.

around. You can see that he has a keen ability to make a person want to be one of the good old boys.

FATHER: Well, he's a very good cheerleader, but that doesn't mean much in my book. I never thought cheerleaders were particularly important. I don't think he has more going on than that.

MOTHER: But he has drawn people in.

FATHER: No. He's been maneuvered, he's been manipulated. He's Charlie McCarthy,[104] he's no Edgar Bergen. Charlie McCarthy could draw people in. But there's nothing there, just a wooden head with a jaw hinge.

MOTHER: Whenever I say that maybe Bush won't win, you always come back to say that he will win, because he has the money.

FATHER: Yes. He can do that. It's a simple equation. Halliburton gets billions and it allots a very small portion of that to win the election. That's so hard for him to set up? I don't see any great genius in that. I see a great deal of crookedness. He's a crook. He's mendacious, he's dishonest, and he's a hypocrite—worse in some ways, because he starts believing it himself.

SON: Did you see that quote? Bush says, "I can't trust the media. So I don't read anything, I have Condi come in and tell me what's going on. Somebody I can trust."

FATHER: Yeah. "I go only to objective sources," he says. So the newsman asks him, "What objective sources?" So he says, "Oh, my staff!"

SON: Yes, but he'll trip up. Events will take him down. Jonathan Schell[105] says that events don't lie and they don't care what the polls say, they just happen.

FATHER: Well, one can only hope.

SON: When Bush says that he himself is personally going to take the responsibility for the outcome in Iraq . . .

FATHER: Yes, the people in this country, they hear that and they think, oh, that's wonderful. I'll vote for him. And then of course everything goes to hell, but they forget all that and then he repeats himself and says, "I'm going to take care of things from here on in." Oh, isn't that wonderful!

---

104 Charlie McCarthy was Edgar Bergen's ventriloquist's dummy, a puppet with a monocle, Bergen's alter ego.

105 Jonathan Schell was a prominent author, journalist, nuclear disarmament activist, and critic of the Iraq War.

And they give him another check. It's all rhetoric—empty rhetoric. But enough of Bush. Again, he's only a symptom of a collapsed republic.

SON: Is there any way to get back on track?

FATHER: No. No, it's got to come out of the fire of civil war or anarchy or some terrible explosion. It has to be nuclear. Metaphorically speaking. People don't want to go back. And what comes out of the catastrophe might grow into something worse that [sic] what we have right now, as it did in Hitler's time, so it's hard to know what to wish for. Things can't change without the catastrophe. And things may change so much for the worse that you'll wish that the catastrophe had never happened. It's like the Arab-Israeli problem. It will never be solved except by something bigger than what you've got now. Well, the bigger problem will cause so much more havoc and death and destruction, you'll wish that you had the old Arab-Israeli problem back.

SON: Do you think an economic crash in this country would do it?

FATHER: Or anything that kills gas supplies and the automobile industry. That would do it.

SON: The car companies aren't doing all that well.

FATHER: The American consumer is doing very well—one American, one car. And now it's more than one car per person. Every American has a marvelous icebox and a marvelous washing machine, but where does it come from? Everything is made of steel and the American steel companies are dead. Well, guess who isn't dead. Japanese steel mills, Austrian steel mills, Chinese steel mills, Russian steel mills—they're doing fine.

SON: And what is America providing?

FATHER: It isn't providing anything except money to buy these things.

SON: Where is the money coming from?

FATHER: The printing press at the mint. Mostly we borrow it from foreign countries. One point eight billion a day from China alone. We have debts piled up beyond our eyebrows. That's where the money is coming from. One of these days the foreigners are going to wonder about the stability of this country, as I am, and pull all their money out and then it will crash. That's the only thing that keeps it afloat and permits this tremendous imbalance in trade. The imbalance in trade is covered by foreign loans. When they stop thinking that this is the place to put their money, interesting things will happen. Next question. [short laugh] The whole business of globalization is so phony as to be beyond belief. The big corporations have given all the little technocratic power to the WTO and the IMF so that they don't have egg on their face when the whole thing goes wrong—which it does every day. So they just point to the WTO and IMF and say oh, those are the guys who did it, not us. And they go merrily on their way. They do all this without taking any responsibility. They know it doesn't work. What we export now are low wages and child labor and all those good things. We import everything else. Neat. All to fuel this increasing discrepancy between the millions that the CEOs march off with and the American worker who isn't earning very much at all.

SON: Did you see that chart? There was a chart in the *New York Times* about a year ago that showed the average worker's wage in 1983 as a little tiny bar at the bottom, and the CEO's bar went a third of the way up the page. And then it said, now let's look at 2002, and there was another chart—again, there was the worker's microscopic rate. But you had to flip the paper open to get the CEO income. It stretched up the whole length of the paper, all the way up to the top of the page. The difference doubled, or tripled, in twenty years.

FATHER: And now it's even worse. And it's not going to get any better. The party's over. And so we come to Gibbon.[106] Gibbon's three signs of a collapsing empire are the use of mercenaries, a general obsession with blood sports, and income disparity. Well, we had a good three hundred years or so, but like the Roman Empire in decline, a too-secure nation rots from within, and doesn't know it until it's too late.

SON: And it's all so petty. The super-rich don't appreciate the stuff anyway—a good glass of wine or a good pair of boots, the afternoon off— they just have them anytime they want. Nothing is special. And they only talk to other members of the club, so they miss out on all the interesting conversations. The effort to survive, the primal taste of life itself, is unavailable to them. They don't experience real stakes. Also, they don't feel appreciated, which is what we all need more than anything else. They become ever more isolated behind their gates and they become deadened, which may be why they're so dangerous. Of course, I choose this point

---

106 Edward Gibbon, one of my father's favorite references, from the late eighteenth century, wrote *The Decline and Fall of the Roman Empire*.

of view because it suits my condition. If I were on top, I'd probably revise my theory.

FATHER: Fat chance. [*laughs*] But you're better off close to the ground.

SON: Yeah . . . I try to be a late worm, to miss the early bird. But poverty has its downside too.

The fact that such a large part of our conversation is taken up with bad news makes me cringe. Nothing can dull the mind like negativity. We should occupy ourselves with the subtler wonders of life, or laugh it all away. If we're going down, let's go down dancing!

We are exiles from Yeats's "deep heart's core," [107] and we want to go home. The ceaseless commercial din, the crush of poverty, and the news of war and suffering exhaust the soul. What amazes me is that the progressive income disparity and the even more provocative foreign policies in Ukraine and the Middle East have not slowed a jot since this conversation twelve years ago, and we seem more passive now than ever. Obama has been a great president in many ways, but even he has played puppet to the burgeoning machinery of chaos. He's a good man in a bad dream.

But Pop's not done for the day:

FATHER: There was Jesus Christ, two thousand years ago, who saw the nuttiness of the human being and how he really ought to behave himself—and nobody paid the slightest attention to him.

SON: Least of all the Christians.

FATHER: Least of all the Christians. [*laughs*] So I don't think you can get any closer to giving the animal a chance to change than that, and he didn't take it. [*He heaves a great sigh.*]

SON: Strange, how we push people around, a lot of it on the basis of some abstract idea about who God is . . .

FATHER: Abstract ideas of any sort.

SON: America, the whole illusion of supremacy . . .

FATHER: It all comes down to the basic fact that the human being is an irrational animal; he's not capable of thinking rationally.

---

107 "The Lake Isle of Innisfree," by W. B. Yeats, 1888.

THE GOD THAT FAILED

SON: Do you know the John Gardner book, *Grendel*?

FATHER: No.

SON: It's the Beowulf story from the monster's point of view.

FATHER: Great.

SON: I'll tell you the story sometime. But I'd like to ask you more about Athens.

FATHER: Athens . . . And the Romans. Look at the Gracchi, the two broth-ers who were the last of the statesmen who gave up their lives thinking that they could save the republic. Who were slaughtered by the so-called senators—and then think of Brutus. What a hero. I don't know that Shake-speare thought he was a hero, but Shakespeare had to be careful. I mean, my God, he had the Caesars looking right over his shoulder. [*laughs*]

SON: Shakespeare was the only playwright of the time that didn't end up in jail one time or another. That's partly why they don't have any records of Shakespeare. Most of the other playwrights got into trouble, like Mar-lowe, who was murdered in a tavern. Marlowe was a spy, by the way.

FATHER: There you go, our bard was very careful. He was sort of like Helms. You could see his mind working: "Uh-oh, I better not say that . . ."

SON: But Shakespeare really did tackle somebody now and then.

FATHER: But in a way that they never got it.

SON: Well, the Puritans got it. The queen's steward, who was the model for Malvolio in *Twelfth Night* . . .

FATHER: Yeah, oops!

SON: . . . who shut down the theaters for the next six years . . .

FATHER: Yeah, yeah. You know that kind of analysis would make a won-derful monograph, Shakespeare as a politician, and the political constraints that he was under and where it showed . . . in any case he didn't portray Brutus as a hero. But there was Brutus trying to save the remnant of a republic by preventing dictatorship. And who knows? It's a bloody place that we live in.

SON: Do you remember the book *African Genesis*, by Robert Ardrey?

FATHER: Ardrey. Yeah.

SON: Who was roundly criticized for suggesting that the human being was territorial, greedy, murderous . . .

FATHER: Which he is, he is. We're just unbelievably mean and bloody. The problem with most Americans is that they live in this funny little dream world. They don't know what's going on. They don't know the terrible deaths, and the lives, the desperate, desperate lives that people are leading all over the world as we speak. You have to put it out of your mind, otherwise you go crazy. And these hypocrites talk about exporting democracy? I mean, it's madness, it's utter madness—and then they think that people hear this crap and believe it.

SON: Well, that fits into the Grendel story.

FATHER: Yeah? [*laughs*]

SON: Well, I'll tell you briefly: the monster is half immortal, born of the mother goddess inside the middle of the earth. He's a hybrid, awkward sort of monster so he comes out and he wants to play. He's the original lonely monster. And he sees these human beings. Great! He's twenty times bigger than they are but he thinks they're wonderful, and they play a little bit, and then he moves a little too fast and one of them gets hurt. And he's horrified and he runs crying back to his mother. And then about five hundred years later he ventures out again and this time the humans are standing there with little sticks with points on them, and they start throwing them at him and he thinks it's a game at first until he gets hit in the eye and then he cries out, *bweh!* and he kills twenty or thirty of them with one swipe of his hand, just as a reflex—and now he's really mortified, "Oh no, what have I done?" And he goes running back to his mother . . . Now of course, over the years the bards have gotten together with the future kings and they've made up epic poems that they sing about the monster . . .[108]

FATHER: And human heroism . . .

SON: Heroism, and the great danger threatening humanity. The kings have managed to convince everybody, through the bard, that they should give all their stuff to the king and he'll build walls, and he'll take . . .

FATHER: Walls, that's good.

SON: . . . and he'll take the hogs they raise, and the swords they forge, and all the jewels and gold, and he'll make sure that everybody's safe! So that when the monster comes the king will protect them. And then it just goes from there, step by step, building a secure fiefdom with a nice big castle in the middle where all the good stuff ends up.

---

108 The Jabberwock and "my beamish boy," drawn by John Tenniel.

But it's not the king type that appalls me, because that has nothing to do with me. It's the bard, making up the stories that'll sell the king's scam, and getting a good spot at the head table. That gives me the heebie-jeebies. We say that storytelling has no purpose, no function anymore, in books or in the theater—but the newscasters, the PR people, they're the new bards. That's where the power lies, still. It's just that we don't think of them as storytellers.

FATHER: Well, a lot of it, I wouldn't say all power, a lot of it.

SON: No, I guess the bards don't wield the power. But they're the ones that cook it up. They create the good guys and the bad guys. They name them—so in a biblical sense . . .

FATHER: The bards are hired henchmen; they're hired guns . . . But this is the animal that ate his brother. Ate him, for God's sake! All because one was a stick creature and the other was a missile creature, terrible story . . .

SON: And we've been doing it ever since. Cain and Abel, Cro-Magnon and the Neanderthal, Troy, the Crusades, the Somme, and then on to the bombing of cities . . . But I think if we just looked at ourselves and admitted that we are all evil, we might start treating each other better. You were talking about Union Square before, where Mishu took you to see the riots.

FATHER: Yes. Of course I have no memory of where it was, just the name of the place.

SON: I went to Union Square after the Trade Center attack. I took my bicycle into the city on the train, and I rode all around the crater, which was still smoking, up and down the avenues. The disaster made people aware of each other in a different way. They were ready to help out, strangers sharing an understanding of loss and humility.

Right after 9/11, Union Square became a living monument. There were Tibetan monks who sang continuously for days without stopping, spelling each other, there were beautiful things sent from all around the world with messages of sympathy and solidarity, and the park was full of people simply being together. Many of them were weeping; the park was full of quiet mourning energy. For a moment it seemed that we could change the world, spend our time recognizing each other instead of blowing each other away. It was like the feeling I got sometimes in the sixties, I am not ashamed to say; a sense of belonging. A deep sharing of grief that brought people together.

FATHER: While you were saying that, I was thinking, the one silver lining in the whole situation, is that Gibbon would give his right hand to be in our shoes.

SON: At ringside?

FATHER: Sitting at ringside, having a ringside seat at the collapse of a republic. Think of how much he would enjoy it, he would have loved to have been here.

SON: It is eventful; that's true. But I like subtler pleasures.

FATHER: No, no, it's fascinating, and much more exciting than . . . Look, the history of a peaceful people is very dull. Whereas what we're going through, it's really interesting. I'm going to miss not seeing the dénouement. But this business of decline is nothing new. It happens all the time. My God, look at Orwell. He has a lot to say about the human animal.

SON: Orwell. There was a man who was driven by emotional forces . . .

FATHER: Absolutely. He was a product of his background, he went to that awful boys' school, which almost did him in, you know, he was so badly treated. And then he went to Eton where things weren't that much better and then he became a policeman out in Burma, and he describes a public hanging that he saw that affected him deeply. And he had to shoot an elephant because the villagers standing there expected him to. Terrible story. And then he went to Spain as an idealistic freedom fighter only to find that those on his side were the worst thugs and murderers that he had ever met. Far worse than those on the other side. That's what finished him off on Communism, especially the Soviet model. He had it when he saw what happened in Spain. They almost killed him; they were out to get him. Goddamn bastards. Never trust anybody.

SON: Do you identify with Orwell in any way?

FATHER: Well, aren't we all products of what we've been through? We all have our quirks and strange ways that are partly a matter of nature and partly a matter of what we've been through. But this nature-nurture thing is such utter nonsense. You've got all these very modern people running around telling us why we do things, helping us figure it out, what's going on up there, [*fingers circling temple*] saying he does that because of this, and he does this because of that . . . but it's too complicated a machine. I think it's beyond human understanding. Any more than a computer can understand itself. There's no way we can get outside ourselves to see what's going on inside ourselves.

SON: And yet that attempt is the most compelling thing we do as humans.

FATHER: Absolutely, we can't let go, but there's no way we're ever going to find out. And there's another thing that's always bothered me. This instinctive agreement with John Donne, his lovely poem, you know, "no man is an island"[109]—again, utter nonsense. Every man is an island; we're all inside a cage, looking out through the bars at the other cages. And we see the eyes looking through the cages across from us—and that's about as close as we can get.

SON: There's a big tension between the individual urge and the community urge.

FATHER: Yes, of course there is.

SON: And both of them are obsolete. The urge to propagate, the urge to kill, to be king, on one side, and on the other, the herd instinct to wipe out anything "other"—all of those things are primal, and totally obsolete.

FATHER: That's it, they may be obsolete, but that doesn't mean that they're not going to continue to go on and be the rule.

SON: Yes. But there may have been a time, when we went to the ancient festivals at Epidaurus, let's say, when there was a collective consciousness that . . .

FATHER: Oh, I think the animal sees the advantage of working together, hunting down the mammoth and killing him and getting the meat, which he can only do if he does it with two dozen of his fellows. He's clever, he's clever enough to know that if he doesn't do it that way he's going to starve, so he does it that way but that doesn't mean that there's any real . . .

SON: But if all of life is the same strand in different shapes, then there actually is a connection. You look at the world from far away, you don't see the islands, you see the globe.

FATHER: Yeah but does the . . . That's an interesting question: does the little coral have any sense that he's . . . or take the ant, does the ant think of himself as a unit of a larger animal that is the ant hill? Does the human

---

109 "Meditation XVII," by John Donne, 1624.

being really think of himself as part of a huge animal made up of all humans? I don't think so, no, I doubt it. And you watch an ant, you know, they go this way and they go that way, and . . . [*laughs*]

We skirted the question: is there a connection between *us*, as father and son? Or: what sort of connection shall we make of it? I was always aware, when we talked in grand terms about politics and humankind, that I was looking for a connection, or more specifically, an acknowledgement of my existence and what it meant to him. I was always looking for a personal meaning in these discourses that he didn't at all intend.

My son Reilly and I were riding in my old truck one day in Boston when he was about five years old. He turned to me and said, "Pop, why do people understand each other?" I tried to conceal my pride, not wanting to spoil the moment, and said, "That's a very good question. In fact, philosophers and scientists have been arguing about that same thing for hundreds of years, and they still don't really know. But what do you think?"

"Hmm . . ." (I could tell that he'd been thinking of the answer before he'd asked the question.) "I think we all used to be the same thing one time long ago, and when we understand each other, it's because we remember it a little bit, in our heart."

He put his hand on his heart. I looked over at him, bouncing along on the road, a very little person on a great ratty old bench seat of a Chevy C-10, full of trust that the truck and I were okay, so he could think about things like this, and I said, "That is a pretty good answer."

I keep wondering why my father took me to the theater when I was young. It was as though he were priming me for what I was to do in life, as though he knew my passion before I did, and secretly shared it with me. For the most part he approved of my zigzag way through life. The days of his deep disappointment in me faded into the past.

When I went to theater school at SUNY Purchase, after spending a few years wandering around and working in manual trades, he told people that I was going to the Rockefeller School for Dance. He hadn't a clue and, I thought, no real interest either. But when he came to see me in a Chekhov play in my third year there, he filled me in on the social history of the time, and showed me how I might have made a crimped cigarette with a torn-off bit of newspaper, as they did back then. Years later, after I came back from Leningrad, where I'd gone to play in *The Seagull*, he hung the Russian poster for the play, lettered in Cyrillic, *Chayka*, on the wall by his bed. Part blessing, part ironic joke on his Cold Warrior days. I brought him a gray-blue fur cap with ear-flaps, with a big Bolshevik red star medallion on the forehead. He was delighted by it and wore it around town during the winters.

I wish I could have been more fun for him as a companion. I could have joined in and laughed with him more than I did. But I remember watching Condoleezza Rice at her Senate confirmation hearings, serving her poison to the senators and the cameras with her best silver. *Do have some more, it's very good!* I had smoke coming out of my ears, like Yosemite Sam.

Then I compare my situation with that of the Iraqi girl coming home from school, standing by a car riddled with bullet holes, in which her father and brother and sister have just been shot to death by Americans in action figure costumes, milling around in the photo, and I can't imagine what was born that moment, in that little girl. She's about eighteen years old now, having lived most of her life in a land almost completely destroyed by us and by the Frankenstein monsters we have created. We call it "collateral damage," but that assumes that the damage is a regrettable byproduct of a purpose that is necessary and good. But is it? If our purpose has been to make the world safe for freedom, or to combat terrorism, have we not curtailed freedoms, have we not terrorized, and bred a far more virulent terrorism?

CHAPTER 9

Alice In Wonderland

"...she could hear the rattle of the teacups as the March Hare and his friends shared their never-ending meal, and the shrill voice of the Queen ordering off her unfortunate guests to the execution—once more the pig-baby was sneezing on the Duchess's knee, while plates and dishes crashed around it—once more the shriek of the Gryphon, the squeaking of the Lizard's slate-pencil, and the choking of the suppressed guinea-pigs, filled the air, mixed up with the distant sob of the miserable mock turtle."

—Lewis Carroll, *Alice in Wonderland*

W e sat at the table in our usual positions.

FATHER: Is there life after espionage? I left the agency in '72; I've been retired longer than I played. [*laughs*]

Behind him was a sliding glass door he'd installed that went out to a small deck he built twenty years before, rotting now—he had not been willing to pay for pressure-treated lumber. Birds chattered and made their rounds. We could hear the sounds of children in the playground across the street. After thirty years of constant relocation, my mother and he stayed there in Brunswick, Maine, for thirty years, rarely going anywhere. My father hated to use the car.

FATHER: So that about sums up everything I've been thinking about. Let's see—I thought a lot today about leaving my goddamned wallet at home. That bothered the hell out of me—an indication of a total loss of mind; then I was looking down at the speedometer and came within an ace of slamming into the back of a car—in the middle of the road in front of me! And if your mother hadn't screamed I wouldn't have slammed the brakes. I just barely swerved around him. I thought about that for a long time too.

I live here in Maine. I've got the library on one side and the playing fields on the other. I don't drive anywhere anymore. I read books and I watch the girls play field hockey in the field behind the house. Boy, they're good, these Bowdoin girls. I get up late and then I make things. I'm a member of the Maine Woodworkers. A couple of years ago they asked me to make an ornament for the Christmas tree at the White House. Sort of ironic. Of course, I make whatever anybody wants, like that half model, or a new mast for Barb's boat. There's always something that needs to be made. The Christmas card, that's always a big slice.

Once every two years, I do a talk at the town-and-college club. It takes me a year to get one of those together. Like the talk on the sex life of the lobster. I had to go out to Cliff Island to go fishing with Bub Anderson, on his boat, and then I had to go up to Boothbay, to all the marine biology centers, and to Portland, to talk to all of the retailers—that took a long time. The sex life of the lobster is fascinating. At least I thought so. The trouble was, at least half the audience fell asleep and the other half left early.

SON: Why, were they offended?

FATHER: No, no, the lobster was just not something that excited them. But the oldest fossil of the daddy longlegs, which is related to the lobster as an arthropod, has for its size the longest penis on record! You see, some things are really interesting. The sex life of the lobster is one of them. But they weren't interested.

SON: Do you have a routine?

FATHER: There isn't any. I do something different every day. I make lists of things to do, like fix the screen and repair the door, and replace the light-bulbs. I take great joy in crossing things off the list. It means that something's been done. Finished. If I'm fixing the mast, then I just keep at it until it's done. For example, the half model is being held up, because I have to get Ben Potter's input on how he wants it, so I wait for that, and in the mean-time I'm making the Christmas card, and it'll take a week to get that done.

Finishing is everything. That was the trouble with espionage, because you never finished it. There's never a package, to say look, here's some-thing I've done . . . everything is ongoing. And if it stops, that means a disaster has happened, someone has gotten killed or the thing has been compromised.

There was a man—he was one of the great boatbuilders in Maine, and he had a shop in Bath. Alexander took me to a lecture he gave about boatbuilding. A magnificent fellow, brilliant in his field, one of the top old geezers that knew everything—varnishes, everything. And he said that in his shop he kept a rocking chair. When he made a mistake he didn't try to fix it right away because to do it right away would have ruined the whole job and he'd have to start all over again. Instead, he'd sit in the rocking chair and wait until the fury had passed, and then he could look at the problem with a certain amount of patience. And boy, that says everything. He had a name for this rocking chair—the anger chair. The Disaster Chair.

SON: That reminds me of Chomsky, do you ever read Chomsky?

FATHER: Uh . . . yes.

SON: He doesn't like the word "intellectual." He was talking about how the man in the factory . . .

FATHER: Yeah, the guy who really knows what's going on is the guy in the shop. Who never puts it on paper, unfortunately—but he's the one who knows. Chomsky was good on that. Yeah. Look at that . . . I'm agree-ing with Noam Chomsky.

*   *   *   *

My parents lived a comfortable, simple life in retirement. My father became an artist! He made "Portraits in Wood," carved figures and symbols, in a frame, arranged to represent a person's life, commissioned by a spouse or board member, to commemorate his or her life and accomplishments. He called them "the boxes." The work combined his investigative skills with woodcarving. He made two or three of them purely for his own satisfaction—one for my mother and one based on Lewis Carroll, also known as Charles Dodgson, a mathematician at Oxford. Pop was intrigued by everything about Dodgson, who some-how protected his secret life by living it quite openly.

My father spent a lot of time in the basement, where he'd built a small shop with a contractor's table saw, a drill-press, a band saw, three or four lathes, and so on. The place was a mess, filled with dust, asbes-tos, and random piles of hardwood. We finally persuaded him to get an air filter system but I'm not sure he used it. He listened to a small radio that was tuned to a country station. He liked Willie Nelson and truck songs. "The Phantom 309," "Convoy," and the one about a parrot that sings "On the Road Again." He worked away down there and carried a steady output of finished things up the stairs. He used cheap glue; because of this his joints sometimes fell apart a few years later, but he had an astounding array of maker skills, and many of his things were wonderful. He received but little recognition for this piecemeal work. Sometimes people inadvertently diminished what he did, but I never saw him wince at it. He had developed a wonderful imperviousness to what the world thought.

The "boxes" became his main focus, and their artistic quality improved as he went along. He became more confident with color and contrast, and the carvings were set more consciously against their backgrounds. He started playing with depth and shadow. The bits and pieces belonged together in a little world governed by his particular logic.

As I grew older and began to resemble him, I was glad that my father's face always looked young. Even at eighty he had a twinkle in his eye, smooth cheeks, and a mouth full of laughter and sadness. Yossi Melman and Dan Raviv, co-authors of *Every Spy a Prince* and two other books in the Israeli/American spy-vs.-spy genre, call him "the puckish spy." The wrinkles were tight. They showed a lifetime of bemused activity. But it was a removed face, in orbit around its own life. His eyes constantly analyzed the scene in front of him in relation to a matrix of selected facts. Sometimes, in the company of people he loved, he let go a little—after a drink or two—and his cynical charm turned bitter. In the evening, having spent two or three hours reading books and articles (he read the *New York Review of Books* cover to cover), and listening to the news about the emerging disasters, his eyebrows started to go haywire. Occasionally, he exploded. He always let rip in the dining room, where it made the most noise, when there was food on the table and someone's dog underfoot. He banged the tabletop; the plates jumped and rattled. He cursed the son-of-a-bitch-of-the-day as though we didn't understand the depth of the problem—as though we were the problem. He erupted with little warning. We all avoided each other's eyes. My mother didn't breathe at these times; she clenched her stomach. I knew from her that this happened just as frequently when the two of them were alone.

During our last interview he watched me and kept himself under tight control. He knew I was looking for something else in him, some sign that there was a reason to keep going as a species, as though there wouldn't be one unless he gave us his blessing. He was rooting for the cockroach! One of his pet refrains. Even at fifty I was overimpressed, and a little afraid of him.

But the simple drudgery of transcribing these interviews started to dislodge the pattern. His voice on tape cranked along in its usual all-knowing, musical growl, but it came from a harmless little plastic box, not from this formidable man. Bit by bit, I robbed his voice of its mystery and power and reduced it to neat rows of words and tidy margins, where I could examine it like a dead insect. When I was in my father's presence, asking the questions, I slid into a reflexive mode, thinking myself a naive utopian, dumber than a stoned hippie. But when I listened to the tape, out of range of the spell he cast, I revised my opinion. I began to notice an unfamiliar confidence in the sound of my voice, and I saw that I let him do most of the talking and that my listening was keen, as his might have been in different circumstances. I began to interpret his caution and his evasions in a new light, in rela-

tion to his inquisitive son. Also: I revised his words. I decided what he
could say.

Meanwhile, we dueled it out.

SON: What is the function of art in our society?

FATHER: Ah, one of the great questions of human history. There have been
wonderful things written. Give me a couple of weeks and I'll remember
some of them. Koestler[110] might have come up with something about the
role of art in human nature. The ones that catch my eye are the ones that
prove that you can't be a great artist unless you're nutty.

SON: Or what other people think of as nutty.

FATHER: Genius takes being crazy. The man we consider to be sane cannot be a great artist. I look at histories of all these guys—you know,
they're cutting off their ears. Jesus Christ! Or they're just terrible people.
Like Wagner—a hopeless, hopeless human being. But then, that's my view.

SON: But you're interested in the subject?

FATHER: Oh yes, I have a very trivial mind. It goes off in all funny directions. I have no control. And I would probably be a much more serious
person if . . . my attitude toward music for example: I'm a totally tin ear.
You could play "The Star Spangled Banner" wrong and it'd sound like
every other "Star Spangled Banner" to me. I can't whistle and I can't
sing. I remember in school: every first former was tested for the choir.
You had to sing "God Bless Us All" or something. And I never got
through the first line. Next! [laughs] And I couldn't drum and I couldn't
play the fife for the fife and drum corps for the May Day celebration;
when I got to West Point I couldn't march to music. I had to watch the
guy in front of me to know whether to . . . you know, it was right foot,
left foot. I can't do it. And I can't dance. That's absolutely hopeless, I've
never been able to do that. See, there's no connection between music
and me. None. It's just a noise. Some noises are very pleasant and I like
them. I listen all day to background noise, which is what music is to me.
Part of it is very painful and I don't like it at all and some of it is rather
nice. I have now learned to recognize some of them . . . like the can-can

---

110 Arthur Koestler, 1905–1983, was a wide-ranging iconoclast and writer. He
was one of the six ex-Communist contributors to *The God that Failed*, 1949, a
book my father often referred to.

guy, *Tales of Hoffmann*.[111] Things like the trademark song for the Lone Ranger, "The William Tell Overture," and the "1812 Overture."[112] I get to know some of these things. And the marches! The German marches are the best. The Badenweiler,[113] all the old Prussian things from the days of 1870 German Nationalism. Marvelous things. Terrible of course, but marvelous. [*laughs*]

But the other night a young friend of ours gave this recital at Bowdoin. Your mother wanted to go, but I had to pick up the Christmas card at the printer's, so the timing was all wrong. But your mother was so interested in this. I thought, well, I'll just stick my nose in the door. And I came in. I had to wait outside until he'd finished the first thing, Schumann. And then he played a polonaise. Wonderful things that didn't mean anything to me. But I sat way over on the left. And the guy's hands—the guy's hands—were absolute magic. To see how he did that. And he not only did the usual thing, you know, taking the left hand and putting it over the right, but he'd take the left hand and put it *under* his right hand. Well—it was captivating. So. That's my connection with art. I think that to see the best of anything is an experience that no one should miss. Whether it's Marcel Marceau doing mime, or Olivier doing something . . .

SON: It's a matter of dedication, isn't it?

FATHER: To see the Oxford guy do *Beyond the Fringe*.[114] The very best is something that one shouldn't miss.

SON: Yes, I agree of course. What I love is to see someone who has two things—great skill that comes from committing one's life to something that barely exists, and a willingness to . . .

FATHER: Yeah, and the same thing goes for Orwell's writing—it was very, very painful but he made it seem utterly effortless. That's the greatness.

SON: For no particular reason.

---

111 By Jacques Offenbach, 1881.

112 Rossini, 1829; Tchaikovsky, 1880.

113 An idiotic Bavarian military march by Georg Fürst to commemorate a German victory in 1914 against France in Lorraine. It was said to have been Hitler's favorite, and was often used as his entrance music.

114 A brilliant cabaret revue by Peter Cook, Dudley Moore, Alan Bennett, and Jonathan Miller, 1960, a precursor to Monty Python.

FATHER: That's right. It's something they have to do.

SON: They don't know where it's going . . .

FATHER: That's right.

SON: And if they're any good it will be something that no one's ever done before.

FATHER: There was this great piano teacher who had a gimmick that took care of that. Young people would come to him with their parents, they would play and he would say, "You're worthless, forget it, do something else! Don't be a piano player." And one young man came back a decade or two later and said, "Look, I've become a very successful piano player. You must have seen that I could be good. Why did you tell me that I was worthless and couldn't do it?" And the man said, "Because if you'd listened to me you never would have made it. If you did have it, you were going to do it no matter what I said."

SON: Or maybe even more so.

FATHER: There you go—exactly. Isn't that a good story?

SON: Yeah.

FATHER: That appeals to me. I can understand that.

This piano teacher is a tyrant and an egotist. It is never useful to tell a student she is worthless. Stamina and resilience in an artist comes from a sense that she is worth something. There are obstacles enough to hone and temper her. Young artists of great promise can be easily crushed. There are wonderfully gifted people all around us who are either working in obscurity or were frightened or abused out of their calling. Often by an embittered, so-called teacher. We need to nourish our artists if we hope achieve any dignity as a species.

We are indeed burdened by the cliché, be it from Puritanism or from twisted ideals of masculinity and authority, or from the near-pervasive mistrust of the "other" mixed with the inherent self-destruction of the artist, that we can only produce the good stuff if we are in torment. It's true that torment can work as a trigger to go beyond, to endure more, to see things from the outside, to wreak havoc, to howl—and that is all good. But without love and beauty, and a profound interest in the possibilities, not to mention the simple aesthetic necessity for range and contrast, the imagination is barren.

Is there anything worth mentioning, particularly in drama, that does not have rending conflict at its core? Maybe not. But it is a cruel spur. The best work comes from a brighter source, a sense of wonder and magic.

Let go, I tell myself. Allow forward movement. Both in terms of my father and in my own work. Release the brake. Look at what he says about the piano player.

My brother Alex is a superb craftsman, a great boatbuilder. He has an intuitive imagination, as well as the willingness to follow an idea to the nth degree, and live with a meager income, like an artist. The other three of us have gone through rigorous training in painting, theater, and bronze sculpting. Together the four of us have spent over a hundred years dedicated to our work. My father recognized some of this, particularly in my sister, Barbara, whose work he admired even when he didn't understand it, and in Alex, whose work possibly intimidated him. But it irritated me that when he spoke to us about artists, he spoke exhaustively and authoritatively, as if of black people, to a black person sitting right there in front of him. Maybe he didn't consider us nutty enough to be called artists. Nutty, but not nutty enough.

I wanted to construct a real bridge between us before he died. I wanted to dispel the sentence of failure he pronounced on the human race—and on me when I was very small. I wanted to get this father-obsession off my back, out of my ribs, and onto the page. I wanted a transformation. I wanted us all to get a huge cathartic laugh out of it.

But we weren't done yet. He growled on:

FATHER: Everybody knows that things aren't as good as they used to be. Nothing is left. [laughs]

SON: Okay.

FATHER: The real thing is that if you can't laugh you're dead. Yeah. And I mean laugh at everything. At every thing. No matter what it is. If you don't think Mr. Bush is funny you'd better leave the country. If you take this stuff seriously, you're going to shoot yourself.

SON: But there are different kinds of laughter. There's derisive laughter, which has a very different effect than say, kindly, participatory laughter.

FATHER: Huh, I've never pulled it apart like that. I don't distinguish between the thing that made me laugh this morning and the thing that made me laugh this afternoon. They may be quite different, I agree, but I never think about that. If I find something funny, I laugh.

SON: Who are your favorite authors?

FATHER: Oh dear, that's a question that you can't answer. But ones that I like? Clarence Day. E. B. White is a brilliant writer. Orwell is a brilliant writer—*The Horse's Mouth* guy . . .

SON: Joyce Cary.[115]

FATHER: Joyce Cary. That really struck me. 'Cause I don't read novels. I don't like novels, especially modern ones. But Joyce Cary was something else. Yeah, that was great. And of course I like all the old stuff. Dickens is great, except it takes a lot of time and nobody has that much time anymore. But Conan Doyle and his character, Sherlock Holmes. Doyle hated Sherlock Holmes, did you know that?

SON: He was trapped by his own creation.

FATHER: Yeah. And parts of O. Henry and Mark Twain have some magnificent stretches—they're all great. Oh, and *Anna Karenina* and *War and Peace* really swept me away. You can really get lost in that world . . .

SON: Tolstoy, amazing. He gave away his estate and became a peasant.

FATHER: Yeah. And the same thing is true of *Les Miserables*. A book to sweep you away. I came to these things very late. I was supposed to read them in school, but I thought they were all worthless. I didn't really enjoy them until I was old. But I like the historians, especially the girls. Barbara Tuchman is unbeatable. *The March of Folly*, do you know that one? [116]

SON: I haven't read it.

FATHER: Read it. And I like Morison. Parkman[117]—if you just have the patience to read Parkman, he's great. But I don't have that kind of patience. I should go back, now that I'm older. But mostly I like trash—detective

---

115 *The Horse's Mouth*, 1944, by Joyce Cary, is a wonderful comic novel about a brilliant but penniless artist in Ireland who is ruthlessly obsessed with finding the right wall for his next painting, an epic mural.

116 *The March of Folly: From Troy to Vietnam.* Tuchman was inspired by John Adams's comment: "While all other sciences have advanced, government is at a stand; little better practiced now than three or four thousand years ago."

117 Samuel Eliot Morison was a prolific and multi-award-winning writer, mostly of military histories. Francis Parkman wrote extensively on French involvement in early American history; he was also a horticulturist and decrier of women's suffrage.

stories. You know, Parker, Eddie Coyle. One a night. That's not reading. I detest the whole idea of the short story as perpetrated by the *New Yorker*. Totally uninteresting to me. They're trying to do something fancy. A storyteller is a storyteller is a storyteller and he ought to tell a story. And the *New Yorker* people don't tell a story anymore. Very modern. Avant and all those good things. Well, they can keep it as far as I'm concerned.

SON: I can't help noticing that you have very strong feelings . . .

FATHER: And I get very angry—oh yes.

SON: Yes. To me, growing up, that was important.

FATHER: Oh?

SON: That you had feelings. I mean, we had an emotional relationship, you and I . . .

FATHER: Usually a very negative one.

SON: Yes. But nevertheless . . .

FATHER: Well, looking back on it—at the time, I was just reacting, not thinking about it—but looking back on it, it was because I cared. I cared too much probably. But when your children grow up, they're not your children anymore, that's gone. The old business of *JESUS CHRIST, WHACK! You can't do that—you're my child!* [eyes me] As you can see, you and I are so completely different. For instance, I don't go in for that mystical stuff. It's a side of life that doesn't interest me in the least.

SON: How would you describe it?

FATHER: It's indescribable—it's the Castaneda approach to life. I think it's all phonier than hell. Like abstract art. My God, some of this stuff. A pile of glass at the Tate: *Look out—don't touch this pile of glass! Because it's an artwork.* They have to tell you for God's sake! You can start right there.

SON: Well, I don't want to be lumped in with a pile of . . .

FATHER: . . . like *Waiting for Godot*,[118] I realize that it's me and not the playwright.

SON: The horrifying thing is that I agree with some of . . .

FATHER: But for me there's nothing there. Nothing. Sorry. But that's me. I'll accept that.

SON: . . . but as long as I can make out . . .

FATHER: There are too many . . .

---

118 *Waiting for Godot,* written in 1949 by Samuel Beckett, is one of the great works of the twentieth century, along with *Endgame*.

SON: . . . as long as I can make out the structure of the . . .

FATHER: Yeah, you see so much more about it . . .

SON:. . . as long as the playwright is consistent with the . . .

FATHER: You know so much more about it than I do, you see what I can't see . . .

SON: . . . and if the play sets up a certain . . .

FATHER: See, that stuff is so . . .

SON: . . . a certain pattern, then . . .

FATHER: . . . so foreign and appalling—I don't have the background—I can't think in those terms. I don't know why I like a play and why I don't, right? I just know—I don't like that one. So.

SON: Anyway . . .

FATHER: Anyway.

SON: So.

FATHER: So.

I have to laugh. The bastard! He refused to hear what I was saying. Especially if I had something different to offer, something that I thought might interest *him*. He interrupted and I pretended that he didn't, so I kept going, and he kept interrupting, and I interrupted his interruptions, until I either lost the thread or I gave up! To him it made no difference as long as he *won*.

At the time it seemed perfectly natural to me. This interview form was nothing new, it was the way we always talked—but sometimes I could feel my blood boiling. I wondered if that's what the Mossad guys meant about my father when they called him the big bastard. *Hamamser hagadol!*[119] I wondered if that's what I'd been squelching all these years, my inner bastard. I could probably use some of that, I thought—and I was right. I need a little more grit in my dealings with the world.

FATHER: You know, white on white. Did you see that play?

SON: No but I know the one you mean. *'Art.'*[120]

---

119 2009 *Newsweek* review of *A World of Trouble,* by Patrick Tyler.

120 Yasmina Reza's 1994 play *'Art'* is about a white canvas, a work of "Art" that is the cause of vehement arguments about art and commerce between two lovers. A theme from "The Emperor's New Clothes."

FATHER: Yeah, it's great. '*Art.*' To me, that says a great deal of the way I feel. Besides being incredibly funny.

SON: I don't want to get into that . . .

FATHER: Don't get into that. [*laughs*]

SON: . . . because there's too much there. There's art, which mirrors the world around us, from the artist's admittedly crackpot perspective, and then there's so-called information . . .

FATHER: That's true enough. Facts are no good without understanding where they come from. Who is speaking them. That's today's disaster. The Americans have created an information world. Information is neither wisdom nor understanding nor anything. Information is worthless—it has to have some purpose. I mean think of how useless history would be if all you had was an endless series of Teletyped messages from every different part of the world on any given day. Just Teletyped messages. You could sit there forever, research it, and it would be absolutely meaningless. In other words, people don't think anymore. The information highway is so busy—they speed down this information highway just the way we do in our cars. I suspect that's where it all comes from—going nowhere as fast as possible. That and the TV. I saw a bumper sticker the other day: *Where am I going? And what am I doing in a handbasket?* I told our minister of the faith that it would make a wonderful theme for a sermon, but he didn't really latch on to it. 'Cause we're all going to hell but we don't know it.

SON: I think the odd thing is that we do know it. Unlike the lemmings. Whom we find so peculiar, racing pell-mell to the cliff edge. We do the same thing, with two big differences: we'll take everything with us, and we know exactly where we're going.

FATHER: No, you have too high an opinion of the beast. We don't know anything. We're ideologues arranging all the information to suit ourselves. It has nothing to do with reality.

SON: You talk about the resurgence of fundamentalism in the Middle East as a binding force. Arabs and Persians for example, very different people . . .

FATHER: Yeah—as it is in this country.

SON: Do you believe there's any kind of intention behind it?

FATHER: Ideologues are obsessed, driven spirits. They don't think in those terms. They don't analyze why they think the way they do. Any more than a born-again Christian thinks about why he thinks about things. It's in the Bible and that's enough. That's it. If you're an ideologue and you've got your holy writ.

SON: It's a replacement for thinking. It gets you out of trouble.

FATHER: Yes, exactly. And no ideologue thinks. He excludes thought.

SON: Does thinking require getting out beyond yourself?

FATHER: What—detachment? Oh, absolutely. How else can you think? The idea of trying to approach something only through your own viewpoint—out of the question. But you can get closer to it than the next guy by being as objective as you can, if you're an historian—and yet you can never be totally objective. Nobody can. We're not that kind of animal. But it's a goal to strive for.

SON: You have to put yourself in another person's shoes, to see things from a different angle.

FATHER: Now you're talking about reaching for the stars.

SON: Is it a useful effort?

FATHER: Useful? Who knows. But we all should. A man's reach should exceed his grasp—a very good aphorism.

SON: Could you imagine calling yourself a pacifist?

FATHER: Goodness, no.

SON: Humanist?

FATHER: I'd like to be. I see that if there's any value in the people who've gone before, it comes through people like, you know, Erasmus.[121] I admire the hell out of him. But I don't think enough of the human being to think he's worth saving. And you have to think of the human being as worth saving to be a humanist, I think.

SON: But you love these little kids who run across the street.

FATHER: Well, they're so funny! They're like birds. I love to see birds. Chirping. And that's what they are. But when they leave that behind, they turn into these awful things.

SON: Unless they become this guy Shmuel, the philosopher.

FATHER: Yeah. Yeah, every once in a while you'll find a raisin. A humanist.

SON: Yeah. And in a sense to be a child . . .

FATHER: . . . is to be a humanist.

---

121 Early sixteenth century Catholic scholar and reformer from Rotterdam.

SON: . . . is to be a humanist. But that doesn't take any kind of discipline. To become a Shmuel, though . . .

FATHER: To remain a child . . . Look, what a thing to be able to do, to remain a child. With all those great things, the curiosity . . . the ability to learn, all those wonderful things. And then they're gone. We mash it all out of them.

SON: I always like to think that our kids will exceed us. We can envision the possibility but we haven't evolved enough to know how. We have to let them take us somewhere else.

FATHER: One can hope. Like a man who remarries—the triumph of hope over experience. 'Cause he always marries the same woman, doesn't he? [laughs]

SON: Okay, so in general you're not concerned about human life.

FATHER: It's case-by-case. This whole business about abortion—I think abortion is a great thing because I think there are too many babies in the world as it is. And that's killing. That's destroying life. And I'm in favor of euthanasia. I think that people ought to be able to choose when they want to go and somebody should be there to help them. I've never understood this business of the sanctity of life. I don't see any difference from the smallest amoeba to the so-called highest mammal. I don't see any crack there at all. I don't see any difference. I mean, we kill cockroaches without thinking about it! We kill flies! What's this about life?

SON: Do you think we're involved in some elaborate sort of self-regulating depopulation, with wars and pollution and so on?

FATHER: No, but I wish we were. The human being . . . I think it's the human being versus everything else. And whatever he thinks about other forms of life, it's always a compromise—we'll meet them halfway. Not understanding that it's all the same. There's no we-them unity. And the human is so constituted that he cannot restrain himself from raping his planet. He has to gouge out every possible resource for personal gain. That's inherent in the human being and I don't think you can get rid of it. The planet's going under if this animal keeps at it the way he has. But I think he's going to kill himself first.

SON: But you enjoy members of the species.

FATHER: Oh sure, sure. I'm one of them. I see all of this in myself.

SON: Do you see any good?

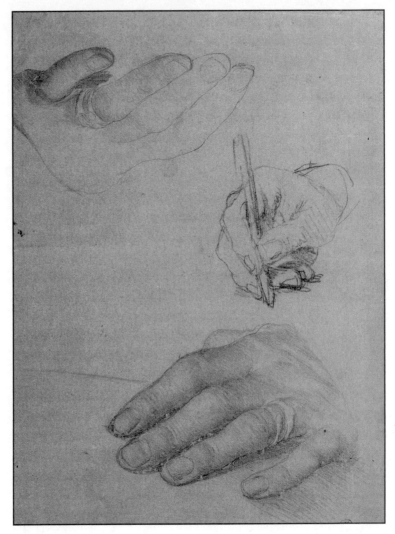

FATHER: Very little. [*laughs*] Not much.

SON: Do you have feelings of love and kindness?

FATHER: I think you have to be very tolerant of the human being to stand him—to move around among them. 'Cause they're pretty awful. If you give him enough food and give him everything he wants he tends to be a much more pleasant animal to lie down with. But my God, put the slightest pressure on him and—oh my! There weren't all that many nice people in the concentration camps. The ones who would give up their last crust of bread to the guy in the bunk below? Minimal. That's why soldiers don't talk about what happened to them in the wars, because how many of them ever behaved properly? How many of them didn't really do everything they could to save their own skins? That's the human instinct. And you can train him so that he will stand and get killed. But by God, he won't like it. And he won't be a hero. There aren't any heroes in my book, no. There are people who do extraordinary things on the spur of the moment without really knowing what they're doing. Many of them do it because of training and then many of them have the ability to be just shit-scared and still do what they think they ought to do—but boy, not many. Not many.

Son: So when you have a surge of feeling, like you did about going to war with Iraq, is that a sentimental, residual biological reaction or do you actually have some . . . ?

Father: I would prefer to think of it as an analytical thought. We could have gone in a variety of directions and we chose the absolutely wrong one. It was a dumb mistake.

Son: But if in the long run the planet is rid of the parasite, then the more mistakes we make the better, no?

Father: Rid of the human being? Yeah, that's true, the sooner the better.

Son: Then why worry about making the mistake?

Father: Because I'm one of them. I'm an American and I'm a human being. I can't divorce myself from that. No one can, can they? We all run our automobiles; we all get what we can. I see this in myself, as I do in everybody else.

Son: I'm still looking for a sign of fellow-feeling here before I throw in the towel. What about Scrooge and the way we listen to *A Christmas Carol* every year?

Father: Every year, tears run down my face.

Son: Why, do you think?

Father: Because I've become a sentimental old geezer.

Son: But what do you think it is that gets you? Scrooge's transformation?

Father: Oh no—it's Tiny Tim. Tiny Tim, Tiny Tim. Oh Jesus. I'm crying right now. No, Scrooge played almost no role except as an alter ego for Tiny Tim. I was much more interested in the earlier Scrooge. As a boy in school. And as the lover of the girl. Scrooge was much more interesting in those two aspects than he ever was as himself. Terrible. [*laughs*] And of course I loved Pickwick—such an evocation of Christmas. Mrs. Wardle smoothing down her skirt: "Things were different when I was a girl!" What a genius he was! And just sloppily sentimental—disgusting.

SON: You told me about a young girl named Margo, who sends you messages in code—why is she so charming?

FATHER: Because a young—I think she is ten years old, isn't that right? To have a young mind that is so acute, combined with an artistic ability— she's mathematical and she's got this wonderful mind that loves . . . She is Alice in Wonderland.

SON: What is your attraction to Dodgson, your interest in him?

FATHER: Oh, my. I'll have to think about that one. I read the books as a kid. The stories are chess games, of course. And . . . what was it that . . . ? Oh, there were so many things about the man that were fascinating. The Jabberwock in German is just mind-boggling. And then you go on and there's the Jabberwock in French and then there's the Jabberwock in Russian and then there's the Jabberwock in Greek for Christ's sake—the man is compelling.

SON: He was a lonely man.

FATHER: Yes. And the business of photographing naked little girls—I mean, what the hell was going on there? And that opens up . . .

SON: Full of ambiguities. And it really reflects more of what people think now than it does of the man himself.

FATHER: Yes. He himself would say, "You ask me these questions. I don't know why. It's in your head, not mine. It's your question; I can't answer it."

SON: But he was greatly trusted by all the parents.

FATHER: Yes. That was Victorian. They couldn't believe that he had any sexual motive. The mothers would come with the little girls and stay while he undressed them and took photographs. And they had to remain absolutely still for minutes at a time. Really, really, really weird. And then there was the wonderful question that he would ask: If I'm standing here with this little girl, and she has an orange in her right hand, and we're looking in a mirror, in which hand is the little girl holding the orange? Is she holding the orange in her left hand in the mirror and her right hand out here with me, or which? [*laughs*] It's that kind of question that entertained him.

SON: I remember that he could only really have a conversation with a child. It was impossible for anyone else to have a conversation with him.

FATHER: Yes. He was a stutterer. And that's why he never got orders and became a priest and a minister—he couldn't give a sermon. But he never stuttered when he was with a child.

SON: I keep going back to your journey—to use a New Age word—if we take these two thirty-year periods . . .

FATHER: It's beginning to interest me that they're of equal length.

SON: How would you say that your outlook shifted during the first thirty?

FATHER: I don't think it did, much.

SON: And the second thirty?

FATHER: Let's go back to the first one. I learned a lot about myself, about America, about other people, other cultures. I got a marvelous education. And I had a lot of fun. But I don't think I changed.

SON: Are there earlier mentors or bosses who would have disapproved of your worldview?

FATHER: I'm sure there were many. But I only took what I wanted and discarded the rest. No matter who it came from.

SON: But you don't want to talk about veering away.

FATHER: I wouldn't know where to begin. I was certainly dumb not to check out an engineering career. But that's the kind of thing you learn later.

SON: And in your post-career, do you think you've gone through a shift?

FATHER: Well look, I was thinking too. You're interested in why I'm a radical. Night hours. There were two things that occurred to me. One was—I wasn't a radical, ever. I just accepted things as they were. Until Barbara shattered her knee and they wouldn't fix it because she didn't have the big insurance policy. That's what radicalized me. When I saw the way society could mistreat somebody as close to me as that and how totally fucking wrong they are in treating people. Health being the biggest example, and a very important example. That radicalized me. I was finished after that.

SON: Do you think you were a latent radical, a supersaturated solution ready to fall out at that point . . .

FATHER: And that was the final blow? No that did it—the whole thing.

SON: Why do you do the Christmas cards?

FATHER: My father.

SON: A tip of the hat?

FATHER: I so loved my father. It's a dedication to him every year. And of course, it's taken over now. [*laughs*] If my father had not had that kind of a mind . . . once he made a cutout model of our Buick touring car. The whole family was inside with a banner saying "Merry Christmas, and you can return your finished touring car to our Specialist" (and he named me) "who will paint it in any color you request." [*laughs*] We would bang ideas off our heads as to what we could do with the Christmas card. I was the one who thought of the one of that mad guy in the *Philadelphia Inquirer* ad, and underneath was written, "Nearly everyone reads the *Philadelphia Inquirer*."[122]

SON: Yeah, the *Bulletin*.

FATHER: Well, whatever it is. And there's this crazy guy, he's the one guy who's not reading it. And we had this card: Nearly everyone reads the Hadden Christmas Card.

SON: How amazing—that guy is one of my constant references.

FATHER: What, the funny man in the middle of all those people whose faces are hidden behind the newspapers?

SON: Yeah, there's always some apocalyptic catastrophe about to happen in the street—a tidal wave, or a building falling over, or a herd of rhinos, and nobody notices because they're too busy reading the news! Except for one guy who's going crazy trying to warn everybody. Are you the guy?

FATHER: Oh, no, that never occurred to me. I just thought it was a horrendously funny ad. Incredibly amusing.

SON: I think of you as that guy.

FATHER: Oh, you're talking about . . . People like Freud think of things like that and try to peel the onion off until you get to it. And you'll never get to that place.

SON: What do you mean by the word *soul*? You write, for instance, about the soul of the Israeli people . . .

FATHER: Yeah, I can't . . . I have no idea. I don't . . . Look, if the cockroach has a soul, we have a soul.

---

122 Cartoons by Richard Decker in the 1950s and 1960s advertising the *Philadelphia Bulletin*, always captioned, "In Philadelphia nearly everyone reads the *Bulletin*."

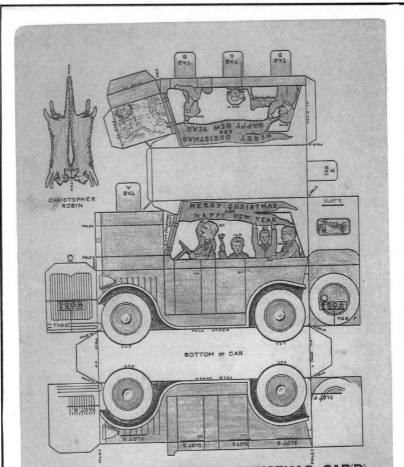

CHRISTOPHER
ROBIN

THE HADDENS' CUT-OUT CHRISTMAS CAR (D)

DIRECTIONS

AS AN ECONOMY MEASURE APPROPRIATE FOR THE YEAR 1932, WE ARE REQUIRING THE RECIPIENTS TO FURNISH THE LABOR OF MAKING THEIR OWN CARS.

READ ALL THE DIRECTIONS THROUGH BEFORE DOING ANYTHING. A WRONG MOVE IN THE BEGINNING MAY DO IRREPARABLE DAMAGE.

IF YOU GET INTO TROUBLE CALL BUTTERFIELD 8-2840 AND OUR EXPERT CAR MECHANIC JOHN HADDEN AND HIS CORPS OF COURTEOUS ASSISTANTS WILL HELP YOU.

FIRST: COLOR THE CAR AND ITS OCCUPANTS WITH WATER COLORS OR CRAYONS. THE IDENTITY OF THE VARIOUS MEMBERS OF THE FAMILY IS INDICATED AS A GUIDE. YOU MAY USE YOUR OWN JUDGMENT IN SELECTING THE COLORS BUT STRONG BRILLIANT HUES WITH VIOLENT CONTRASTS ARE RECOMMENDED. FOR EXAMPLE, IT IS ENTIRELY PERMISSIBLE TO MAKE THE BODY OF THE CAR RED—AND RED IS MORE SUITABLE FOR

CHRISTMAS CARS. COLOR SAMPLES MAY BE SEEN AT OUR SERVICE STATION, 206 EAST 72ND STREET.

SECOND: CUT OUT, WITH KNIFE OR SCISSORS, AROUND THE ENTIRE PERIMETER OF THE CAR ASSEMBLY. CUT ALL THE TABS AND SLOTS CAREFULLY, AS INDICATED; ALSO CUT THE UNDER PARTS ONLY OF THE FOUR WHEELS. THE MORE INDUSTRIOUS WORKERS MAY ALSO CUT OUT THE BLANK AREAS AROUND THE FIGURES ON EACH SIDE OF THE CAR, BUT THIS IS NOT NECESSARY.

THIRD: SCORE ALL FOLD LINES LIGHTLY WITH A KNIFE. FOLD THE VARIOUS SIDES AND PARTS AS INDICATED AND FIT EACH TAB INTO ITS RESPECTIVE SLOT. THE ENTIRE ASSEMBLY CAN BE COMPLETED WITHOUT USING PASTE.

FOURTH: CUT OUT CHRISTOPHER ROBIN, BOTH SIDES, FOLD ALONG BACK AND STAND IN A LIFELIKE ATTITUDE, BESIDE OR BEHIND THE CHRISTMAS CAR.

FIFTH: READ THE MESSAGE ON THE BANNERS AT THE SIDES OF THE CHRISTMAS CAR.

SON: This is a word that you use in your papers.

FATHER: Well there you are then, the cockroach has a soul.

SON: But what do you mean by it? Is it a habitual . . . ?

FATHER: No. I suppose it's shorthand for the German word *Geist*. The Polish word *Ducha*. See, it's an important word—the Israeli word *Ruach*. And of course in the Hebrew it has meanings far beyond . . .

SON: Breath?

FATHER: Who?

SON: *Ruach*, isn't it also the word for breath, in Hebrew?

FATHER: Probably, but it's spirit. And that's what I mean by soul. The driving spirit that gets people to do things—whatever it is.

*   *   *   *

Journal entry:

Yesterday, weeping. Watching Joan Plowright in *The House of Bernarda Alba*, the film of the Lorca play with Glenda Jackson, directed by Camus. So often life in the theater seems a waste of time—frivolous, ego-driven—but when I see good work, there is nobility in it again. Again it seems clear: if we could all respect each other, everything else would take care of itself; it would be so simple. If we could break the idea of status, of superiority. If we could recognize one another's gifts, encourage ability, skill, and wisdom, and demand no reward beyond a sense of satisfaction and community and respect. The idea of material wealth would grow obsolete, ridiculous. The idea of having more than someone else would prove deeply embarrassing. We would rely on elders for guidance, on artisans for our daily needs and on artists and our children for glimpses of the Beyond and for Delight.

The hard tone that my father sometimes took on left me cold. But what did I expect? I was after his soul. He resisted it, he became harder and colder, and the effect was painful to me. But then, when I least expected it, when I'd given up, he would open up. As he did when he talked about how he felt when my sister shattered her knee. It was such a different side of him; he showed his sense of moral decency, his feeling for someone he loved, admitting that the structural unfairness to her had shifted his view, that he was shiftable. Amazing!

As we went on, he began to invest more in the interviews. He became more articulate, he held the tape recorder closer to his mouth and he went on and on. I got about thirty pages per ninety-minute tape, single-spaced.

Often it was grueling. One day I was in gales of laughter—over his description of Dr. X, for instance—and other days I'd start to freeze. His laughter was telling: when he threw up an absurd image of himself, going down with Mishu, his chauffeur, to watch the riots, for example, to watch people beating each other up, his laughter was harsh. But other times he laughed gently, as though opening up to a new thought, as though stepping innocently into a clearing in the woods.

I read the book *Inside the CIA*, by Philip Agee. It disturbed me, as Agee no doubt intended. There were whole sections I couldn't even read, about codes and cryptonyms. The rest of the book portrayed his work for the CIA as a stupid game, elaborate and obsessive, and clubby—in which the recruit, and then the seasoned worker, played the part of professional bastard. Deception, of course, was key, and that bred paranoia. Nobody knew what anyone else was doing—and yet they all did the same basic work. The broken record played over and over: penetrate other groups, find out what they're doing, mess with people in every conceivable way, make them hurt, ruin their equipment, throw chemicals all over the place, into people's cigarettes, into their food, on their steering wheels, in meeting halls. Fuck with people: fuck with their bloodstreams, their respiratory systems, the things they make, the places they live, the people they trust, the food they eat. Damage their credibility, their cause, their families—and knock them off if necessary.

I could have spent a lifetime studying the awful truth and even then I wouldn't have known anything, really. But the research is possible. As Pop said, it's all out there. I printed ninety pages straight off the Internet on the Manchurian Candidate program alone. There was a mad Canadian doctor, Donald Cameron, who had testified against Nazi scientists at Nuremberg, some of whom were soon afterward recruited for his own program, who led a team of scientists and doctors at universities (fifty-four of them), research foundations, drug companies, hospitals, and prisons that received practically unlimited funds to run experiments on human subjects, many of them unwitting, with LSD, electroshock, torture, induced comas, some of them permanent—not to mention operations overseas . . .[123] The subject bored me to death. The very idea of putting that much effort into screwing other people up seems almost too base to be human, and numbingly tedious to boot.

One morning I woke from a dream about a performance at a summer arts camp for kids. The camp is next to a brook that runs through a beautiful wood. Children who are from all parts of the world play a concerto. Some of them are refugees from cities that have been destroyed; some are from our own broken places—and the rest are from prosperous American families. After the concert, we eat an exquisite dinner in the sunlit evening under sycamore trees; everyone talks animatedly about music, dance, and poetry and their effect on our lives. Someone fires up an old film projector to show a silent film from the early days. The light and the sound of the flickering images are so beautiful that I weep.

To celebrate my mother's eighty-fourth birthday, we fixed up a "movie machine" in the guest room. With Pop's mischievous encouragement, the lifelong ban on TV was lifted. We brought the magic lantern into the house. None of us could quite believe it.

My mother was giddy with happiness. She went to the library the next day and came home with Chaplin's *City Lights*, and *Cabaret*, with Liza Minelli and Joel Grey. My father was patient and attentive throughout. We hugged each other on departure, for the first time, with simple affection.

If a shift can occur on a little street in Maine on a day in mid-February, it is surely occurring in other places. Is there any chance that we can slow down the juggernaut of destruction, hatred, and fear we have created? Run it into the ditch for good, to rust as a memorial to our dangerous folly?

---

123 The program, begun in 1953, was codenamed MKUltra. Richard Helms destroyed the files before they could come to light in the Church Committee hearings, but 20,000 documents that had been misplaced later surfaced to fill in the details.

*   *   *   *

SON: So I lay there last night—I couldn't sleep—and I wrote down sixty questions.

FATHER: Oh my God, last night? Holy Christ . . . One thing I want you to find out for me: Why do I cry all the time now? I think of something and I cry, I go to the goddamn movies and I cry . . . I mean, the most sugary, unsophisticated stuff—it's terrible . . .

SON: Well, I've noticed—like when I told you at dinner about Union Square . . .

FATHER: Well that was probably my first memory of New York. Mishu.

SON: No, I mean later, after the towers fell—I noticed out of the corner of my eye that your face changed, you dropped your head—and you were overcome . . .

FATHER: How we blew it—Christ, the whole thing! We had all that sympathy and we just threw it away. Destroyed it! Funny, that's not usually the kind of thing I would . . .

SON: So I read all of the stuff you sent me . . .

FATHER: Uh-huh, uh-huh . . .

SON: . . . and listening to the tapes—there's a thing that keeps coming up about how bare facts are no good without knowing . . .

FATHER: Yes. A fact is no more useful in itself than a piece of wood.

SON: That's what I'm asking you about, not just the facts, but what it means. I'm looking for . . .

FATHER: [*shouting illogically to the rest of the house*] The gate's open! Goddammit.

SON: . . . what it means to you—and me . . .

FATHER: Shall we turn this off?

SON: No, you know what I'd like is . . .

FATHER: Oh. I think we ought to turn this off . . .

SON: No, because I'm right in the middle of a thought . . .

FATHER: [*shouting*] There! That's better! [*to me*] Bob's your uncle! Yeah, okay . . .

SON: I want you to come with me a little bit on this.

FATHER: You realize that I can't come up with anything without being provoked by a question—or reminded of something because these are all buried logs and they're down in . . .

SON: So you have no interest in any of this on your own.

FATHER: Not in that sense, no. But I think I'm remembering more things as you remind me; it's kind of a chain reaction. You start with a few neutrons, and you . . .

SON: So you'll keep doing this?

FATHER: Whatever you want. I told you about the event in Hamburg, when the Germans came to me and . . . ? Well, this is the story of what happened in Hamburg . . . but I went through that, didn't I?

SON: Yeah, but we haven't put it on tape. And I don't mind if we repeat things.

FATHER: Oh, okay. I'm likely to do that, so cut me off, 'cause I can't remember what I've said and what I haven't. Your mother complains bitterly about this. She's just like my mother talking to my father, *you know, my dear, you never get it right. That's not at all the way it happened.*

SON: She ought to be interested in the newest version of it.

FATHER: Yeah! Well, no. It has to be the right version. Did I tell you about Mishu?

SON: Yes. But tell me again.

FATHER: Well. Shall I turn this off?

SON: Sure.

FATHER: I don't know how. You do it.

Epilogue

"And make our Father's business ours. Amen."
—Groton School Hymn

My father appreciated his "opposite numbers"—their ruthlessness, their skill and evil genius, their dark humor, and their long tradition of struggling against the odds, but he abhorred the grim and bloody tyranny of Stalin. He had a keen patriotism, but it suffered erosion. The basic ideals he stood for were gradually compromised beyond measure, and he saw his country betrayed by his countrymen. He felt isolated, found it impossible to play along, and eventually he was marginalized. This brings us again to his pet peeve about Donne—that Donne was wrong, that every man *is* an island. I think what is closer to the truth is that my father became an island. Neither patriotic nor treasonous, just an island of his own in his own orbit.

But Donne is right, no man is an island, like it or not (though, in truth, we are more isolated if we only consider "man"). We are all connected under the water by land. We're protuberances of land, separated by water. And that can be quite lovely. But he didn't experience it that way. He couldn't give over to the connection. He was lonely; you could hear it in his voice. He was a precocious child; the adults never paid any attention to him. Somehow he got into this club in Berlin, where it was really fun for a while. He and his friends played hard and they thought they would be blown to smithereens any second. They loved it; they had a great time. But after that, when he wanted to go to Poland, and set up his station in Hamburg, he became a lonely, wandering child.

He retired before he reached fifty. His career took up a young third of his life; at the end of which he was stuck in Washington, crazy old-boy bureaucrats looking over his shoulder.

He sometimes took great pleasure in encounters with complete strangers. I remember arriving home one day with an older hippie who'd given me a ride in his VW bus. It was a classic scene: I invited this guy to come home and meet the folks. I'd only known him for a few hours, but the peace movement made all longhairs brothers back then. He was way off his route, a long way from home, he'd driven me several hundred miles and I said, "C'mon over to my house, meet my family; they'll welcome you in." My father got into a conversation with him that excluded the rest of us, and it went on for hours. As long as he wasn't responsible for a person, Pop could let go and enjoy some fellow-feeling. And he loved the unexpected gesture of kinship across social gaps.

In my kid's unfiltered perception, which was uninformed but often accurate, I could feel my father's sadness and maybe that softened me toward him. Otherwise he was pretty hard. But he was so fantastic! His stories and his gesticulations were so theatrical, and he was elegant, knowledgeable, and powerful—and free. He'd go streaking around the world doing whatever the hell he wanted. At someone else's expense! He lived like a king and he had a lot of fun. So it seemed.

He started a little film group with a few of the British officers stationed in Israel, including an MI6 guy who was a good friend, and I was included in these evenings. We watched old films from a noisy projector. I remember Margaret Rutherford reciting "The Shooting of Dan McGrew" in a hilarious Miss Marple movie. Every now and then I tried out some riposte with those middle-aged buffaloes and they laughed! I felt a heady sense of belonging. I can imagine how a steady diet of that kind of approval might warp a young man's life.

*　　*　　*　　*

My father's voice always banged around in my head. I hear him now, though he died two years ago.

I'd led the charge to bring him home from the hospital, with the help of hospice workers who finally allowed us to stop the chemo and the other meds and let him come home to die. We'd moved a hospital bed into the living room, which he was never again to leave except for an occasional trip around the dining room table, and then loaded him in. My sister went back to her house-painting, exhausted and apprehensive for us, and for the next several days and nights I continually lugged him up and down off the bed, and changed his clothes and sheets. After a few days one of the hospice workers saw that he needed a catheter. It made things much easier, but he was never convinced that it worked. I kept him company, caught him in my arms whenever he lurched up to go to the bathroom, to keep him from falling. I poured him whiskey once a day and took naps whenever I could, between crises of restlessness.

He started to go in and out of reason. Ghosts visited him and he didn't know where he was sometimes; he thought that they were watching him, that he was in prison and was going to be tortured. His watchful untrusting eyes.

I'd been the hero briefly, his fellow soldier to get him out of the hospital, where these fantasies had begun, but when we got him home I was the problem. I was the one to give him drugs, feed him, change his diaper, empty his colostomy bag, and clean him up. The hospice nurse came once a day: I learned techniques and some things got easier. But I had to lug him around a lot, and my lower back started to go out.

I stayed busy and felt useful, feeling neither worried nor sad. After four days of no real sleep I was beginning to think I was pretty good at this. Patient, adept, learning quickly the arcane nuts and bolts of dying.

After a few days he started to get stronger and I felt a secret panic that he would reverse the process and survive for another month, maybe a year. What then? *No!* I thought, *Turn back, old man! Don't come back! You've set your tiller and it's steering true—keep going!*

I was a coward to think this, and a traitor. I kept it to myself. One morning he'd asked me to call the CIA to find out about death benefits for my mother. I was on the phone for a half hour, bouncing from one operator to another—staff cuts—but finally I got the right office. At that moment my father started to get up again, to go to the bathroom. It was his final campaign and he was obsessed with it. I'd explained, I'd made drawings, I'd talked about gravity flow . . . "Gravity flow," he muttered, with perfect contempt. I asked him to wait just this once for a moment so I could talk to the woman on the phone. "No, now! Now!" It was a lost cause. I asked the woman to wait a moment. I tried to explain to him that I finally had someone who could answer his question but he waved me away and started to get up again.

He'd fallen that morning. I came in to find him sprawled in every direction upside down, holding the arm of the nearby sofa pathetically, as if he were still in danger of falling into some abyss. He pretended that nothing was wrong when I came in, as if he was inspecting the fringe of the rug. My mother had said she would look after him for a moment so I could take a nap, but it was hard for her to be present during that time. After that I'd attached a clip to his shoulder, with a string to an alarm, so that if he tried to get up, the alarm would go off and I would get there before he fell.

He wouldn't let me get back to the phone. Everything spilled over in a moment. I lost my cool. Everything I'd held in, as if all my life, just cracked open. "You're such a fucking asshole!" I shouted with my big strong voice, and I meant it. "And you always were one," I spat at him.

"Just go away," he said, ignoring me, waving me away, getting up. Finally I stood there again, holding him up, in that horrible embrace, two disgusting bears in the woods.

I decided I would stop trying to convince him that he didn't have to pee, that I would hold him up as long as he wanted to stand, before falling back, catch him, help him up again, let him down again, up, down, whatever he wanted, until he was exhausted. Whatever he wanted. He was dying. I had a long swath of life ahead of me. Give him a break. He's going to lose this one.

But it was too late. I'd cursed him and I would never be free of it. It would ring in my ears for the rest of my days. There was no way out. I couldn't apologize; that would have been an insult. We knew each other well enough to avoid that catastrophe at least. Just as I was beginning to see myself as a pretty good guy here with my dying, hard-ass father, I'd blown it. I was, in fact, a pain in the ass myself, much worse than he, a total fuckup.

We sulked for a few hours.

Then he asked for a drink. Scotch, with ice and bitters. I said sure, and started to make the drink. "Are you having one?" he asked.

It was an opening, but I ignored it. I wanted him to take in how fried I was, how badly he'd beaten me. I said, "No, I'm in no shape to have a drink."

No answer. I said, "Do you want it in a glass or a sippy cup?"

In a glass, I'd have to hold it with an iron grip to prevent it from spilling when he dropped it on his chest. I would hold it from underneath, near his lips but out of sight, so it would seem like he was holding it. In a sippy cup (what a horrible word!) he could have it all by himself without the charade of me holding the glass, pretending that he was holding it, so that when he dropped it, it would not spill and I could recover it and he could have another sip. His one remaining act of sovereignty.

He waved away the question. It was beneath him. I would know what to do.

I decided he should hold it on his own, in the sippy cup. I got it ready and presented it to him. Maybe now, a moment of ease?

No. He waved it away as if to say, that's not it, you dimwit! Not the goddamn cup!

"Okay. I'll toss it down the sink if you don't want it." He shrugged. I tossed it, with an extra vicious toss.

A few days later, my brother Jamie came from the West Coast with his wife and I handed Pop's care over to them. They came in the door during one of his up-and-down bouts, around two in the morning. It was a good bit of timing. I could show them what to do and then get some sleep at last.

Jamie stood there with tears in his eyes. I hadn't felt anything for many days. My dog seemed relieved. Now at last there was another being who could help carry the feeling of all this.

The next day I gave him his first morphine and he went into a long period of quietude that seemed more restful. His eyes were clamped shut and his breathing started to go into a cycle in which he seemed hardly to breathe at all for long moments. Then he would gasp for breath, breathe quickly a few times, slow down, and seem to stop breathing again. This went on for the next few days.

I slept and prepared to go back home to meetings and projects. The others could take care of him. They would spend time with him in his last days without me always there. It seemed to me he was almost done, and one of the nurses agreed. His feet were turning blue, she said. That's a sign.

I said good-bye to him, asked him to save a place for me, that I was going. He heard me, I thought, so there it was. I was done.

Three hours later I still had not gone, lord knows why. I was helping the nurse who'd come to give him a wash. We got his favorite shirt and cut it down the back so we could simply drape it around him. My mother didn't want us to cut it because she thought he would need it, but we told her he needed it now. An old silk scarf. The nurse shaved him and we started to wash him, pushing him over to one side a bit. He cracked one eye open and looked at me. He hadn't opened his eyes that day. "You're still here," he said, and a tear rolled down his beautiful cheek.

"Yes. I couldn't go yet. I'm sorry I shouted at you. I didn't want to. But I was so pissed off!"

A little smile crept across his face. He was happy. He'd won, really won, this time.

He died three days later. My sister had gone back to see him again, unexpectedly, and she had her hand on his chest when he stopped breathing for a long time. "He's gone," she said.

Jamie was standing there. Pop lunged with his shoulder and took one more big breath. "He's proved you wrong again," Jamie said. But then he really was gone.

*   *   *   *

Son: Well, this morning I went back to Escher and the puddle. So you've got this tire rut.

Father: I don't remember it as being a tire rut.

SON: We'll have to look.

FATHER: I'm sure you're right—I just don't remember that.

SON: So here's this machine. It's just a dumb machine, going through this glade; it makes these tire ruts in the mud. And boot tracks, I think. Then rain fills it up. And what's left, mirrored in the surface of it . . .

FATHER: Why there are leaves I don't know.

SON: It's because they're mirrored. The trees above are reflected in the surface of the puddle.

FATHER: I'm wondering if some leaves weren't floating on the . . .

SON: Maybe!

FATHER: The interesting thing about that puddle was that it was so different than anything else Escher did. Those things were sort of gimmicks, the birds flying in both directions, the steps going up and down—but the puddle was a work of art.

SON: Yes, I agree!

FATHER: That's why it sticks!

SON: And the fact that you pulled that image out of thin air—there's an apocalyptic thing about the inception: A *truck!* has gone through the mud but what's reflected in it—the aftermath—is beautiful.

FATHER: Hmm. You're reading this into it. In my head none of that exists—or if it does, it's so subliminal for me that I don't know it's there . . . That's your input!

Acknowledgments

First and foremost, thanks go to my father, John L. Hadden, whose presence challenged and tempered all my convenient ways of thinking. He became a skeptical but committed partner in this project, and our conversation seems to have intensified since his death. He can still make me laugh.

My mother, Kathryn Falck, kept a steady hand at the helm, and she and my sister and brothers, Barbara, Alex, and Jamie, lived through it all with more patience and wisdom than I was able to muster, and gave me proof that it was all real.

Friends who supported me in this expedition include Andrew Bundy, with whom I share a lifetime conversation about fathers; Bruce and Sally Odland, who brought these conversations to their dining room table many times through the years; Mary-Ann Greanier, who supported the work in ways astute and heartfelt; and Normi Noel, whose conversations at tea are a comfort. Bill Ballou and Cecile Bouschier gave me time in Berlin, where I began to write in earnest, and Sara Greenfield, Tom Melcher, Revan Schendler, and Christopher Hudson gave me invaluable feedback as second readers. Eric Darton, my teacher and guide, told me to go look at a diorama at the Museum of Natural History in which a shaman in a small hut hauls back the dying spirit of a sick person. An assistant holds a chain around his waist to anchor him to the earth. Eric Darton did that for me. Ellen Ogden has held my hand through much of this process, and fed me in more ways than I can count.

Roger Mattson generously shared his interest and expertise, particularly concerning the NUMEC affair, and Tom Segev told me to write about my father when I met him in Washington ten years ago, at the unveiling of the US State Department's official history of the Six-Day War.

Thanks are due to *American Letters & Commentary*, where an early excerpt of this material appeared, and to Benjie White, Al Miller, Anna Shapiro, Ava Roy, and Kevin Coleman, who invited me into their theaters (Hubbard Hall, The Theater Project, Firehouse 13, We Players, and Shakespeare & Co.) to try out a stage version. Kate Holland, Steve Boss, Dhira Rauch, Toby Bercovici, and Sandy Klein all lent their theater eyes to this project.

I feel tremendous gratitude toward Peter Sichel, who, among other kindnesses, gave an early manuscript to Jeannette Seaver, who took me on and performed miracles as my editor. Her wisdom and tenacity gave this book the light of day, as did the deft efforts of her team at Arcade/Skyhorse, including Maxim Brown, Jerrod MacFarlane, Leah Zarra, Ashley Albert, Cal Barksdale, and Michael Onorato.

Finally, my thanks to Reilly Hadden, who helps me break the cycles.

Appendix

John L. Hadden's Notes on the Apollo/NUMEC Affair Prepared for DOE and US Congressional Committees in 1978

On October 7, 2014, I met with Roger Mattson, a nuclear safety engineer and investigator,[1] at my house in Vermont to talk about conversations I'd had with my father about the Apollo/NUMEC affair. We also went through several boxes of documents that my father had given me before he died. Included in the boxes was an envelope lettered in my father's hand: "Washington Trips." The envelope contained a September 1, 1978 invitation from the Inspector General of the Department of Energy (DOE), the successor of the old Atomic Energy Commission (AEC), asking him to come to the Germantown, Maryland, office of DOE "to meet with representatives of my office to discuss freely and in complete detail your knowledge of matters relating to your knowledge of Israel's nuclear power capability . . ."The

---

1 Roger Mattson is a mechanical engineer with a doctorate in Mechanical Engineering from the University of Michigan and fifty years of experience in government and private sectors concerning the safety of nuclear power plants and nuclear weapons production facilities. In 1977 he led an investigation of the Apollo/NUMECC affair for the Nuclear Regulatory Commission that was reported to the US Congress, the National Security Council, and the Central Intelligence Agency. Mattson has taken an interest in the Apollo/NUMEC affair since that time. He and Victor Gilinsky authored two papers on Apollo/NUMEC that were published in the *Bulletin of the Atomic Scientists* in 2010 and 2014. Mattson has a book on the Apollo/NUMEC affair in publication.

envelope also contained a September 1, 1978 letter from Stansfield Turner, Director of Central Intelligence: "The scope of the [DOE] Inspector General's inquiry may encompass information which you have pledged not to reveal pursuant to the terms of the secrecy agreement which you executed when you entered on duty with the Central Intelligence Agency. You are hereby released from the terms of that secrecy agreement, for the purpose of the Inspector General's inquiry, within the limitations set out below . . . You may disclose classified information pertinent to specific intelligence sources or operational methods only with the express approval of my personal representative." Based on his travel voucher, my father met with the IG staff of DOE on September 6, 1978.

Separate documents in the files show that he interacted with Peter Stockton of Congressman John Dingell's (D–MI) staff in March 1978 and Henry Myers of Congressman Morris Udall's (D–AZ) staff in July 1978.

There also are documents related to my father's interactions with DOE and Udall staff members in the papers of Morris Udall in the University of Arizona's Special Collections Library, Tucson, Arizona. Those documents include a May 22, 1978 memorandum from Udall staffer Dr. Henry Myers to Morris Udall, which refers to the "Washington Meetings." It reads in part,

> Last week I talked by phone about NUMEC with John Haddon [sic], purportedly top CIA person on Israeli matters in years 1968-1972. While Haddon was elliptical in manner, I inferred there is little doubt in his mind that a diversion did occur. He was evasive on the question of why the matter had not been more intensively investigated by the FBI and AEC; he implied this was a matter he would discuss with you but not me. In recent weeks he has met with [US Congressman John] Dingell and [US Senator John] Glenn. In addition he talked to Dingell staff [Peter Stockton] for more than 20 hours. Staff were excluded from the Glenn meeting. Dingell staff says that Haddon is authentic and that discussion with him is essential to gain an understanding of the affair.

My father's papers show that he met with Henry Myers on July 13, 1978 and with William Knauf, an investigator in DOE's Office of the Inspector General, on July 15, 1978. These two meetings preceded the September 1, 1978 formal invitation to meet with the IG of DOE – and Admiral Turner's September 1, 1978 waiver of his CIA security oath, described above. Those two documents led to my father's meeting with the IG staff on September 6, 1978.

In the "Washington Meetings" envelope, there were five pages of notes in my father's tight handwriting, clipped together with a 3x5 card, also in his handwriting. These documents were apparently an outline of what he conveyed to DOE's IG staff and to the Congressional staff. The notes are transcribed below. Roger Mattson's interpretations of the notes are provided in italics. The symbol (?) indicates where the handwriting is unclear.

I include this appendix not only to provide more detail about my father's efforts to report on his findings about NUMEC, etc. (to do his job), but also to demonstrate, in these cryptic notes, how my father organized his thoughts, and how he often made his points by asking questions.

Notes, interpreted by Roger Mattson, PhD

3x5 Card Clipped to the Notes
1. Sonneborn, Arms for '48 War [*Based on my research and review of John Sr.'s documents, I believe this note refers to the Sonneborn Institute formed by American Zionist Rudolph Sonneborn in the late 1940s and early 1950s to coordinate and fund military aid to the fledgling nation of Israel.*]
2. Use of J. Agencies for cover [*J=Jewish*]
3. Agency contact owing (?) to rolls of film
4. No reports on I except orally [*I=Israel*]
5. Construction of nuclear warhead—US Technician [*Based on what follows on the legal-sized papers, I think this brief note refers to Raymond Fox, a Jewish designer of nuclear weapons from Livermore National Laboratory, who immigrated to Israel in 1957.*]

6. Relationship Between AEC & NUMEC. AEC & I affairs [*I=Israel*]

7. Financing—Leadership = J connection with I direct [*Research by Avner Cohen, Seymour Hersh and others has shown that wealthy Jews in America, Canada and Europe contributed tens of millions of dollars for the construction of Israel's plutonium production reactor known as Dimona.*]

8. Nuclear Technology:

9. California Assn = recruitment [*In the following notes, Hadden said more about the California connection.*]

10. Recruitment from Livermore [*This is probably another reference to Raymond Fox.*]

Further afield: Delivery System—J [*Based on John Sr.'s writings, I conclude that this note refers to the Jericho missile, which Israel developed to deliver nuclear weapons. See more about this, below.*]

Final worry: Are the Soviets in the pipe line?

A notation on side of the 3x5 card apparently is a phone number: 466-4226 [*I found that when James Woolsey was examined by the Senate Select Committee on Intelligence on February 3, 1993, he listed in his resume the phone number of Richard Helms as 202-466-4226. Helms was the Director of Central Intelligence when Hadden was CIA station chief in Israel.*]

Page 1 of 5 Pages of Notes on Yellow Legal Paper

1956 begin (Nasser's weapons of 1955) [*This appears to be the starting point of Hadden's narrative.*]

Clarence Kelley [*Kelley was FBI Director from 1973 to 1978. I know of no connection between him and the Apollo/NUMEC affair. It is well established by FBI documents that Kelley's predecessor, J. Edgar Hoover, was convinced that NUMEC and Shapiro were connected to the Israeli bomb.*]

IAEC resigned in 1957 [*Histories of the Israeli atomic energy program say that all the members but one of the Israeli Atomic Energy Commission resigned in 1957 over their chairman's (Ernst David Bergmann) insistence on developing nuclear weapons.*]

①

1956   begun (Nasser's weapons of 1955)   Chaim Killer
         IAEC resigned in 1957
      Bergmann Peres 1961 Dimona

1960-1963 UAR Missile Program

         Brookhaven - Livermore + Training

Warhead   French help linked to Jews in US (This may have tipped off the Soviets)
to take home
weapons   US Inspection of Dimon + Question of French Aid Col to WGov

Numec   California weap- Sci Att. Livermore
Shapiro   who arranged?
             WGM- Perm. only non-govt. receiving but products whether need

                 Subsidiary firm - in Israel ("eg. isotopes")

Fox case   Connections with AEC
in Livermore
ship channel to which Losses - dipl. pouch. (100 Kg)
he; men access to tech.
             visiting La. nuc. plgs.
Hijacked Shipment   who paid?
of Euro Material   Fine of 1 million dollars- check all banking records

                 Fire

Use of Brain Bank   Cover-up in AEC
for SIS operation
             False shipping close to non-Israel addresses

                 Bunay

      Stopped inspection opening up chem avenue. Gas centrifuge
      Rupture of centrifuge- arms samples.- US- report suppressed
      Uran from Arab - Yellow cake from Argentina. So. Af.

② Research?
      Small - non - Jewish
      Remember Sonnenborn Inst   The Pledge
      Need for intercepts.
      Soviet agent
      of all contacts of Sci Att - plus head of firm.
      Consider many cases as excuses in preventing proliferation as appropriate obtaining connection

Bergmann Peres 1961 Dimona [*Research by others has shown that by 1961, the US knew for sure that Israel's plutonium production reactor at Dimona was under construction by the French. The Israeli Minister of Defense Shimon Peres and the Israeli AEC Chair Ernst David Bergmann oversaw the secret deal with the French to build the reactor.*]

1960–1963 UAR Missile Program [*I think Hadden concluded that this program and the threat that it represented are what motivated Israel to build the bomb. UAR = United Arab Republic*]

Brookhaven—Livermore = Training [*It is well known that Israel arranged to have nuclear technicians trained at National Laboratories in the US, such as Brookhaven and Livermore.*]

French help linked to Jews in US (This may have tipped off the Soviets)

US Inspection of Dimona + Question of French aid to WGM [*Weapons Grade Material*]

Sidebar: Warhead to take nuc weapon [*I think Hadden knew that the Jericho missile's warhead could be nuclear.*]

California Group—Sci. Att. Livermore [*I believe that this is a reference to Avraham Hermoni who Hadden knew well. Hermoni was the onetime Israeli scientific attaché, who worked for Israel's secret nuclear espionage organization called LAKAM, was a leader in Israel's weapons development authority called RAFAEL, and organized contacts throughout the US to gather information on nuclear weapons and other scientific matters for Israel.*]

WGM—Perm only non-gov't receiving hot products—who arranged? Who financed? [*Based on my research, Hadden was referring here to the fact that NUMEC was a private company permitted by the US AEC to hold and process weapons grade materials, i.e., both plutonium and highly enriched uranium. Recent research by others (e.g., Grant Smith in his book* Divert*) has established that the original financing of NUMEC involved David Lowenthal, an American Zionist with connections to Israeli intelligence and the Sonneborn Institute.*]

Subsidiary firm in Israel ("e.g. isotopes") [*From AEC and FBI records, I know that in the early 1960s, NUMEC established a joint venture company with the Israeli AEC. It was called ISORAD. Zalman Shapiro, president of NUMEC, and Ernst David Bergman, Chair of the IAEC, formed ISORAD.*]

Sidebar: NUMEC Shapiro *[It is a mater of public record that Dr. Zalman Mordechai Shapiro was founder and president of NUMEC from 1957 to 1970.]*

Connections within AEC *[Documents form the Justice Department and the FBI show that there were concerns by the president of the United States that Shapiro might have had connections in the US AEC that enabled him to get away with large losses of highly enriched uranium (HEU) from NUMEC's uranium processing plant in Apollo, Pennsylvania. Investigations by the FBI and the Department of Justice failed to confirm these allegations, but doubt persists.]*

Sidebar: Fox case in Livermore *[My research shows that this note refers to Raymond Fox, Jewish nuclear weapons designer, who left Livermore National Laboratory for Israel in 1957. His story has not been widely documented, but it is summarized in Seymour Hersh's book* The Sampson Option.*]*

Losses—dipl. pouch—(100kg) *[My research discloses that there have been various alternatives considered for how the Apollo HEU might have been transported to Israel. One idea is that the 100 kilograms of HEU found to be missing at Apollo in 1965 (more went missing later) were smuggled to Israel in diplomatic pouches.]*

Visiting Is. Nuc phys. *[AEC and FBI records show that Baruch Cinai (a.k.a. Dr. Bernard Cinai), an Israeli metallurgist, was loaned to NUMEC by Israel. At NUMEC he had access to advanced materials processing technology for plutonium and uranium, despite concerns by the US AEC.]*

Sidebar: slip changed in Wash re: access to techn. *[It is not clear to me what this means.]*

Fine of 1 million dollars. Check all banking records—who paid? *[I have learned through recent releases of formerly classified FBI files that NUMEC was fined a total of about this much for a portion of the 100 kilograms of HEU found to be missing from Apollo in 1965. Communications between the AEC and the Joint Committee on Atomic Energy show that this $1 million was in addition to fines of about that much paid previously by NUMEC for missing uranium. It is known today that the fines were paid through bank loans to NUMEC that were later repaid by Atlantic Richfield Company when it bought NUMEC in 1968.]*

Fire *[I have reviewed public records showing that a fire in a vault at Apollo in 1963 destroyed records and left a few kilograms of HEU missing.*

The fire exacerbated the investigations of NUMEC because of the missing records.]

Sidebar: Hijacked shipment of EUR Material [*This note refers to the Plumbat affair wherein Israel illegally diverted 200 tons of natural uranium from the European Community in 1968. The Dimona reactor is fueled by natural uranium. The Plumbat affair is the subject of a book of that title.*]

Cover-up in AEC [*I have reviewed formerly classified AEC records from the late 1960s and the memoirs of Glenn Seaborg, former AEC chairman, showing that the AEC commissioners conspired to downplay the seriousness of the missing HEU and avoided dealing with the possibility that the materials were diverted to Israel.*]

Sidebar: Use of Binai Brit for IIS operations [*B'nai B'rith is a Jewish service organization. I have reviewed records from the National Archives showing that President Eisenhower knew that American contributions for the construction of Dimona were laundered through Jewish charitable organizations.*]

False shipping docs to non-Israeli addresses [*This is another postulate for how missing HEU got to Israel.*]

Ramey [*It is a matter of public record that James Ramey was a lawyer who worked for the AEC then was Executive Director of the Congressional Joint Committee on Atomic Energy and later served as an AEC commissioner. Records form the National Archives show that Ramey first was informed about Dimona in January 1961 while serving with the Joint Committee. Seaborg's memoirs say that when he could not get the Nixon administration to approve an upgraded security clearance for Shapiro in 1970, Commissioner Ramey arranged a job for Shapiro at a division of Westinghouse that did not require a clearance.*]

Stopped inspections opening up new avenue—gas centrifuge

Rupture of centrifuge—urine samples—US—report suppressed

Uranium from Arial—yellow cake from Argentina—So Af. [*I think that these three notes refer to various ways and places that Israel acquired and enriched uranium. Certainly the South African connection is well established. It came as news to me that Hadden thought someone in the US secretly aided recovery from an accident in a gas centrifuge enrichment plant in Israel. Vanunu said the enrichment plant originated at Dimona in 1979 or 1980.*]

Sidebar: IV—Research? [*A bit of research by me indicates that the IV Hadden placed in the sidebar of his notes at this point probably reminded him* to say that Israel established Institute Number IV near Haifa as its center for nuclear weapons development.]

Small—non-Jewish [I don't know what Hadden might have been talking about here.]

Remember Sonneborn Inst. The Pledge [The Pledge is a book by Leonard Slater about the Sonneborn Institute. Hadden kept coming back in his writings to the idea that Hermoni had reactivated the idea of the Sonneborn Institute to provide American support for the Israeli bomb.]

Need for intercepts

Soviet aspect

All contacts of Sci Att—plus head of firm [This note is probably a reference to Israeli scientific attaché Avraham Hermoni and NUMEC President Zalman Shapiro. My review of declassified FBI records shows that both of these men recruited expert assistance to Israel and were monitored by the FBI when they did so.]

Consider using case as exercise in preventing proliferation as opposed to obtaining conviction. [Hadden appears here to be saying that the government should not prosecute Shapiro under the Atomic Energy Act but should use the Apollo/NUMEC affair as a learning experience. Records from the late 1970s indicate that is what the Nuclear Regulatory Commission did.]

Page 2

1952 IAEC—Heavy Water [I have collected AEC records showing that Bergmann of the IAEC sought heavy water for the Dimona reactor from the US AEC in the mid 1960s. When AEC declined, he turned to Norway, as documented in the works of Cohen and Hersh. I don't know why Hadden uses the 1952 date since the deal with Norway to supply heavy water for Dimona did not occur until about 1959.]

Dostrovsky [I think this note refers to Israel Dostrovsky, head of the Weizmann Institute and director general of IAEC. He headed the radioactive isotopes group at the Weizmann Institute. Hadden must have made a connection between him and the Israeli bomb. I know of no connection to Apollo/NUMEC.]

Material Unaccounted For [This is a term of art (MUF) that Hadden probably used to describe the losses of HEU from Apollo/NUMEC.]

1956—Discussion in Israeli leadership after 1955 Soviet Arms deal (Policy of Deterrence) [*It appears Hadden extemporized here on why Israel decided to go for the bomb. I think Ben-Gurion knew from the outset that Israel should go for the bomb.*]

Relationship with the French as a result of 1956 [*The Suez crisis occurred in 1956. Memoirs of Peres and writings of others say that Israel's support of the French during the crisis earned later French cooperation in building the Dimona reactor.*]

Bergmann—R&D—(1) young scientists—Training in US— like Einstein—Relationship with B.G. (Arab use of European missile experts) [*B.G. stands for David Ben-Gurion, first Prime Minister of Israel. There is a record of his asking Einstein to succeed him and Einstein's refusal. Here Hadden may have likened US support for Israel's bomb to European support for Arab missiles.*]

Lead time? + possible bombing of facilities? + embargo? [*From his other writings, these appear to me to be Hadden's thoughts about why Israel would want to supplement the production of plutonium at Dimona with the acquisition of HEU from Apollo/NUMEC. That is, plutonium and HEU were alternative paths to the bomb.*]

Brookhaven +Nahal Soreq (US!) [*Nahal Soreq is a research reactor built by the US for Israel in the late 1950s pursuant to President Eisenhower's Atoms for Peace program. It is fueled by HEU and has been the subject of international safeguards inspections throughout its lifetime.*]

(2) Reactor—reasons for French help. Info + Algeria = Dimona [*I think Hadden was again, in this reference to Algeria, citing motives for Israel's pursuit of the bomb.*]

(3) Delivery System—Marcel Bloch = Jericho [*Public records show that Jericho is the name of an Israeli ballistic missile. Bloch, who changed his name to Dassault, was head of a French aircraft manufacturing company. It has been shown by others that development of the Jericho missile was a joint project of Dassault Aviation and Israel.*]

Sidebar: Costs: 100 million for bomb project, 100 million for missile, 20 m/yr. [*I think these are Hadden's estimates of the cost of these two elements of Israel's nuclear deterrent.*]

Several paths theory a la Manhattan: viz Sonnenborn Institute + Czech Arms deal (The Pledge) e.g., El Al [*Hadden apparently likened*

Israel's alternative paths approach to the bomb to the alternative paths chosen by the US in WW II, i.e., development of both plutonium and HEU for bomb materials. The Pledge *was a book by Leonard Slater proclaiming the accomplishments of the Sonneborn Institute. The Czech arms deal was an agreement between the USSR and Egypt in 1955 to supply Egypt with more than $250 million worth of modern Soviet weaponry, through Czechoslovakia.*]

(4) New Sonneborn in US—compartmented. Coordinated by Sci Attaché—Hermoni e.g., man working the delivery system [had] no knowledge of nuclear warhead (He knew from design) [*Once again Hadden appears to me to be talking of his conviction that Hermoni used the Sonneborn approach in his solicitation of American help for the Israeli bomb.*]

(4a) US Technician recruited for work in Israel—Livermore (Fox). Who falsified report? [*This is another reference to Raymond Fox, the Livermore nuclear weapons designer that immigrated to Israel in 1957.*]

Top priority: WGM [*I think Hadden was recommending that top priority in investigating Israeli nuclear weapons be given to the supply of Weapons Grade Material from outside, i.e., where did Israel get its HEU?*]

Recruitment of US key personnel. Note Cal. Outfit. [*Hadden's repeated references to the California recruitment of assistance to Israel probably included Raymond Fox. I wonder if Hermoni might have recruited billionaire Hollywood producer Arnon Milchan who recently wrote a book about his secret assistance to Israel in the acquisition of triggers for atomic bombs.*]

Set up NUMEC with Shapiro: only non-gov't facility. Where did he get funds? Who authorized hot products? [*These are central and oft-repeated themes of Hadden's concern with Apollo/NUMEC. Hot products apparently refers to HEU.*]

Subsidiary firm in Israel (min of Def) incl Ag com. [*This is another reference to ISORAD, the joint venture between NUMEC and IAEC described above. The tie to the Israeli Ministry of Defense was Bergmann's reporting arrangement with Peres. I think Ag com refers to the cover story for ISORAD, i.e., irradiation of agricultural products.*]

"Losses" sent through pouch—100 kg. [*This is repetition of the above mentioned route for stolen HEU to reach Israel.*]

Visiting "physicist" Israeli

MUF discovered—1 million fine. Who paid?

Fire destroyed records

False shipping documents—no receipts—no checks possible [*It is well known that in the 1960s the AEC did not inspect packages of radioactive material that NUMEC and others shipped abroad.*]

1971 NUMEC closed out—Shapiro nervous [*My reading of the totality of Hadden's musings on Apollo/NUMEC convinces me that he thought Shapiro left NUMEC in 1971 because of fear that his role in the diversion of materials and know-how to Israel would be discovered. The death penalty was associated with violations of the Atomic Energy Act of the type that have been alleged.*]

Possible use of Soviets [*I have no knowledge of this matter.*]

Processed bomb material sent back. AEC informed [*This possibility is intriguing, but to my knowledge it has not been confirmed by the US government documents so far released to the public.*]

No action. Why? [*I think Hadden, like others, wondered why Shapiro was never prosecuted.*]

Problems [*Hadden listed some problems and questions, below.*]

Inspection of Dimona [*Records of the National Archives show that there were several inspections of Dimona by the US during the Kennedy administration. The results were documented. One can see with hindsight that the Israelis managed the inspections and the inspectors were duped. Historians have shown that President Johnson stopped the inspections.*]

Page 3 (Apparently a Summing Up)

1957 resignation of IAEC—leaves Dimona under Min of Def
   a. Increase in time between inspections
   b. Instead of separation plan—gas centrifuge (Dutchman worked for Siemens in Paris in WWII) Case of the ruptured cylinders—Rsr. Dr. to US. Uranium Fluoride
       Why was report quashed?
   c. Uranium extraction facility at Arial
   d. Yellow cake from Argentina
   e. Uranium Ores from South Africa (for Israeli Technology)
   f. Liberian Freighter—20 tons of uranium processed material. From N. Sea to Med. Who shut off investigations?

Final moves:

- Air Force Officer
- Tulipman—1st Head of Division—secretly transferred 1965 to Institute No. IV—highest award by Minister Def Dayan 1971 [*My research shows that Tulipman formerly was head of Dimona.*]
- Top Soviet Agent—can pinpoint people for Israelis & get take without having to recruit

Page 4

I   Atmosphere:

1. Pressure from the Arabs 1955 Arms Deal. Deterrence + Reprisal = Military Superiority. Later: use of EUR techn. for missiles 1962–1963. SCVD. US Reactor?
2. Belief in Technology
3. Several Paths [*Hadden believed the Israelis took two paths to the bomb, plutonium from Dimona and, at least initially, HEU from Apollo.*]
4. Experience of Sonneborn
5. Lead Time—Embargo—Bombing interruptions
6. Pressure of JFK Inspections—1962/63

II   General

1952 Heavy Water

Late 50s early 60s Training at Brookhaven, etc.

1957–critical 1964 [*I think this is Hadden's estimate of Dimona's construction period.*]

Facts:

1. 100 million for French Reactor at Dimona—no research purpose—under Min of Def—Bergmann (1957 resignation). Use of increased time between inspections.
2. 100 million for Jericho Missile 1968—known nuclear warhead design (600 million over 10 years—½ yr's budget) (Reasons for French Aid)

3. Nuclear Physicist from Livermore + endless raft of US Techs.
4. Shipments of Uranium: Argentine Yellow Cake, South African, Domestic production at Arial. Hijack of nuclear material
5. Experiments in gas centrifuge (Results of Testing)
6. Cal: Am Isr Tech Aid program [*I think this refers to Hermoni's work in California, above.*]
7. Hijacking [*I think this refers to the Plumbat affair, above.*]
8. Resistance to Inspections—no NPT [*NPT=Nonproliferation Treaty*]
9. Interest in Gas Centrifuge
10. Transfer of Personnel
11. Warhead of Jericho
12. Flying maneuvers [*Hadden and others surmised that bombing runs practiced by Israeli F16 aircraft were indicative of the ability to deliver nuclear weapons. Hadden said as much in interviews with journalists in the late 1970s.*]

V   Dangers:

1. Anti Semitism?
2. Will spur Arab efforts w/perhaps Soviet Aid?
3. Make more difficult aid to Israel?
4. Idea that US responsible?
5. Encourage other small countries to go nuclear?

Page 5 of 5 Pages of Notes on Yellow Legal Paper

III   Facts NUMEC

1. Loss of WGM—100# by NUM
2. Shapiro's background
3. Subsidiary in Israel
4. Visiting Israeli Scientist
5. Fire at NUMEC
6. Shapiro warned of investigation
7. Intense resistance of AEC to investigation

IV   Questions

Who authorized NUMEC to get material as 1st Civ facility?

Who gave money to start NUMEC?

Who paid the fine?

Who quashed the Urine Sample report?

Who falsified the Fox report?

Who was against investigation?

Who was the "Israeli Physicist"? (background)

What records were destroyed in the fire? (Precise details re fire)

Who warned Shapiro?

What was reason for shipments of radioactive material into US?

Who warned the Israelis to knock them off?

Why was investigation of hijacking closed off by West German?

(Survey of all Hermoni contacts in AEC indicated Soviet not Israeli interest.)

(French operations certainly known to Soviets—Parque/Prague (?) Case)

What John Hadden Did Not Include in His Outline

[Mattson:] Hadden left something important out of his briefings described above. Or else he added the information extemporaneously. He was the source of what some have called the "smoking gun" in the Apollo/NUMEC affair. He and his colleagues at the American embassy in Israel are credited with searching for plutonium particles in the environment of Dimona and finding, unexpectedly, a unique brand of HEU that was enriched at the Portsmouth, Ohio, plant of the AEC and processed into naval fuel by NUMEC at the Apollo plant. There is no other explanation for its presence in Israel. This discovery occurred in late 1967 or early 1968. Hadden told others of this find, but he did not include it in his outline of remarks to DOE and the Congressional staffers.

For example, Hadden told journalists Melman and Raviv about his efforts to collect radioactive samples in the environment near Dimona. "He would make a point in driving as close as he could to the nuclear reactor and occasionally stopped his car to collect soil samples for radioactive analysis. Shin Bet was obviously tailing him, and an Israeli helicopter once landed near his automobile to stop it. Security personnel demanded to see identification, and after flashing his US diplomatic passport Hadden drove off, with little doubt there were big doings at Dimona."[2]

John Hadden, Jr. recalled a time in 1965 when his father took the family on a picnic in the Negev Desert where the dome of the Dimona plant could be seen. While he and his siblings ate peanut butter sandwiches, John Jr., aged twelve, watched his father clip branches from the shrubbery and put them in the trunk of their car.

Seymour Hersh told it this way: "In an attempt to determine whether the chemical reprocessing plant was in operation, the CIA began urging attachés to pick up grass and shrubs for later analysis."[3] As a senior DOE scientist told journalist John Fialka, the American embassy personnel in Israel were "walking through the daisies," collecting dust on their shoes for later radiochemical analysis. They were looking for traces of fission products, including plutonium, which would appear in the environmental samples as soon as the reprocessing facility began to operate. They did not expect to find the unique brand of HEU produced only at the Portsmouth facility.

2 "Spies Like Us: Spy vs. spy intrigue between the CIA and Israel, centered around the US Embassy in Tel Aviv," Yossi Melman and Dan Raviv, *Tablet Magazine*, Netbook Inc., April 8, 2010.

3 *The Sampson Option*, Seymour Hersh, p. 57

Illustration Credits

Frontispiece: M. C. Escher's "Puddle," © 2015 The M.C. Escher Company-The Netherlands. All rights reserved. www.mcescher.com.

Page 3: "Poolside view3," by I, בוט-םוי. Licensed under CC BY-SA 3.0 via Wikimedia Commons. https://commons.wikimedia.org/wiki/File:Poolside_view3.jpg.

Page 5: "Mom jumping," photographer unknown.

Page 18: "Volunteers of America Soup Kitchen WDC," by Franklin D. Roosevelt Presidential Library and Museum—Franklin D. Roosevelt Presidential Library and Museum. Licensed under Public Domain via Wikimedia Commons—https://commons.wikimedia.org/wiki/File:Volunteers_of_America_Soup_Kitchen_WDC.gif.

Page 24: "Alice 05d," by Sir John Tenniel—"Alice's Adventures in Wonderland" (1865). Licensed under Public Domain via Wikimedia Commons—https://commons.wikimedia.org/wiki/File:Alice_05d.jpg.

Page 29: "Dog with mask WWI," by Halsey, Francis Whiting—"The Literary Digest History of the World War," vol. V, p. 333. Licensed under Public Domain via Wikimedia Commons—https://commons.wikimedia.org/wiki/File:Dog_with_mask_WWI.jpg#/media/File:Dog_with_mask_WWI.jpg.

Page 34: "Hadden crest," courtesy of David Hadden.

Page 39: "Close view of West Point cadets as they pass in President Truman's inaugural parade.—NARA—200046," by Abbie Rowe—US National Archives and Records Administration. Licensed under Public Domain via Wikimedia Commons—https://commons.wikimedia.

org/wiki/File:Close_view_of_West_Point_cadets_as_they_paass_in_President_Truman%27s_inaugural_parade._-_NARA_-_200046.jpg.

Page 50: "Berlin Square," by John Hadden.

Page 55: "Mom dancing," photographer unknown.

Page 60: "Bundesarchiv Bild 183-1983-0121-500, Berlin, Bar 'Eldorado,'" by Bundesarchiv, Bild 183-1983-0121-500/CC-BY-SA. Licensed under CC BY-SA 3.0 de via Wikimedia Commons. https://commons.wikimedia.org/wiki/File:Bundesarchiv_Bild_183-1983-0121-500,_Berlin,_Bar_%22Eldorado%22.jpg.

Page 67: "C-54landingattemplehof," by USAF—United States Air Force Historical Research Agency via Cees Steijger (1991), "A History of USAFE," Voyageur, ISBN: 1853100757; USAF photo 070119-F-0000R-101 [1]. Licensed under Public Domain via Wikimedia Commons—https://commons.wikimedia.org/wiki/File:C-54landingattemplehof.jpg#/media/File:C-54landingattemplehof.jpg.

Page 79: "08 Workers Revolt in Berlin—Flickr—The Central Intelligence Agency," by The Central Intelligence Agency—08 Workers Revolt in Berlin. Licensed under Public Domain via Wikimedia Commons—https://commons.wikimedia.org/wiki/File:08_Workers_Revolt_in_Berlin_-_Flickr_-_The_Central_Intelligence_Agency.jpg.

Page 88: "Salzburg," by John Hadden Sr.

Page 90: "Boy with pirate flag," by John Hadden Sr.

Page 92: "Krampus," drawing by Reilly Hadden.

Page 104: "Ford Falcon," drawing by Jamie Hadden.

Page 110: "Israeli F-4 Phantom—Flickr—The Central Intelligence Agency," by The Central Intelligence Agency—Israeli F-4 Phantom. Licensed under Public Domain via Wikimedia Commons—https://commons.wikimedia.org/wiki/File:Israeli_F-4_Phantom_-_Flickr_-_The_Central_Intelligence_Agency.jpg.

Page 119: "Desert, barbed wire," by John Hadden Sr.

Page 135: "President Nixon walking with Kissinger on south lawn of the White House—NARA—194731," by Oliver F. Atkins,

ILLUSTRATION CREDITS

263

1916–1977, Photographer (NARA record: 8451334)—US National Archives and Records Administration. Licensed under Public Domain via Wikimedia Commons—https://commons.wikimedia.org/wiki/File:President_Nixon_walking_with_Kissinger_on_south_lawn_of_the_White_House_-_NARA_-_194731.tif.

Page 153: "Harry St. John Bridger Philby," photographer unknown—Image from *The Heart of Arabia, a Record of Travel and Exploration* (London: Constable and Company, 1922) by H. St. J. B. Philby: http://www.archive.org/details/heartofarabiarec01philuoft. Licensed under Public Domain via Wikimedia Commons—https://commons.wikimedia.org/wiki/File:Harry_St._John_Bridger_Philby.jpg.

Page 159: "Traditional carnival mask of Nuoro, Sardinia, during the Feast of Saint Anthony of Fire. [NB: Or Sant'Antonio del Fuoco]" https://commons.wikimedia.org/wiki/File:Issohadoreandmamuthones.jpg.

Page 164: "Issohadore and Mamuthones," by Cristiano Cani—http://www.flickr.com/photos/cristianocani/2199949849/sizes/l/. Licensed under CC BY 2.0 via Wikimedia Commons—https://commons.wikimedia.org/wiki/File:Issohadoreandmamuthones.jpg.

Page 187: "Son to partisans," originally uploaded by Irpen at English Wikipedia—Transferred from en.wikipedia to Commons. Licensed under Public Domain via Wikimedia Commons—https://commons.wikimedia.org/wiki/File:Son_to_partisans.jpg.

Page 197: "George W. Bush walks with Ryan Phillips to Navy One," White House photo by Susan Sterner—http://georgewbush-whitehouse.archives.gov/news/releases/2003/05/images/20030501-15_d050103-2-664v.html. Licensed under Public Domain via Wikimedia Commons—https://commons.wikimedia.org/wiki/File:George_W._Bush_walks_with_Ryan_Phillips_to_Navy_One.jpg.

Page 207: "Jabberwocky," by John Tenniel—Copied from English Wikipedia. Licensed under Public Domain via Wikimedia Commons—https://commons.wikimedia.org/wiki/File:Jabberwocky.jpg.

Page 213: "Alice par John Tenniel 25," by John Tenniel—*Alice in Wonderland*, Illustrator: Tenniel 1st Russian Edition. Licensed under Public

Index